More Praise for

HEAVEN'S COAST

"Both an invitation and a gift. In this dazzling memoir, Mark Doty has achieved nothing less than a miracle."

—Philadelphia Inquirer

"The same exquisite sensibility that informs Doty's poetry is at work in this magnificent memoir. . . . *Heaven's Coast* is more than the memory of the dying of a body; it is a record of the birthing of a spirit." *—Seattle Times*

"In *Heaven's Coast* [Doty] has sung a lyric to his love, a rhapsody. *Heaven's Coast* is both a journal of mourning and a memoir of heartache, an attempt through language to manage unmanageable grief. . . . Profoundly sad, yet somehow hopeful."

—Newsday

"[A] luminous study of love and loss." *—Publishers Weekly*

"Day-to-day details are often transformed by beautiful or cutting verse." *—Out*

"A wonderfully written book . . . a work of humility."

—Hartford Courant

"With a poet's precise economy of language, Doty meditates on his relationship with his dying lover. . . . He has a gift for coaxing insight from the seemingly commonplace." *—The Nation*

"Doty's is that rare book about death and dying that reading it makes us glad to be alive in this world and able to love someone, even while knowing that someday we will lose them."

—*Asheville Citizen-Times*

"A heart, a soul sing of love and loss in this beautifully and powerfully wrought remembrance given us by one of our finest poets. Mark Doty's lyrical, deeply affecting voice, so poised and compelling in his poems, sustains itself wonderfully over the long, brave haul of this venture of his into prose. Always he is warm, honest, generous—a writer with so very much to tell us, teach us, give to us."

— Robert Coles

"Mark Doty understands the rhythms of language, riding them like a gull on the wind. *Heaven's Coast* is just that graceful, but also rich in sturdy earthbound wisdom. It broke my heart, then somehow made it stronger."

—Armistead Maupin

"*Heaven's Coast* is a radiant and profound work of art. Reading it was a transforming experience, so much so that I'm afraid I may need months or years to fully comprehend what it's meant to me. For now, all I can say is that I'm astonished by Mark Doty's command not only of language but of the shifting, nearly inchoate mortal conditions language seeks to illuminate. During the time I was reading *Heaven's Coast* I found myself wanting to call everyone I knew and say, 'Stop whatever you're doing and read this book.' I suspect it will prove to be an enduring accomplishment."

— Michael Cunningham

HEAVEN'S
COAST

Books by Mark Doty

Turtle, Swan 1987

Bethlehem in Broad Daylight 1991

My Alexandria 1993

Atlantis 1995

WALLY ROBERTS AND MARK DOTY, 1992

HEAVEN'S COAST

a memoir

MARK DOTY

HarperPerennial

A Division of HarperCollins*Publishers*

Grateful acknowledgment is made to HarperCollins Publishers for permission to use extracts of poems from *The Only World* by Lynda Hull, copyright © 1995 by The Estate of Lynda Hull.

Grateful acknowledgment is made to HarperCollins Publishers for permission to use an extract from *The Book of Job* by Stephen Mitchell, copyright © 1979 by Stephen Mitchell. Revised edition copyright © 1987 by Stephen Mitchell.

Portions of this book appeared, in earlier versions, in *Provincetown Arts* and *The Yale Review*, and in *Wrestling with the Angel: Gay Men Write About Faith and Religion* (Riverhead Books, 1995) and *In the Company of My Solitude: New Writing from the AIDS Pandemic* (Persea Books, 1995).

A hardcover edition of this book was published in 1996 by HarperCollins Publishers.

HarperCollins books may be purchased for educational, business, or sales promotional use. For information please write: Special Markets Department, HarperCollins Publishers, Inc., 10 East 53rd Street, New York, NY 10022.

First HarperPerennial edition published 1997.

Designed by Caitlin Daniels

ISBN 0-06-092805-0 (pbk.)

99 00 01 ❖/RRD 10 9 8 7 6 5 4

CONTENTS

PREFACE

This book was written in the flux of change; I wrote it not from a single still point but in the forward momentum of a current of grief. I wanted to allow for shifts in my perspective as time moved forward, as what we think of as healing began. What is healing, but a shift in perspective?

Almost eighteen months after Wally died, I know a little differently. I see a little more broadly than the man who wrote these pages, adrift in the sea-swirl of shock and loss. But something's gained by allowing the voice of those hours, the long days of new mourning, to have its say. In a way I know less now, too. The Lakota Sioux say that when nature gives one a burden, one's also given a gift. Loss brought with it a species of vision, an inwardness which was the gift of a terrible time — nearly unbearable, but bracingly real. I felt I was breathing some strange new air, the dizzy-making oxygen of an unfamiliar altitude. The long days of Wally's illness were a period of increasing tension, everything in the world closing down to one little point of dread, a fear assuaged only by the lightness and acceptance of his spirit. When he died, all that tension began to uncoil in me. My perception opened again, but where was I then? Some vague lunar place, a winter shore lit only by starlight, an icy marsh. In memory, what I did most of that year was tramp and tramp, in freezing salt places, cold expanses of beach over which the clouds moved in great luminous shrouds. I am glad I do not have to live, now, in quite the porous state these pages try to capture, but I am lucky to have been there, and to have been able to make some record, however halting, of those days.

A host of people helped to carry Wally and me through the last part of his life; they enabled us to live well, and their assistance helped us to face those days together with dignity. I am especially grateful to Darren Otto, a host of loving and strong home health aides, the Provincetown AIDS Support Group, and the Family Care Program of Cape Cod Hospital.

I could not have written this book, nor indeed made it through the days described here, without the help of real and invaluable friends. Michael Carter and Rena Blauner have been essential to me, irreplaceable spirits and close readers; my friend and editor Robert Jones trusted me, believed in this book, and read it with enormous responsiveness and acuity. Rudy Kikel, Marie Howe, and Brian Bouldrey helped me to get started. Amy Bloom, Martha Christina, Richard McCann, and Maggie Valentine read closely and deeply, and offered wise suggestions. Alfred Corn, Kathryn Davis, Margaret Erhart, and Nancy Lagomarsino generously allowed me to incorporate portions of their letters here. Finally, Paul Lisicky not only helped with the book, but helped me remember just how good it is to live.

I am grateful for extraordinary support from the Ingram Merrill Foundation, the National Endowment for the Arts, the John Simon Guggenheim Foundation, and the Mrs. Giles R. Whiting Foundation. My gratitude, as well, to the Rockefeller Foundation's Bellagio Center, for a residency in Italy which enabled me to finish the volume.

This book is for every man and woman living with AIDS, for every man and woman gone, for anyone who's loved them.

HEAVEN'S
COAST

Prologue: Is There a Future? April 1993

~~~

In 1989, not long after my partner Wally and I took the HIV test, the pain in my back—which had been a chronic, low-level problem—became acute. I went to a chiropractor I'd seen before, a rough-and-tumble kind of guy with a strange, cluttered little office on a shady part of Main Street in the Vermont town where we lived then. Dr. Crack, as I thought of him, was his own secretary, and furnished his office with all manner of cast-offs and inspirational posters, along with many implements of vague and mysterious use. In general, he did not inspire confidence. He snapped me around with considerable force, and though I felt much better after being treated by him, I also felt a mounting sense of nervousness about the degree of force he used. One day the crack my neck made as he whipped it into place was so loud that I resolved to see the new-age doctor my friends had spoken so highly of instead. She had cured one friend of a nervous tic in the eye simply by massaging a spot on her spine; others swore by her gentler style of manipulation.

On my first visit, as I lay on my stomach in a room full of ferns and charts marking the locations of chakras and pressure points, she touched one vertebra which throbbed, seemed almost to ring, painfully, like a struck tuning fork. I felt she'd touched the very center of the pain in my sacrum, the weak spot where my ache originated. When I told her this, she said that the particular vertebra she was touching represented "faith in the future."

Under her tentative touches—delivered with less pressure than one would use to push an elevator button—my back simply got worse, but her diagnosis was so penetratingly accurate that I never forgot it. After a while, I went back to Dr. Crack, and my back got better, but not the rupture in my faith.

The test results had come back negative for me, positive for Wally, but it didn't seem to matter so much which of us carried the antibodies for the virus. We'd been together eight years; we'd surrounded ourselves with a house and animals and garden, tokens of permanency; our continuance was assumed, an essential aspect of life. That we would continue to be, and to be together, had about it the unquestioned nature of a given, the tacit starting point from which the rest of our living proceeded. The news was as devastating as if I'd been told I was positive myself. In retrospect, I think of two different metaphors for the way it affected me.

The virus seemed to me, first, like a kind of solvent which dissolved the future, our future, a little at a time. It was like a dark stain, a floating, inky transparency hovering over Wally's body, and its intention was to erase the time ahead of us, to make that time, each day, a little smaller.

And then I thought of us as standing on a kind of sandbar, the present a narrow strip of land which had seemed, previously, enormous, without any clear limits. Oh, there was a limit out there, somewhere, of course, but not anywhere in sight. But the virus was a kind of chill, violent current, one which was eroding, at who knew what speed, the ground upon which we stood. If you watched, you could see the edges crumbling.

Four years have passed. For two of them, we lived with the knowledge of Wally's immune status, though he was blessedly asymptomatic; for the last two years, we have lived with AIDS.

His has not been the now-typical pattern of dizzying descents into opportunistic infections followed by recoveries.

Instead, he's suffered a gradual, steady decline, an increasing weakness which, a few months ago, took a sharp turn for the worse. He is more-or-less confined to bed now, with a few forays up and out in his wheelchair; he is physically quite weak, though alert and responsive, and every day I am grateful he's with me, though I will admit that I also rail and struggle against the limitations his health places upon us. As he is less capable, less present, I do battle with my own sense of loss at the same time as I try not to let the present disappear under the grief of those disappearances, and the anticipatory grief of a future disappearance.

And I struggle, as well, with the way the last four years have forced me to rethink my sense of the nature of the future.

I no longer think of AIDS as a solvent, but perhaps rather as a kind of intensifier, something which makes things more firmly, deeply themselves. Is this true of all terminal illness, that it intensifies the degree of what already is? Watching Wally, watching friends who were either sick themselves or giving care to those who were, I saw that they simply became more generous or terrified, more cranky or afraid, more doubtful or more trusting, more contemplative or more in flight. As individual and unpredictable as this illness seems to be, the one thing I found I could say with certainty was this: AIDS makes things more intensely what they already are. Eventually I understood that this truism then must apply to me, as well, and, of course, it applied to my anxiety about the future.

Because the truth was I'd *never* really believed in a future, always had trouble imagining ongoingness, a place in the unfolding chain of things. I was raised on apocalypse. My grandmother—whose Tennessee fundamentalism reduced not a jot her generosity or spiritual grace—used to read me passages from the Book of Revelation and talk about the immanence of the Last Days. The hymns we sang figured this world as a veil of appearances, and sermons in church characterized the human world as a flimsy screen behind which the world's real actors enacted the struggles and dramas of a loftier realm.

Not struggles, exactly, since the outcome was foreknown: the lake of fire and the fiery pit, the eternal chorus of the saved — but dramatic in the sense of scale, or scope. How large and mighty was the music of our salvation!

When the Hog Farm commune came to my town in an old school bus painted in Day-Glo colors swirled like a Tibetan mandala, the people who came tumbling out into the park had about them the aura of a new world. Their patchouli and bells and handmade sandals were only the outward signs of a new point of view. We'd see things more clearly, with the doors of perception cleansed; fresh vision would yield new harmony, transformation. I was an adolescent, quickly outgrowing religion when this new sense of the apocalyptic replaced it with the late sixties' faith in the immanence of Revolution, a belief that was not without its own religious tinge and implication. Everything promised that the world could not stay the same; the foundations of order were quavering, both the orders of the social arena and of consciousness itself. I couldn't articulate much about the nature of the future I felt was in the offing, but I could feel it in the drift of sitar music across a downtown sidewalk, late summer afternoons, and in the pages of our local "underground" newspaper, *The Oracle*, with its sinuous letterhead as richly complicated as the twining smoke of the Nepalese rope incense I used to burn. I was sure that certain sorts of preparation were ridiculously beside the point. Imagine buying, say, life insurance, or investing in a retirement plan, when the world as we'd always known it was burning?

One sort of apocalyptic scenario has replaced another: endings ecological or nuclear, scenarios of depleted ozone or global starvation, or, finally, epidemic. All my life I've lived with a future which constantly diminishes, but never vanishes.

Apocalypse is played out now on a personal scale; it is not in the sky above us, but in our bed.

In the museums we used to visit on family vacations when I was a kid, I used to love those rooms which displayed collections of minerals in a kind of closet or chamber which would, at the push of a button, darken. Then ultraviolet lights would begin to glow and the minerals would seem to come alive, new colors, new possibilities and architectures revealed. Plain stones became fantastic, "futuristic"—a strange word which suggests, accurately, that these colors had something of the world to come about them. Of course there wasn't any black light in the center of the earth, in the caves where they were quarried; how strange that these stones should have to be brought here, bathed with this unnatural light in order for their transcendent characters to emerge. Irradiation revealed a secret aspect of the world.

Imagine illness as that light: demanding, torturous, punitive, it nonetheless reveals more of what things are. A certain glow of being appears. I think this is what is meant when we speculate that death is what makes love possible. Not that things need to be able to die in order for us to love them, but that things need to die in order for us to know *what they are*. Could we really know anything that wasn't transient, not becoming more itself in the strange, unearthly light of dying? The button pushed, the stones shine, all mystery and beauty, implacable, fierce, austere.

Will there be a moment when you will die to me?

Of course you will cease to breathe, sometime; probably you will cease to breathe before I do, though there's no way to know this, really. But your being, your being-in-me, will last as long as I do, won't it? There's a poem of Tess Gallagher's about the aftermath of her husband's death, one called "Now That I Am Never Alone." Of course.

Is my future, then, remembering you? Inscribing the name, carrying the memory? Remembering is the work of the living, and the collective project of memory is enormous; it involves the weight of all our dead, the ones we have known ourselves and the ones we know only from stories. It is necessary to recall not just names but also faces, anecdotes, incidents, gestures, tics, nuances, those particular human attributes that distinguish us as individuals. A name, after all, stripped of contexts, is only a name. Lists of them, like the ones read at ceremonies around the Quilt, remind us of enormity, scale, the legions of the dead. Details, stories, remind us of the particular loved body and being of X and Y or—say it—W.

Even photos, after a while, lend themselves to speculation. When I was a child we had a big metal fruitcake tin, the kind printed with golden trellises and scrolls, full of family photos. Many of them were inherited, and even though there were names penned on the back—Alice, Lavinia, Mary—over time an increasing number of them went unrecognized, anyone who could identify them gone. Although we had names for them, and faces, they had lost their particular humanness when we no longer had their stories.

Let this, then, be one more inscription, one version of my and Wally's story. We have been together a dozen years, fused in a partnership that felt, after a while, elemental, like bedrock. If I write about it as if it's already done, that's because so much of it *is*—W. is less present, each week spends more time asleep, and is less and less capable of involvement in the stuff of mutual life. We're pushed into a different kind of relation. (Those sentences were true when I wrote them, but this week he's much more alert—still unable to walk but ready to get out of the house, ready to shop for new shoes and magazines. It's only Wednesday and this week we have already been out three times, me pushing the wheelchair to town, to restaurants where we can sit outside, along the rough street and rougher sidewalk. We are laughing a lot, full of the pleasures of reprieve. Nothing about who we are together has changed. We have a present again.)

"Look, I am living," Rilke writes in the *Duino Elegies*. "On what? Neither childhood nor future/ grows any smaller." Like most great poems, I guess, this is both true and not true. Certainly the past is accomplished, complete; what has been is over and nothing can change it now, nothing can change except our perspectives, the way we interpret or understand. And the future *is* infinite, if not our personal fates then that great flux of matter and spirit which goes on, in which we will in some way participate—as energy if not as individuals.

Mourning contracts the eye like a camera lens in strong light; the aperture of the soul shrinks to a tiny pinpoint which admits only grief. The past *feels* diminished when the future seems to shrink. When I am overcome—as I am, about once a week—by the prospect of losing my lover, I can't see any kind of ongoingness; my vision becomes one-pointed, like looking through the wrong end of a telescope, and the world seems smaller, further away, sad, a difficult place which no one would much want to inhabit.

The grief which sweeps over me is the grief of anticipation. It is a grief in expectation of grief, and it carries with it a certain degree of guilt, since one feels that what one really *should* be doing is enjoying the moment, being together *now* while it is possible to do so, rather than giving in to some gloomy sense of incipient loss. And while most of the time I can maintain that sensibility—the preciousness of the present, the importance of not projecting too far ahead, not trying to feel my way blindly toward the future—I can't sustain it all the time. The future's an absence, a dark space up ahead like the socket of a pulled tooth. I can't quite stay away from it, hard as I may try. The space opened up in the future insists on being filled with *something*: attention, tears, imagination, longing.

The more one tries to live in the present, it seems, the more one learns the inseparability of time, the artifice of our construction of the trinity of experience; yesterday, today, tomorrow meld into one another, blur in and out. We move between them at the speed of memory or of anticipation. Trying to remain in the moment is like living in three dimensions, in sheerly physical space; the mind doesn't seem to be whole unless it also occupies the dimension of time, which grants to things their depth and complexity, the inherent dignity and drama of their histories, the tragedy of their possibilities. What then can it mean to "be here now"? That discipline of paying attention to things-as-they-are in the present seems simply to reveal the way the nature of each thing is anchored to time's passage, cannot exist outside of time.

Take, for instance, the salt marsh where I walk near Wood End Light, out beyond Herring Cove Beach. That marsh is perhaps my favorite place in the world; it feels inexhaustible to me, in all the contradictions which it yokes so gracefully within its own being. It is both austere and lush, wet and dry, constant and ceaselessly changing, secretive and open. I have never, in years of walks, grown weary of looking at it, perhaps because there is no single thing which constitutes "it"; the marsh is a whole shifting confluence of aspects. At low tide it's entirely dry, a Sahara of patterned sand and the tough green knots of sea lavender, beach grass around the edges of the beds of the tidal rivers gleaming as it bends and catches light along the straps of its leaves. As the tide mounts, twice a day, this desert disappears beneath the flood. It is a continuous apocalypse; Sahara becomes sea becomes sand again, in a theater of furious mutability.

Its lesson—or at least the lesson I draw from it today, since this teacher's so vast and has so many possibilities hidden in its repertoire—is that what one can *see* is the present, the dimension of landscape which is in front of us now. But now is shaped by the past, backed by it, as it were, the way the glass of a mirror is backed by silver; it's what lies behind the present that gives it color and sheen. And now is always giving way, always becoming. It is this progress into the future which gives things the dynamic dimension of forwardness they could not have were they composed solely of a past and a present. If past and present are the glass and its silver backing, then future is what is coming-to-be in the mirror, the image that presents itself, intrudes into the frame. I mix my metaphors with abandon, because I am talking near the edge of the unsayable, at the difficult intersection of what I can feel but barely say.

Wally is in my body; my body is in this text; this text is light on my computer screen, electronic impulse, soon to be print, soon to be in the reader's body, yours—remembered or forgotten, picked up or set aside, it nonetheless acquires a strange kind of physical permanence, a persistence. My friend Billy, hearing about what I'm writing, says, "long-term survivors, you've got to address long-term survivors." It's a message of hope he wants; hope is perhaps simply a stance toward the world, finally, a stance of participation, or inseparability. That which cannot be separated cannot perish. The world has one long-term survivor, which is the world.

This is how I see through the wider end of the telescope, when my perspective's wide enough to see us as part of this vast interchange of being, not its center. On other days, the water of grief—deep, impenetrable, dark, cold—pours over everything and I am lightless, unseeing.

Whether or not I have faith in the future, whether there is a personal future for Wally or whether I am all there will be of us (and then those who might read or remember me later all there will be of me)—well, whatever I believe today, whatever my marsh and my study convince me of, the future does go on without us. The world doesn't need us to continue, although it does need us to attend, to study, to name. We are elements of the world's consciousness of itself, and thus we are necessary: replaceable and irreplaceable at once. Someone will take our places, but then again there will never be anyone like us, no one who will see quite this way; we are a sudden flowering of seeing, among the millions of such blossomings. Like the innumerable tiny stars on the branching stalk of the sea lavender; it takes how many, a thousand, to construct this violet sheen, this little shaking cloud of flowers?

"Eternity," Blake said, "is in love with the productions of time." Perhaps, in fact, eternity inheres in the things that time makes; perhaps that's all of eternity we'll know: the wave, the flower, the repeated endless glimmerings and departures of tides. My error, which perhaps really *does* express itself in that pain in the fifth vertebra, lies in thinking the future's something we can believe or disbelieve, trust or doubt. It's the element we breathe. Our position in time—ungraspable thing!—is the element in which we move. Our apocalypse is daily, but so is our persistence.

Part One

COASTAL
STUDIES

Sweet Chariot: February 1994

I grew up in two religions.

The first one—comforting, strange, rigorous, in its way—was comprised of an astonishing and lovely set of images. It was a religion given to me primarily by my grandmother, whose East Tennessee faith had the kind of solidity and rock-depth upon which Jesus must have intended to found His church. *She* was Peter's rock, unshakable, holding us all up—or at least holding me up; I was too small to have much of a sense of what she meant to my parents or to her husband, my cantankerous and difficult grandfather who outlived her by twenty years. My memories of her are very particular ones: a day out behind our house when she and I picked dandelion and poke greens, sunlight filtering through the thin flowered rayon dress she wore—this would have been 1957 or '58—and she showed me the right leaves to pick for the greens she'd boil with fatback to serve with the chicken she plucked and set to roast in a black graniteware pan sparked with a whole firmament of stars. In that house, where she and my grandfather lived with us, their room was a secret source of meaning and depth. I didn't like him much but I liked his things: a drawer full of beautiful useless old fountain pens with marbled cases, cigar boxes full of rubber bands, stuff saved for the day it would surely be needed. I loved her with all my heart, and everything that was hers: the green rocking chair, a fruitcake tin filled with swirled peppermint candies, the Bible with the words of Jesus printed in red, like holidays on a calendar. She would set me up on her lap and, rocking all the while, read Bible verses to me. I'm not sure if I remember especially her readings from Revelation or if it simply feels to me now, whenever I hear someone mention a phrase like "last days" or "apocalypse," that the scent of her—lavender, peppermint, and clean old dresses—and the texture of her clothes, the Bible's leatherette cover and onionskin pages, are forever commingled with those words; some essence of her imbues them. It was she who presented me with my first religion, which was the religion of images, and they were given to me in Bible verses and in the songs we sang on the porch swing, summer nights: the sweet chariot coming to carry us home, the moon turning to blood, the angels sounding the trump so that all the dead would clap hands and arise, the thin veil of this world—thin as her sprig-scattered skirt!—parting at last and opening into a world we need not fear, though it would be awesome, a world made true and just and bright and eternally resonant as the songs we sang.

I loved the word *chariot*. I couldn't sing it without thinking of the cherries in my uncle's orchard, which I'd seen once, and where my father had lifted me up into the branches so that I could pick the half-ripe fruit. Sweet chariot, sweet cherries, gold and red and green, a kind of glowing flush like heat on the skin of the little fruit, which was smooth and cleft and satisfying on the tongue as the word: *chariot*. This was the way the images invited us to dream into them.

I don't think I had any awareness of the second religion, the codes of explanation and prohibition, until after her death. I was five. She died of a heart attack, throwing her bedroom window open, in winter, and gasping for air. I remember most vividly being wrapped in a quilt, one she made, I imagine. I watched TV very early in the morning, at an hour when I wasn't usually awake, and saw the minister come in his black jacket and collar, his odd flowery scent. And then gladiolas around her coffin, and again that sweet essence of peppermint and lavender, and little ribbons decorating the flowers on her grave. I dreamed that she came to see me, in the night, and stood beside a cane chair in a circle of lamplight to speak to me—very softly and intimately and comfortingly, though I haven't any memory at all of what she said.

My understanding of a more worldly religion began after that. One Sunday there was a sermon especially for children— I believe this was in a Presbyterian church in Nashville, or perhaps in Memphis—instead of the usual Sunday School Bible stories accompanied by big colored pictures. (What were they? I want to say chromolithographs, or engravings, perhaps because the pictures and their sense of the world, an ancient and quaint exoticism they portrayed, seem so firmly of the nineteenth century.) This Sunday, no "Baby Moses in the Bulrushes" or "Joseph in His Coat of Many Colors." Instead, the minister told us a story about the terrible dangers of desire.

A little girl's mother had baked a particularly beautiful pie, and set it on the dining table to cool, saying to her daughter, "Make sure that you do not touch this pie." The girl thought about this, and tried not to touch the impossibly attractive thing. But after a time, overcome by her longing, she simply could not resist anymore, and she decided that if she snitched—that was the word he used, *snitched* (a particularly pinched, ratlike little word, it seems to me now, full of disdain and pettiness)—just one little piece it would be all right. So she did, taking the little bit of pie into the closet and eating it in the dark where no one could see her. The morsel eaten, she was still filled with hunger; the pie was so good, she wanted it so badly. So she would snitch just one more piece, and eat it in the dark surrounded by the comforting wool of her parents' coats. But, of course, that didn't satisfy her either; once a contract with appetite had been entered into, there wasn't any turning back. And standing in the dark, her hands and lips covered with the evidence of her need, the little girl felt, suddenly, seen. She was watched and she knew it, and so she turned her face upward into the dark from which that sense of witness came, and there, floating above her, was the eye of God: enormous, missing nothing, utterly implacable.

My parents told me that when we came home after this sermon, I hid under my bed and wouldn't come out. I don't recall that now, but I do remember inventing a new game, which I used to play alone, since my sister was ten years older and I might as well have been an only child. We lived that year in a big old farmhouse on a horse farm we rented. The horses used to wander on their own business—nameless, cared for by others. In my new game I marked off some portion of the yard by the abandoned chicken coop and named it Hell, and I'd play devil, racing about the perimeter with my pitchfork, poking at souls, meting out punishments, keeping them in line. With a girl who lived down our road I'd play a game in which we took turns dying and going to heaven, which I imagined as a kind of garden with a maze, a rose garden, where I would meet a blond and milk-pale Jesus. *I come to the garden alone, while the dew is still on the roses . . .* But that game, which was soon forbidden to us by a relative who said, "You mustn't play that, it might come true," was a game of images, of peace and stillness. My game of Hell was an enactment of energy and ferocity, of power and defiance. I think I have responded to the religion of prohibition in this way ever since.

Perhaps if my grandmother had lived, and if we'd stayed in Tennessee, my two religions would have merged, and I would have grown away from the images I was originally given, or felt oppressed by them. But because I was split off from that world, the landscape of my childhood and of the songs seems permanent to me, sealed, untouchable, a mythic landscape of hymns, with their rivers and flowers, their cherry trees and blood and moons. We moved away from my parents' families, on to suburbs in Arizona and Southern California and Florida, and into a succession of increasingly polite Protestant churches which finally evaporated into a bland social gesture which was easily set aside. My mother, late in her life, found a religion of imagery again in an Anglican church so high and so influenced by the architecture and pageantry of Mexican Catholicism as to be a kind of spiritual theater. I came, after a while, to seek the images of comfort and challenge and transformation in art. My mother, with her love of painting and music and beauty, had helped me to look there, but I think I understood intuitively that there was no sustenance for me in the religion of explanation and prohibition.

The explanations were never good ones—the world as trial by fire, proving ground to earn God's love or His forgiveness for having been human—and it was apparent to me even at an early age that the notion that anyone around me actually *understood* God's will or could articulate it was patently ridiculous. There's a wonderful line in Charles Finney's quirky book, *The Circus of Dr. Lao*, which I read as a kid, an Americanized version of a speech of Hamlet's: "There are more things in heaven and earth, madam, than even a lifetime of experience in Abalone, Arizona, could avail you of."

The prohibitions were worse than the explanations. They suggested that the divinity had constructed the earth as a kind of spiritual minefield, a Chutes and Ladders game of snares, traps, and seductions, all of them fueled by the engines of our longing; the flames of hell were stoked by human heats. As if desire were our enemy, instead of the ineradicable force that binds us to the world.

I cannot be queer in church, though I've tried, and though I live now in a place where this seems to be perfectly possible for a great many people. Here in Provincetown we have a wonderful Unitarian church, with a congregation largely gay and lesbian, and it pains me a bit to have to admit that when I have gone to services there I have been utterly, hopelessly bored. There's something about the absence of imagery, an oddly flaccid quality of neutrality in the language of worship. I long for a kind of spiritual intensity, a passion, though I can certainly see all the errors and horrors spiritual passions have wrought. I don't know what I want in a church, finally; I think the truth is that I *don't* want a church. My friend Phil has sweetly and politely informed me that it's a spiritual experience for him to be in the company of his fellows, worshiping together at the U.U., and that my resistance to it is really a sort of aesthetic snobbery, a resistance to its public language and marriage of spirituality and social life. I don't want to judge anyone's way of finding a soulful commonality, but nothing puts me less in mind of ultimate things than the friendly meetings held within my local church's square-boned New England architecture and flourishes of trompe l'oeil.

Perhaps my discomfort has to do, still, with issues of desire. Wind, glimmering watery horizon and sun, the watchful seals and shimmered flurries of snow seem to me to have far more to do with the life of my spirit. And there is somehow in the grand scale of dune and marsh and sea room for all of human longing, placed firmly in context by the larger world: small, our flames are, though to us raging, essential. There is something so *polite* about these Sunday gatherings of tolerant Unitarians that I feel like longing and need must be set aside. Isn't the part of us that desires, that loves, that longs for encounter and connection — physical and psychic and every other way — also the part of us that knows something about God? The divine, in this world, is all dressed up in mortal clothes, and longing and mortality are so profoundly intertwined as to be, finally, entirely inseparable.

My lover of twelve years died just last month. It astonishes me to write that sentence. It astonishes me that I am writing at all; I have not, till now, and I didn't know when the ability to focus might come back to me. I haven't yet been able to read, and there are many other things I haven't even begun to approach, in the face of this still unbelievable absence. I will be sorting out and naming the things I learned from Wally for years to come, probably for the rest of my life, but here is one thing I know now.

All the last year of Wally's life, he didn't stop wanting. He was unable to walk, since some kind of insidious viral infection which his useless doctors didn't seem to know the first thing about gradually took away his ability to control his body. But he wasn't ever one of those people who let go. Oh, he did, in the sense of accepting what was happening to him, in the sense of not grasping onto what he couldn't have, but he lived firmly in his desires. From the bed where he lived all that year he'd look out onto the street at anything in pants walking by and be fully, appreciatively *interested*. I never for a minute felt hurt by this or left out; it wasn't about me. It was about Wally's way of loving the world. I think in his situation I would have been consumed by frustration and a sense of thwarted desire, but he wasn't. Because his desire wasn't about possession, and his inability to fulfill it wasn't an issue; it was to be in a state of wanting, to be still desiring beauty and grace and sexiness and joy. It was the wanting itself that mattered.

A couple of months before Wally died we heard about a couple in the city, one of whom was ill, who needed to give up their little dog, since they felt they couldn't take care of him.

Wally talked and talked about this until it became clear that what he really wanted was for Dino to come to live with us. We already had a dog, Arden, a calm black retriever with a meditative, scholarly disposition, but Wally had his heart set on a new dog who'd sleep next to him and lick his face.

The day that I went to Manhattan to pick up Dino, Jimi and Tony changed their minds; they weren't ready to let him go. Wally was so disappointed that I went to the animal shelter with the intention of finding a small, cuddly dog who'd fit the bill.

What I found was a young golden retriever with enormous energy, a huge tongue, and a phenomenal spirit of pleasure and enjoyment. He didn't just lick Wally's face, he bathed his head, and Wally would scrinch up his face and then grin as though he'd been given the earth's brightest treasure.

Sometimes late at night he'd tell me about other animals he wanted to adopt: lizards, a talking bird, some fish, a little rat.

I don't know many men who would want a new dog, a new pact with domestic life, with responsibility, with caring for the abandoned, in the final weeks of their lives. There's a Polaroid I took of Wally with golden Beau curled up and sleeping in our rented hospital bed beside him. He could barely use his hands then—our friend Darren and I would feed him, and give him drinks to sip through a straw—but he's reaching over with his beautiful hardly functional hand to stroke Beau's neck. That is how I will always see my love: reaching toward a world he cannot hold and loving it no less, not a stroke less.

Desire I think has less to do with possession than with participation, the will to involve oneself in the body of the world, in the principle of things expressing itself in splendid specificity, a handful of images: a lover's irreplaceable body, the roil and shimmer of sea overshot with sunlight, a handful of cherries, the texture and weight of a word. The word that seems most apt is *partake*; it comes from Middle English, literally from the notion of being a part-taker, one who participates. We can say we take a part *of* something but we may just as accurately say we take part *in* something; we are implicated in another being, which is always the beginning of wisdom, isn't it—that involvement which enlarges us, which engages the heart, which takes us out of the routine limitations of self?

The codes and laws fall away, useless, foolish, finally, hollow little husks of vanity.

The images sustain.

The images allow for desire, allow room for us—even require us—to complete them, to dream our way into them. I believe with all my heart that when the chariot came for Wally, green and gold and rose, a band of angels swung wide out over the great flanks of the sea, bearing him up over the path of light the sun makes on the face of the waters.

I believe my love is in the Jordan, which is deep and wide and welcoming, though it scours us oh so deeply. And when he gets to the other side, I know he will be dressed in the robes of comfort and gladness, his forehead anointed with spices, and he will sing—joyful—into the future, and back toward the darkness of this world.

Cold Dark Deep and Absolutely Clear

A week and a few days after Wally died, my friend Michael and I stood on the shore at Hatch's Harbor, which is just where Cape Cod Bay and the Atlantic intersect in a roiling line of watery activity called the Race. At Hatch's Harbor the sky always seems enormous, the horizontals of dune and marsh and shoreline particularly vast and dazzling. It is especially pristine because the place isn't easy to reach, accessible as it is only after a long walk through a fire road in the dunes, along a dike built across a huge stretch of marsh, and then round the sandy tideflats skirting a lighthouse whose foghorn tends to sound in all weathers, even the brightest sunlight. The once-manned house is operated by remote control now, the switch apparently off in Connecticut someplace.

In the water that afternoon I saw first one oddly shaped dark form, a sort of mound a few feet from the foaming edge line. It was a seal in the shallow surf, floating on his or her side, eyeing us curiously. My two dogs were with us; I think seals seem to sense them as distant but unlikely cousins, and want to study them. In a moment the watcher submerged, and then rose again a few yards away, a wet black marble bust, the perfectly erect head held with marked dignity and poise. It was joined shortly by another pair of heads. And then another pair, and then another rolling on her side, enjoying the wave of her body and the quick flip of tail. And then there were dozens of watchers, looking toward us with as much curiosity and surprise as we brought to our study of them. The alien world of the water might as well have been, for me, the other world of the spirit; I felt I was looking into the realm of the dead, which I could not enter or know very much about. I thought of Elizabeth Bishop's poem, "At the Fishhouses," in which she describes the seawater of the Nova Scotian coast as

> *Cold dark deep and absolutely clear,*
> *element bearable to no mortal,*
> *to fish and to seals . . .*

Miss Bishop's marine creatures endure what no other mortals can; they seem more like spirits than living things. This other world was both clear and impenetrable, visible and unknowable. Although dozens of likable faces looked back at me, any one of which might almost have been his.

So began a chain of encounters with seals.

Seals are coastal creatures, citizens of two elements. Though most at ease in the water—where gravity's unmoored and their bodies arc and tumble freely, somersaulting and floating on their sides, supported by the movement of just one flipper, the flick of a tail—they bring some of that undulance with them to land, on the rare occasions when one sees them out in the winter sun.

I have always associated seals with Wally, through a chain of private associations with the sort of complexity and irrationality that characterizes the way a poetic image twists together a clutch of meanings, fibers spun into a single, complex yarn, various in texture, glinting with strands of separate and intermingling color. Something in the handsome cast of his head, the depth and clarity of his brown eyes. Something about playfulness and a freedom of spirit—which, however obscured by circumstance or by self-doubt—could also break through unclouded, pure. There's a film called *I've Heard the Mermaids Singing* in which the heroine fantasizes a kind of erotic freedom underwater, an unfettered aquatic *pas de deux* with another woman, which she imagines to the music of Delibes, a ravishing duet from *Lakmé* called "Dôme Epais." This aria is an invitation—one woman inviting another to stroll along an Indian river and pick jasmine —and it is pure fluidity, the unmistakable text of a kind of joy, the pleasure of swimming, of free movement, of floating in an untroubled suspension. Wally loved that music, and I imagine that in part this was because he was not, in his body, a comfortable swimmer, though he longed to be; in his spirit was a latent seal.

Seals bear a noticeable kinship to dogs, which Wally loved, and with which he felt a deep and immediate connection. "You like dogs," a tea-leaf reader in a Boston tearoom once told him, "and dogs like you."

I've just read an Inuit tale, which a friend has sent me, the story of a boy who left his parents behind to live with the seals, and in their camps at the bottom of the sea (where they gather around their fires!) heard their tales of ancient days and times to come.

And I've been thinking of Bishop's seal, who floats, in her poem, in an element like knowledge, and likes to listen to her renditions of Baptist hymns.

And then there's the notion of the seal as merman, of the creature which embodies the two worlds, unlike us, who live firmly in one medium, despite our brief visits to the other. To be of the coast, a mer-being, is to partake of the liminal, that watery zone of possibility where one thing becomes another, where the rules of one world are suspended as we enter into the next. The coast is the shifting zone of change and transformation. A coast is not a line really but a borderland, site of a continual conversation between elements which transforms both.

Movements between the worlds are limited, and often extraordinary. This is Ludovico Guicciardini, writing in *Description of all the Lowlands*, a seventeenth-century guide to Holland:

> They also claim that, around the year 1526, a mer-man was taken in the Frisian sea, formed in every way like the rest of us; they say that he had a beard, hair on his head and other hairs that we have, but quite setulose (that is, resembling the bristles of a pig), and harsh, and that they accus-tomed him to eating bread and other ordinary foods; they say that in the beginning the man was very wild, but that later he became gentle, though not totally tame, and he was mute. He lived for several years and finally, having once escaped the same illness, died of the plague in the year 1531.

Travelers between worlds are mute; they cannot tell us what they know. The language of the other element is untranslat-able, though here it seems that, accustomed to solid ground, the mer-creature is also susceptible to its epidemics.

The wounded seal is young and startlingly silvery in the February sun. Its injury is a small bloody line along the tip of one side of the graceful little tail, as if perhaps it's been bitten; it doesn't look terribly serious, but of course I don't know how to read their pain, their expressions. He's alone on the shore, a fact which in itself doesn't seem to bode well. Why is he no longer part of the group? When I've seen them in the water or, once, in a sunning herd on the edge of the shore, they seemed happily grouped, like a pack of dogs. Do they abandon the injured or dying, perhaps to divorce themselves from the smell of blood that marks an animal as prey? I've heard that sharks come in, this time of year, to feed on the young ones.

Beached on a low rise of sand, maybe thirty or forty feet from an outgoing tidal river, he is not pleased to see us, partic-ularly the two dogs who are full of curiosity and longing for a game. The seal raises his head and barks and makes a noise like a hiss of warning; my worry for it is mixed with wondering what those teeth are capable of. Though it seems, distinctly, young—the look on its face suggests that we'd say, were it human, this child is lost. I am busy restraining the dogs; their excited noises, and mine, rouse the seal to action. I fear that it's incapable of much movement but it awkwardly flips and starts to scoot down the rise toward the water, picking up speed. At the edge of the tidal stream it looks back to us, then slips into the water. It's no less awkward in three inches of water than it is on sand, but as soon as it reaches a foot-deep stretch of sea it's gloriously fluid, like a heron taking to air; what was compromised and lurching is suddenly capable of splendid and effortless motion.

A body that was wounded sits stranded, incapacitated. Gone into another element, that same being takes gorgeous, ready flight. I am filled, entirely, with the image of my wounded lover leaping from his body, blossoming into some welcoming, other realm. Is it that I am in that porous state of grief, a heated psychic condition in which everything becomes metaphor?

Or does the world consent, in some fashion, to offer me the particular image which imagination requires?

Metaphor is a way of knowing the world, and no less a one than other sorts of ways of gaining knowledge. Years ago, in Boston, I used to go to weekly meetings of the American Spiritualist Church—something like a Quaker meeting for psychics, or potential ones. After some meditation and singing, people would spontaneously give one another the messages they received. Many of these were incredibly detailed, elaborate pieces of perception about other people involving problems, opportunities, advice. Often the messages involved communication from the dead, who would be described to the receiver in exacting detail. I was never much good as a fledgling psychic. Where others saw clear and detailed pictures, I would perceive just a rush of images, seldom organized into anything coherent. But every once in a while I would see a sort of scene, usually a cryptic one, and feel that it related to a particular person in the group. If I told that person my images, I would usually discover that they made sense to her, even if I didn't understand them.

Could metaphoric thinking, the sort of work that artists do to apprehend their reality, be the same function of the mind, applied in a somewhat different way? My way of knowing experience is to formulate a metaphor which describes or encapsulates a particular moment; it is a way of getting at the truth. And a way of paying attention, of reading the world.

My seal said, The wounded one's gone free, gone swimming into what is familiar to no mortal.

The second seal bears no visible wound, but its face is full of distress and exhaustion; the eyes seem enormous, entirely dark, defenseless, world-weary. All of which might be construed as anthropomorphizing, but how could one look into that gaze without empathy? This seal, near the same stretch of beach, was up much higher, a week or two later, where the last stubborn snow held on in the shadow of a dune. Had an especially high tide brought it there? Did it pull itself further from the water, in order to rest on shore? This time the presence of me and my attendant animals wasn't enough to rouse the creature to return to the water; we were simply enough to cause it more pain. The younger and more aggressive of my dogs, the buoyant golden, didn't take long to figure out that the seal was feeble, a fine subject to pester. I got him on the leash, hauling him away, and resolved to call the Center for Coastal Studies as soon as I could get home to see if they couldn't effect some kind of rescue. We rounded the dunes that line the wide marsh, headed back toward the dike and the fire road and home, far enough from the seal for him to be out of the adolescent dog's mind, I thought. I let him off the leash.

But I'd miscalculated, expecting that his usual scattered attention would hold sway. The seal was too thrilling—too vulnerable—for him to forget so easily. He ran back, and I ran after him, to find him yelping madly at the creature, who was barking back and looking at me with a kind of bottomless exasperation. I leashed the dog and hauled him away again, this time keeping him on the lead until we were far away, into the marsh, a half-mile of dunes in between us and his prey.

Which did not turn out to be enough to stop him; when I made the mistake of letting him loose, he took off straight across the tops of the dunes, abandoning the curvy edge of the marsh for the shortest distance to further torment. I ran right across the dune-tops after him, my older and calmer black retriever loping behind me. When I thought I couldn't run anymore—dry-mouthed, heart pounding—I made it to the last crest of dune to find him yelping and leaping perilously close to the seal's head, both of them flashing teeth at one another.

This time the seal's face seemed to convey a kind of helplessness and desolation that cut me to the core. I wanted a way to apologize for bringing this yapping annoyance, this petty grief, into what was already clearly a deeper pain, a silent and solitary occupation. I felt as if the seal were doing some grave work and I not only couldn't help, I couldn't help but harm; I couldn't even keep my brutalizing pet from making things worse.

We left. Beau stayed on the leash at least a mile, till we were well in the middle of the dike that keeps the tide from washing away the modest ambitions of this town's airport runways. Even then, released, he thought of running back, and began to, but I was given from someplace the sudden wise impulse to run in the other direction, toward home; making a game of it convinced Beau to run after me, instead of after his own wildness. It was a moment of choosing between loyalties to different aspects of himself, and he chose domestic partnership.

The woman who answered the phone at the Center for Coastal Studies said they'd had several reports of exhausted seals beaching themselves, resting, then riding out on the next high tide when they recovered. Exhausted from what? I asked.

The work of finding food, she said. I didn't know why then, more than any other time, they'd be weary. I described the seal's look of distress and exhaustion, I said I feared it was ill. She said she didn't know if there was anyone who could get out that day and look, but perhaps there was. She took my phone number, but they didn't call.

So my attempts at helping didn't seem to. The fact of the exhausted, incapable body—the fact of illness?—was intractable. I walked or ran on the wide expanse of marsh and dune, under that huge sky, around the single immovable fact.

The wide elemental landscape seemed to heighten and emphasize the lesson. Do what you can, nothing avails; it even seemed, with my panting, excited companion, that I'd made things worse.

The dead seal is an emblem of perfect repose; it lies like a yogi who's left the body for a time, gone completely into himself, the beached body left behind in a state of great quietude, utter silence. The head's turned to the right, so that one cheek rests against the sand. The small flippers lie peacefully at either side, and the perfectly straight spine ends in the symmetrical flourish of the tail. But there is no sense of movement or fluidity in the body, despite the grace and economy of its lines. Could it be one of the same seals I've seen? I think the first one was smaller, the second larger, but who can tell, really, since animation changes the scale of things. Does everything look smaller, in the stasis of death? The seals I'd seen had such purposeful fluidity of movement—beings of water, but of fire, too, the electric liquidity of the body as it turned and flipped, the sleek head raised, the eyes full of fear or defensiveness or exhaustion or—was it?—sorrow.

The eyes. Besides life, they are all that is missing from the body, and it is this absence that finally makes the form before me seem not at rest but dead. Gulls have taken the eyes away with their insistent beaks; their footprints are stamped all around the head like ancient letters on the clay tablets of

Babylon. The law which they inscribe is that of hunger; what is soft, what is unguarded, what yields to them is what sustains those white engines, all wings and throat, which carry an appetite so large it obliterates all else. At first when I see that the eyes are gone, I think this is terrible and I imagine I will be unable to keep looking, but it isn't like that. Having been with Wally at the end of his life and then with Wally's body—form in repose—there is something new and unflinching in my looking at flesh. The spaces where the seal's eyes were. . . *sockets* doesn't seem the right word, these are little caverns of bone, reddened with a bit of blood, their depths not entirely visible. They enter deep into the sleek face, beneath the whiskers and the sweet upward curve of the mouth which one wants to read, in the living animal, as a smile. In death the mouth is relaxed, as blank and unreadable as the face of a sleeper.

Wally's body was almost unspeakably beautiful to me. All the last months of his illness, his head had been turning to the left on his pillow in a way that looked uncomfortable or rigid; people were forever straightening him out. This seemed intended to make him comfortable, but perhaps had more to do with the helper's need for a more familiar kind of alignment. In a moment, the muscles in his neck would pull again back to the left, and over time they became so stiff that it was difficult to bring his head back to center. This was something to do with whatever unnamed thing was happening in his brain; as happens after a stroke, the sides of his body behaved in different ways, not quite in concert. After he died, his head lolled to the right freely and loosely, as though the tendons could at last compensate for the time they'd been taut. There was a deep calm to his face; he seemed a kind of unfathomable, still well which opened on and down beneath the suddenly smooth surface of his skin. Which seemed polished, as it cooled, though not stiff; it was as if his body moved toward the condition of marble, but marble that's been palmed and warmed, touched until it picks up something of human heat. The heat in him lasted a long time. I loved that heat. I don't know how long I held his face and his shoulders and stroked him; as he began to cool I kept my hands on his belly, where the last of his warmth seemed to pool and concentrate. Here the fire of the body came to rest, smoldering longest, down to the last embers.

It is strange now to write this—after eight weeks—with the kind of odd detachment that language can lend us. It's as if I am watching myself—not in the plain light of film or the factual journalistic one of videotape, but as if through some kind of antique instrument, one which preserves the luster of the moment, the beauty of its peculiar light. Which seems to me now like the light of Dutch still life: rainy, northern, gentle, interior light that has itself a kind of resonance and presence. The instrument through which I look at that night (curious now that it seems instead like a deep winter afternoon, a snow-locked day at the very heart of winter, far inside the body of time) holds me at enough of a distance that I can describe what I see, that I can bear to look and to render, and yet it preserves the intimacy of those hours. That quality, their intimacy, is perhaps more firmly unassailable than any feeling I've ever known. I have never felt so far inside my life, and Wally's.

A week after he died, a book displayed in a shop window stopped me in my tracks on the sidewalk. It was a volume of reproductions of Michelangelo, and on the cover was a nude man, a figure from the Sistine ceiling, his eyes closed, his fine malleable flesh a kind of ash gray, the gray-white of porcelain clay. Looming behind the surface of his skin, especially in his face, were other colors; a blue like the hinge of a mussel shell, a coppery green. I felt as if I were seeing Wally there, the dead body held up for us to contemplate. The body dead is, in a way, our world's great secret. We see always flesh in motion, animated, disguised beneath its clothing and uniforms, its signals and armatures, its armor of codes and purposes. When do we look at the plain nude fact of the lifeless figure? Pure purposelessness—and thus, in the absence of the spirit, strangely and completely present. Never having a chance to see it, to assimilate our horror of it and go on to actually *look*, how would we know that the lifeless body is beautiful?

And empty. As empty as these spaces where a seal's eyes were, which contain now a little March sunlight, and wind off the surface of the marshy harbor, and the fluid music of shifting bird-cries counterpointing the regular exhalation of the foghorn. Which seems to be warning us, this clear day, for no earthly reason.

Wally's body was the vehicle through which I knew him. All other knowledges proceed through the body, *after* it, as it were. His was a wonderful vehicle, a beloved one, but it was not him. This fact seems so strange to me, so heavily laden, a deep vein of the incomprehensible. I find myself repeating it, trying to formulate it: we are not our bodies. The body is not me. I am my body, but I extend beyond it; just as my attention laps out, as my identity can pour out into the day. I have learned more about this, living beside water; as if the very fluidity of the landscape gets inside us, and encourages our own ability to slip our fixed bounds and feel ourselves as extended, multiple, various. Walking the shore, a warm day in March, toward that huge headland of cloud hung above and ahead, one pure white cliff above the dunelands, I become, momentarily, cloud, running dog, the raddled sonics of gull and wind and breaking wave. The wave seems a separate thing, yet it's a product, an effect, of that which is waving; gone into my elements, I am equally fluid.

The plainness of the poor abandoned body became more plain to me when I encountered Wally's ashes. The week after his death, while I anticipated receiving them, I imagined the relationship I might have to them. It had been terrible, to let the body be taken; had I not been so certain that it was not him I couldn't have done it at all, I could never have allowed it. But even though it was only his body (*only!* as if that were some minor thing) I couldn't allow him to go naked, without something of home, so I sent with him a quilt I'd made for him, years ago, a red and white geometry splashed with starlike red leaves. I am not much of a quilt-maker; my clumsy stitches were done in honor of my quilting grandmother. First I'd thought it would be a November birthday gift, then Christmas—and then eventually the thing spread across my lap and legs kept me warm all winter and into a Vermont spring while I worked on it. The stitches were rough but they were mine, every one of them. His body left wrapped in it. I didn't watch. I took the dogs down to the harbor, beneath a great wheeling starry void, the air so cold and sharp and still it seemed it might crack.

The next day I had to sign papers at the funeral home, and I began to look at different sorts of urns and vessels (everything made for this purpose seemed obscene, or banal, or at least achingly and inappropriately bland). And I began to think what it would be like to receive the ashes, the commingled evidence of body and of fabric. Which did not come and did not come; the day before the service, a week from the night of his death, the funeral director told me the ashes might not arrive, that they were "somewhere between Brockton and the post office." I wasn't very understanding; I told him I wanted him to know how much it meant to me for the ashes to be at the ceremony. I told him I expected that, and after a hesitation he said he'd have them there. "You understand," I said, "how much it means to me." I wasn't sure he did; my statement was an imperative, as though if I ordered him to recognize the magnitude of my need, he would.

In fact, the package arrived at the post office on Saturday morning, and the man from the funeral home arrived in my kitchen at ten-thirty, where a host of friends were getting ready for the day. I went by myself into the bedroom, the room where Wally died, with the plastic box and a kitchen knife to break the sealing tape. I sat with the thing on my lap, cut the binding, and slid the brown polymer coffer—coffin?—open. Sealed there in a plastic bag, strangely cold from its journey through the mails, were the remains of my darling: little pearled bits of gravel, almost like ground clay. There was a moment of piercing,

utterly abject grief—*this* is what is left—and I swear it was fol-
lowed, in less than a minute, by the clearest sense that what I
held was inert, only a material, not even alive in the way that
clay or soil is. If it was clear that Wally's body wasn't him, then
it was even more clear that this sack of—what to call it?
stone?— was even less so. The funeral directors have a word
for this stuff, one of those deeply debased late twentieth-cen-
tury words which do disservice to what they name, or rather
what they avoid. "Cremains," they call it. It makes me shudder,
aesthetically, still, but I admit I understand better the impulse.
They may want language to serve to distance us (or them) from
the fact of the body's burned residue, but the plain fact is that
there is about the material *itself* a kind of distance, a lack of
relation to what it was.

In the ancient epic of *Gilgamesh*, the oldest poem in the
world, there is a heartbreaking declaration of a beloved's
death: "The companion Enkidu is clay." A beautiful and bitter
irony, since the poem which preserves the love of Gilgamesh
and Enkidu is itself inscribed on tablets of clay. But clay has so
much more soul and presence, such a quality of heaviness and
sorrow to it, such a definite scent and taste. In that same poem,
clay is described as the food of the unmourned dead; its heavi-
ness and moisture perfectly evoke the humor of grief. But
ashes have a kind of anonymity, a quality of no-life which feels,
at last, vacant, without essence.

So I wrapped the stuff in a silk Japanese kerchief and
placed it in the brass box I'd bought. Which I carried, that
afternoon, to the service, and which I think only a few people
noticed anyway, in the rush and swell of the speaking and the
music, the spinning intensity of the day.

I had thought that the ashes would somehow be the service's
center of gravity; the place where everything deepened, open-
ing into the darkness of grief. But it wasn't like that; they
seemed a sort of afterthought, an extra. When people asked,
before that day, what I was going to do with them, I said I'd let
them go eventually, scattering them, but in truth I couldn't

really imagine it, couldn't think I'd ever really be ready. But once I encountered the lifeless sack of what once carried his life, I could think of dispersing them—thought, in fact, that perhaps then they'd be more alive, mingled again with water, soil, and stone, the rising yeasts of the world. They are going, this spring, out to Hatch's Harbor, where my seal lies, a body resolving even as I write into thousands of things which are not the body—entering into gull and tide and the unseeable tiny lives inside the sand.

I lay my hand on the seal's back. The spring sun has warmed the fur, which catches the light. I want to caress it; I want to lie down beside it. I am stopped by some nagging sense of what is clean and sanitary (voices from elementary school in my head, I guess, about touching dead animals), and perhaps more by some sense of propriety, of the dignity and unapproachability of the dead. It would not be right to pretend we could approach their bodies, that we could hold them. I held Wally's body for a long time, and I could feel as I did, as I let my hands know him for the last time, that the body was moving away from me, sinking into itself. Perhaps that is one thing the soul is: our outward attention, the energy and force in us that leaps out of the self, almost literally, into the life of the world. The spirit is that in us which participates. It moves alone, like air or fire, and it moves with the body, lifting the body's earth and water into gesture and connection, into love.

Without spirit, the body closes back into itself like an old piece of furniture, an armoire whose ancient wood is still fragrant, resinous, whose whorled grains and steady sleep refer back to the living tree. The cabinet is an elegy to the tree from which it arose, the body a brief unkeepable elegy to the quick and shining self.

Is the body a shell?

A few days ago, on the dogs' morning walk along the harbor—when I am mostly not awake—I picked up a green crab's shell. Or a portion of one; the legs were gone. The body contained within the central carapace had become a sweetmeat for a gull. What was left was this patinated green husk about the size of a soda cracker, a tiny breastplate. It resembled, in fact, something retrieved from a sunken Greek or Roman ship, lost armor pulled from preservative Mediterranean brine.

The reason I put the shell in my pocket was the color of the interior, a startling Giotto blue, a sky from heaven or Arizona rinsed and shining. At home I left the fragment on top of the refrigerator; by afternoon the blue had faded to a kind of milky lacquer, a faintly skyey mother-of-pearl. By the next day it was a pale, iridescent opal. A lovely color, but far in power and register from that initial cerulean. Imagine living surrounded by that blue, bearing in one's own body the most brilliant wash of the summer firmament.

What color is the underside of our skin?

The fragment made me think of Rilke's archaic torso of Apollo, whose head "we cannot know" since it's long since gone; in the power and presence of the fragment a whole sense of spiritual life arises. Broken, the god speaks to us more clearly.

This morning I picked up a second crab. I do not know why this one died; there is no visible sign of damage. It is about the same size as the first. But this one's intact, centered on a white saucer on my desk. Are crabs subject to rigor mortis? If so, this one has only left the world just a little while ago. Move him in any way and the legs shift into a pleasing, vaguely Chinese pattern, the weight of the—torso, is it?—balanced by the two larger claws which reiterate, even in death, their message of menace and power.

It smells of seaweed and ruin.

I will not open this shell; I am less squeamish now about the tumbled mess of the flesh, but I'm no scientist. Yet there is something I love about placing this body next to the fragment of shell whose dry lavender interior reminds me of what was there: even in the smallest chamber, a sky.

Seal Coda

I'd made the seals into metaphor, made them *my* seals. Somehow I thought that because I had given form to my experience and thus, in a way, let go of it, I wouldn't be confronted with the lifeless body again. Arrogance! Writers try to make the world into themselves, and then when they return to the outer life they expect to have changed it.

But there, half-covered by sand, lay another seal, also already eyeless. *Make all the meaning you want*, Death says, *shape it how you will. Open the limits of your thinking or feeling, make room for me, accommodate how you will, nothing touches the plain truth of me.*

Hold your grief, release it, come to terms or don't—nothing touches the fact of the lifeless body.

A week later, walking the same stretch of marsh and harbor, I began to imagine what it would be like to scatter Wally's ashes there, in that shining expanse, or in the higher wind-harried space of dunes around the gleaming lighthouse. I cried harder than I had for weeks, thinking of letting go this portion of the evidence of him. Whatever I think ashes are, the notion of flinging them into the blue and white emptiness of that place made me weep all the way from the depths of myself, sobbing from the bottom of my lungs, from some place inside the body light never reaches.

And out on the shore that day, the seals were swimming—

the first I'd seen alive and unthreatened for weeks, and the last I would see that season. They were watching me and the dogs, floating there in their untouchable pack, beautiful faces looking back at me from the other world, which I was not allowed to reach.

115 Beacon Street

Being in grief, it turns out, is not unlike being in love.

In both states, the imagination's entirely occupied with one person. The beloved dwells at the heart of the world, and becomes a Rome: the roads of feeling all lead to him, all proceed from him. Everything that touches us seems to relate back to that center; there is no other emotional life, no place outside the universe of feeling centered on its pivotal figure.

And in grief, as in love, we're porous, permeable. There is something contagious about this openness. Other people sense it and respond to us differently, since our unguardedness seems to invite them in.

I went back to Boston for a day, a few weeks after Wally died. The reasons for this trip weren't entirely clear to me when I decided to go. I knew I wanted to walk around the old neighborhood, where we first lived together, and I thought perhaps I'd take some pictures.

In grief and in love — so allied, perhaps, as to be severe gradations of *one* state? — the places and things associated with the beloved take on a shine, a numinosity which radiates out all the energy, the depth of emotion and meaning with which they have been invested.

It wasn't as if we hadn't been back often, since the years in the early eighties when we lived together and apart in a neighborhood of brownstones and brick rowhouses, iron fences, and lampposts and April's splendid flowering trees. After we moved to the suburbs south of Boston together we'd gone into the city constantly, for real life; after we moved to Vermont we'd come back often for a badly needed dose of urbanity, acceptance, and style. But in those days it wasn't as if we were returning for our past; our visits had more to do with the present, with dipping into the city we could enjoy *now*, then hurrying home, glad we didn't live there anymore, in the speed and abrasion of it.

Our trips back to the city, the last few years, had been trips to the hospital, for appointments with the doctor who was supposed to be more knowledgeable than anyone in Provincetown; the medical care in Boston had a reputation for being cutting-edge, and all the technical arsenal of the industry—MRIs, CAT scans, electronic and nuclear wonders—were located in the city's cluster of hospitals. These regular visits were maddening, in their blandness and lack of news or insight or even good human commiseration. Each time was the same: we reported symptoms, the doctor wrote them down, said something equivocal. We'd combine these unsatisfying episodes with some shopping, with dinner and a walk. But it seemed, quickly, too tiring to do anything but drive into the hospital parking garage, get to the appointment, and get home again so Wally could go back to his couch, or, later, to bed. And then there were months we no longer bothered to go, since the travel seemed a needless undertaking, an investment of energy Wally didn't have, pain and aggravation caused for no good reason. We'd see our local doctor, and he could talk to the high-powered experts on the phone.

So it had been a long time since I had walked through the original neighborhood of our union. Perhaps, before Wally died, it wouldn't have been possible to return in quite this way. Coming to the end of a novel pushes our attention back to the earliest chapters. We think back through where our characters have been, reexamine their experience in order to see its shape. As a life continues, we can't know what turns and surprises its narrative will take; we can't know what we'll be able to see in the new lights the future will provide.

Death requires a new negotiation with memory. Because the story of Wally's life came to a conclusion, at least those parts of the story in which he would take an *active* role, the experiences of our past needed to be re-seen, re-viewed. Not exactly for his story to be finished, but in service of the way his life would continue in me, braided with the story of mine. Which is going on, at this moment, on the Red Line, intermingling with the unreadable narratives of my fellow travelers passing through neighborhoods of dull-colored three-deckers into the city center. This is the train, I remember en route, Wally used to take home from work, when we were first together and he worked doing displays for a department store in Quincy, on the South Shore. And then I know where I'm going first, to the Charles Street Station, which is where I used to come to meet him, sometimes, in our first months together.

After the deep tunnels of downtown, the train rumbles up into daylight as it approaches the river, the elevated track passing a strange, narrow brownstone apartment I used to love to daydream about whenever I passed it. What it would be like to live there, days and nights threaded by trains? I think Wally told me he'd looked at an apartment once in that skinny Victorian tower, and considered taking it until—luckily—the train came thundering along just outside the windows, a scheduled thunder to drive any resident mad. Then the doors open on the platform and I'm out and onto the concrete footbridge, and there are the metal stairs down to Charles, the handsome and gentrified street along the foot of Beacon Hill. Suddenly I am feeling Wally's body descending them, maybe a bit weary after the long day, the crowded train ride home, but glad to see me anyway. I'm in him, a dozen years ago, and I am in myself, on an almost forgotten day when I am leaning against the fence by the sidewalk, dressed up to meet him in—what? overalls, I think, and a scarf and a black umbrella, something a bit too self-conscious, done-up to meet my new lover as he comes home. And I'm in my body, not my twenty-eight-year-old body but my forty-year-old self, watching us both. *Fluidity* doesn't seem quite the right word for what time does; if experience were a film, it would be one that doubles back on itself, looping, superimposing, one moment coming to stand beside another, layered over it, though they're years apart.

A dozen years dispensed with, at least for a little while, I am on the Charles Street we knew. Here Romano's bakery, where we'd go for coffee and napoleons, layered confections done up like presents in creamy glazes and pipings. Here the realtors with their windows full of photographs of expensive apartments, the upscale grocery with its windows full of perfect food, the florists' and antique dealers' windows: promises, everywhere, of the dream of occupying, the hope of home.

I am strangely, buoyantly happy, though there is a ragged edge to it, like the torn spring clouds of late March or early April; it is the sort of joy that might become tears at any moment. It seems to be contagious; people are oddly friendly, emotionally available in a way that doesn't usually characterize this—or any?—city. At the corner of Charles and Beacon, the Public Garden opens out, wide and inviting in the grand scale of its accomplished trees, severe in its colors (the day's a dozen shades of gray) but greening, the faint haloes of the outer branches a haze of bud. Here is the pond where the swan boats will soon be doubled beneath the arching footbridge; here the angel on the corner (did she always face in this direction? memory reorients her) whose motto enjoins: Cast thy bread on the waters . . .

And I know what the joy is.

It wasn't that I'd ever stopped loving him. But the years had shifted things, as years must, adjusting the focus. Twelve years is time for a river to try a variety of positions, to adjust itself and settle and adjust again, defining the channel in which it flows. After an initial year and a half of fireworks and jealousy and consuming passion—far too volatile to sustain—our union modulated, happily, into something more durable, the beginning of a long, comfortable time of partnership. That is the movement, I guess, from being "in love" to *living* in love, which is quite another thing. Still with its intensities, its pleasures and depths, but marked also by trust and elasticity, the kind of relaxation which allows a couple to be both profoundly engaged with one another and turned outward, involved in the life that surrounds them.

In the years before Wally's death, our life together came to center around his illness, and whatever questions or issues might have arisen between us, whatever evolutions might have occurred in the normal course of a relationship, were simply covered over or set aside, obscured by the reality of a more pressing condition. That, I think, is one of the real tragedies of illness; you cannot know the life you might have had. Epidemic forces us to multiply this loss a thousandfold, a hundred thousandfold: had AIDS not appeared among us, what lives, what works would we have had?

After Wally died I realized there was a new quality in my feeling for him, something that didn't have anything to do with taking care of him. It was, in fact, not something new, but the reemergence of an original feeling, from years before: I was falling in love with him again.

I am taking a walk with my lover, in the place that was ours, which is imbued with that early intensity, where dramas of passion and sexual obsession were played out, dramas of doubt in ourselves and in one another, dramas of jealousy. It's ironic, since he spent the last nine months of his life in bed or in a wheelchair, that *now* we can walk together, now that he's dead. Beacon Street, Berkeley, what Robert Lowell called "hardly passionate Marlborough Street" and my friend Lynda would later revise to "*harshly* passionate Marlborough Street." No other landscape, in the history of neighborhoods in which we lived, can hold quite the resonance that this one does, perhaps because no other is quite so far away, and no other's yet become so emblematic and so completely interiorized, the city surface transformed into the surface of dream. There is a wonderful little poem of Cavafy's, "In the Same Space," as heartbreakingly plain and direct a poem about memory as I can imagine:

> *The setting of houses, cafés, the neighborhood*
> *that I've seen and walked through years on end:*
>
> *I created you while I was happy, while I was sad,*
> *with so many incidents, so many details.*
>
> *And, for me, the whole of you has been transformed*
> *into feeling.*

Cavafy's Alexandrian neighborhood is remade within the perceiver through the transfiguring power of long inhabitation. But that which we leave behind is transfigured in us, too; my city's a location of memory and desire, and I can plot in this neighborhood points of rapture and longing and wonder. Here a corner where a particular magnolia, in flower, tattooed the sidewalk, and us, with the shadows of its blooms, the street lamp glowing through them tinting our passage beneath to a warm flesh tone. Here the portico of a church—little private space—we'd duck inside to kiss, happy transgression. Here the marquee of the old theater—since then become a big housewares shop, and now a fancy bookstore—where we emerged one winter night into an enormous snowstorm, which completely buried us both in big wet flakes while we fought all the way home. What we were arguing about? I have no idea, but I remember the wet snow breaking against Wally's red down vest, my wet shoes, my misery; it was still those early days when one thinks each fight means it's over, that it's all been a mistake.

Here the doorway at the Butera School of Art, where a homeless woman whose life I always used to try to imagine lived, huddled in many scarves and hats, a shopping bag filled with. . . what? No more school of art now; looks like it's become condos. And no homeless woman, at least not today; did I think I'd see her here, twelve years later, when half the people I knew who *had* roofs over their heads are gone? Across the street, in one of these buildings, was the office where Anne Sexton's psychiatrist had been; I used to like to imagine her coming here for sessions, then walking, afterward, on the Esplanade, along the river. Here, a mailbox a tall, broadly built black man claimed for his own. He used to dress in black plastic trash bags, in inclement weather, and he'd use a pushbroom to clean his piece of sidewalk, the space around the mailbox he claimed as his. He seemed to own nothing but the pushbroom.

And here is the doorway of the building where we lived: 115 Beacon Street. It looks—well, untouched, except perhaps the double doors' black paint peels a bit more, the windows of the bay fronting the sidewalk (once they were *my* windows!) grimy and unrevealing, sealed as they are with heavy venetian blinds.

I've brought along a camera. I'm standing at the foot of the steps, trying to get the entryway framed just right in the lens, when a dark shape enters the frame—the back of a man in a black coat forging brusquely into my view. He doesn't look back as he says, "Don't photograph me going in here."

I tell him I won't. "I used to live here," I explain, "years ago."

He hesitates a moment, deciding whether or not to talk to me, and then turns, halfway up the steps, so I can look up into his face. "You know," he says, "the old girl's in a nursing home now. She's a hundred and two."

The "old girl" is Miss K., the landlady, already ancient and close to senile when we'd known her a dozen years before. Her father bought a string of Beacon Street brownstones in the Depression, elegant bow-fronted rowhouses, which had fallen, over fifty years, into various states of disrepair, as their condominiumed neighbors were polished till they shone. She lived in the front room of one of the apartment houses, a bay-windowed parlor stuffed with her father's immense Renaissance-revival furniture, a virtual warehouse of Chinese porcelain: blue and white ginger jars, umbrella stands, big tureens and platters swimming with carp and chrysanthemums and clouds. She slept on a grayed cot in the corner, and sat at a little work-table in her housecoat receiving rents and writing receipts. The huge mahogany armoires and china cabinets—with their carved profiles of Dante and Beatrice, their claws and beaks and garlands of fruit—blocked the windows, absorbing the light, so she'd sit beside a scholarly little lamp which illumi-nated nothing much besides her account books. She was quar-relsome, suspicious, and easily confused. She ran her houses like the rooming houses of another era, collecting rents by the week, but by those days she had a hard time knowing who was who and who lived where. Her tenants—whose boyfriends came and went, who shifted between apartments in new con-figurations of friendship and romance—didn't help matters much. And because she was losing both her sharpness and her eyesight, people began to cheat her, bringing back the same rent receipt again and again with the dates changed to show her they'd already paid. And carrying and selling off the heavy Victorian stuff that furnished the apartments, replacing it with things found on the street. Wally said that Miss K. still had an attic, in the brownstone of which she herself was dowager empress, stuffed with princely beds and sideboards, unwieldy configurations of walnut and marble, sphinx-headed and brass-footed extravagances—useless now, in days of diminish-ing rooms, when what used to be a dining room or a second-floor parlor was someone's whole apartment.

The man I'm talking to is in his sixties somewhere, I guess, with a slightly furtive quality that begins to relax as we talk. I explain that I lived on the first floor, alone, and then on the third-floor front (I can see the beautiful built-in shutters we lived behind, up above my head, closed over windows which seem to me now almost legendary) with Wally. I explain that Wally died in January, that I'm back to see the old places, and by confiding in this man I open a conversation.

He says he was afraid I'd come from Miss K.'s lawyer, or a real estate agency. "Her lawyer," he explains, "is running everything. But he can't kick us out, since he'd have to find us apartments in the neighborhood at the same rent. Which don't exist. So he just doesn't rent out the apartments as they open up." And open up they have; out of the ten or so places in the building, only two tenants remain. Where have they all gone? Disappeared, moved away, and mostly, of course, died; this was a house full of gay men, in 1981, and now it's a house full of no one.

First there was Bobby, Wally's best friend for years, who lived on the first floor, in an apartment he painted and wallpapered a dozen times just in the years I knew him. He and Wally had been lovers for a short while, as kids, when each had first come to the city; their relationship had simply drifted into a friend-ship which sustained both men for years. They'd worked together at Laura Ashley, selling cozy sprigged and flowered fabrics and clothes and wallpaper, so they shared a private lexi-con of pattern and colors. "R–22," one would say to the other, and they'd both dissolve into laughter. I was jealous of him, at first, and it took me a while to understand that Bobby simply came with the deal, like a favorite aunt or a big unsightly piece of family furniture. Not that he was unsightly, exactly, but whenever he was around he was a *presence*, someone to be accounted for: center of attention, storytelling, raconteuring, singing show tunes, not listening much. He was absolutely devoted to Wally and hardly listened to him, a duality which would, eventually, distance them.

After we moved away from Boston, we gradually saw less and less of Bobby, though every Christmas he'd appear with armloads of gifts, mostly things for which we had no use, things people had given to him, or stuff he'd stolen from the stores where he worked. The dishonest streak in Bobby's char-acter seemed to grow more pronounced as he grew older; he'd give Wally a new watch—something we both knew he himself would never pick out—and weep crocodile tears, moved by this beautiful present he'd chosen especially for his oldest friend. He wanted to give us so much that he'd be indispensable to us, that we would be wildly and forever grateful, that he'd have a permanent home in our lives. Which he already had, though never an entirely easy one.

Though you can grow weirdly fond of those traits in friends you don't admire, so much do those aspects seem like essential parts of someone. It was impossible to separate Bobby's dishonesty from his generosity, somehow; his falsehoods were often so touchingly transparent, and the size of the lies seemed allied to the size of his heart. Bobby moved away from the Beacon Street apartment when he found a lover, a man he clearly did not love, another instance of the dishonesty we couldn't abide. The lover was someone Wally and I detested, but they were together for years, living in a big house in a well-heeled suburb of the city. When Bobby came back from the hospital after his first bout with pneumocystis, the lover told him to pack. Homeless, ill, he tried the patience of his parents and his friends, and lived with us for a hellish month in which we arranged our lives around his suddenly burgeoning needs. In a month he'd made a considerable recovery, and felt well enough to be really impossible. (I still think I hear his ghost sometimes, over my shoulder, when I'm at the stove, complaining about my cooking.)

He wound up living in the YMCA in Cambridge, in Central Square, in a place I can only think of as the end of the road, the very walls and floors redolent of hopelessness. The last time Wally and Bobby saw one another was at Mass General Hospital; both there for tests, they met in the hospital lobby. Wally couldn't walk well; Bobby couldn't see well; without the energy to go for lunch, they sat in the waiting room and talked, two men in their forties who might as well have been seventy. At the end of the visit, Bobby asked Wally for cab fare; he accepted the ten that Wally offered and then ducked out of sight down the hospital steps, heading for the train, not the taxi stand, so that he could use nine of the ten for other things—a final moment, in Wally's eyes, of dissembling, fully in character.

The fellow I'm talking to on the stairs had moved into a basement apartment while Bobby was still upstairs pursuing a life of continual redecoration. Less guarded now, he starts to tell me about himself. He's a retired antique dealer, he says, with a knowing look. He lives downstairs, in what was once the kitchen of the great house, its big iron stove still filling one entire wall; it was the apartment where Doug lived once, with Wally's brother Jimmy. Doug, who moved away to San Francisco, was the first person I knew to die of AIDS, the first from the building to vanish.

"Did you know David?" my new friend asks. I did. David and Bobby had been boyfriends for a while, and used to sing together at a rather fusty neighborhood bar called Napoleon's, a piano bar wrapped in red-flocked wallpaper where it was not uncommon for the patrons to wear suits. Since the men there were mostly of a certain age, Bobby could enjoy feeling youthful there, and his singing and stories made him a social star.

"Is David still here?" I ask.

"Oh no." Then a lowering of the voice, a confidential angling of the head. "Rumor has it that he has a terrible disease."

I wince, internally; I hate the covering up, the notion of AIDS as shameful or unspeakable. But I remember this man's age, imagine years of the closet; it's not up to me to tell him how to deal with the epidemic. I ask if he knows where David is now.

"There was a terrific storm one evening," he says, "and we found water pouring down the steps"—the great marble stair that winds down the spine of the building—"and it was pouring out from under his door, because his windows were all open in the rain. We had to break in—we thought he was dead in there—but he was gone. Just the windows open and the rain pouring in. Then we heard he's in a hospice somewhere."

I'm remembering David's old apartment, big paper fans—

red?—spread out on his marble fireplace, and his red face lit up with cocktails and show tunes and the ambient glow of Napoleon's ruby wallpaper. David and Bobby, both of them out of work, watching TV in their bathrobes at eleven in the morning.

Before I can think what to say, my new friend says, "You can come in if you like."

He opens the heavy black doors with his key, and suddenly I am almost overcome by a sense of wonder and strangeness. It is as if he were opening the gates of a tomb, some ancient place, little disturbed, still containing the artifacts left with the dead.

It's dark in the big vestibule, under a dusty chandelier. The building might as well have been sealed a thousand years, only a wraithlike tenant or two slipping in and out because they have somehow retained the magical property of moving back and forth between realms. A sideboard upon which Bobby used to lay out everyone's mail is still here, its dark varnish gleaming Victorian in the gray light, but now there's only one yellow envelope waiting there, someone's electric bill. The black and white marble floor is dirty, the staircase stained where rainwater from David's abandoned windows streamed in. And here's the door to the studio where I lived when I first met Wally, my little white room—probably once where the parson used to wait to be received—mostly occupied by an enormous mirror-topped fireplace. A room in which *I* was mostly occupied with love; in memory, in that room, I am always waiting for Wally to come home from work. Or I've been away to teach, and I come home to find the room decked for my homecoming—candles and streamers and shiny letters of metallic foil hung on a wire across the room saying—what? HAPPY BIRTHDAY, probably, I can't recall. I was twenty-eight, and this was my first great passionate love as a gay man, my first headlong risky adventurous union with somebody my own age, for whom this love was as risky and new and full of promise and threat as it was for me. I'd staked everything to be with Wally—given up my job and apartment in New York (admittedly a dumb job and an unpleasant apartment) and landed myself in Boston, living downstairs from him, not much money, no job but temp work, my eyes huge with stars.

Which were not quite bright enough to keep me from being miserable—oh, I was gloriously alive then, in those months of risk and passion, right on the edge, but it was also terribly hard, since I'd entirely rearranged my life (such as it was) to come to a new city, to live with a man I barely knew.

It happened like this. At twenty-eight, I was between lives. ("How many lives," my friend Lynda wrote in another poem, "have fountained through my own . . . ") I'd spent most of my twenties in a heterosexual marriage, living in the Midwest. I'd married young, in flight from both my family and a sexual orientation that scared me half to death. In 1971, I'd been a freshman in college when I met Ruth, and I was dazzled and fascinated by her. The fact that I'd never met a self-identified adult gay person was also, of course, a serious shaping factor; I didn't *know*, living as I did in a place and time where gay people were hidden, erased, what kind of life I could have. I thought maybe lots of men felt the way I did, and then went ahead and lived the way they were expected to anyway. Maybe if you ignored homosexual desire, it would go away.

Reality, of course, proved opposite. When the marriage ended, I stayed in Des Moines for another year, teaching, catching my breath after this dizzying change, and discovering what it was like to have a boyfriend, to enter into a new planet of activity. At twenty-seven, the divorce final, my temporary teaching job over, I realized I could go anywhere. With six hundred dollars to my name, and the kind of energy that springs from knocking down the closet walls and seeing around one a wide and unknown world of possibility, I put what I owned in the back of my little yellow Chevette and moved East, headed for the myth and actuality of Manhattan.

Young Gay Man Leaves Stultifying Midwest for the Urban

World of Romance and Permission: a classic American story, and I won't retell it here. Suffice to say it was thrilling, though the excitement was mostly about finding out that I could do it, that I had enough nerve and inner resources to land on my feet in a new realm. Though, truthfully, my days didn't involve very *interesting* forms of struggle: finding an apartment was the hardest part, as mindless though reasonable work as a typist was everywhere available. I'd work every hour of overtime I could get, typing reports for marketing consultants in a glamorous firm on Park Avenue. I didn't have the money to buy clothes I needed to wear to work, so I'd go out to a shopping center in New Jersey to use the one credit card I owned—a Sears charge, left over from my days in Iowa—to buy shirts. Of course I told no one.

The practical aspects of the day-to-day—how does one *live* in this city?—seemed to occupy all my time; New York, on a secretarial pool salary, was more about survival than pleasure.

I was lucky to have a part-time teaching job, in a program for writers in Vermont, a graduate school where students and faculty come together only for two weeks each summer and winter. It wasn't enough to live on, but it helped, and it meant being able to feel like a writer instead of someone who did other people's typing. This meant a trip north to Montpelier, and I decided to make the journey into at least something of a vacation, knowing there wouldn't be many of those for a while. I went briefly to Provincetown, but it was rainy and cold, and I didn't feel connected to its gay resort culture; I didn't know how to thread my way in that unfamiliar world. (Strange to think that I walked then, another person, on the streets and beaches that have become, now, the landscape of my daily life.)

So I went on to Bellows Falls. In those days, in this little railroad town outside of Brattleboro, there was a gay hotel called the Andrews Inn, an imposing-looking brick building that sat square on Main Street, next to the Oddfellows Hall and a diner called the Miss Bellows Falls. This was very odd;

the gay traveler is used to finding his hotels and guest houses out of the way, and—less so these days, but for most of my life, anyway—his bars black-fronted and lacking signs. But the Andrews Inn was centrally located in a town which resembled a set for a Frank Capra movie, and somehow it seemed to work. Restless in my room, early in the evening, I tried to read student poems in preparation for my residency up north. No good; I couldn't concentrate. I went to the bar downstairs, had a gin and tonic, and tried not to look too much at the two or three others sitting around the bar. Eventually, bored, I went back to my room for another go at the poems, but they hadn't developed any new nuances in my absence. So I decided I'd take another walk down to the bar, without it ever occurring to me that this decision would change my life. After the fact, we look back at such moments, the thoughtless time before something momentous happens; how odd it seems, not to have known then, when afterward we can hardly imagine ourselves without such knowledge.

A few more people had gathered at the bar and around the tiny dance floor and jukebox. While I stood ordering another gin, I noticed a man who was standing by the dance floor, his back to me. Tall, his hair close-cropped, he was wearing jeans and a blue football jersey with white sleeves. (A jersey I have still, packed in a trunk. Years after it was too small for Wally, it seemed important to keep it, and now it's a precious thing, if also a terrible one.)

I walked over in his direction, emboldened—because I liked the shape of him—enough to go and stand behind him. When he turned around, as he did in just a moment, he looked directly into my face, his own countenance open and friendly and somehow with hardly any veil across it. What he said was, "Hi."

This is another classic story, one that's particularly difficult to tell because the externals of it hold little to distinguish it. In truth I can't *remember* much of what we said then, though I remember that we were soon having a wonderful time, and dancing, with an increasing sense of energy and connection.

And if in fact I *could* reproduce here our conversation, I imagine it would be perfectly sweet but also thoroughly banal, on the surface, just like the surface of any such encounter.

All the life of such moments lies in what doesn't show, in the buzz and sparkling within—or shows not in words much but in the gaze, in the look of a face opening to another, in all the little ways we communicate the fizzy stirrings of attraction, into which both of us were falling more deeply and thoroughly as we talked and danced. An excitement, the pulse-quickening buzz of flirtation, the pleasure of discovering that talk didn't dispel the mutual attraction but deepened and strengthened it. Then, after I don't know how long, we decided to go out to the balcony for some air.

We wound up various staircases and back ways to arrive at a broad metal platform on the top of the building, looking out over the backside of the town, a wide span of railroad tracks with a steaming engine, the gleaming black ripple of the river. Wally leaned against a brick wall, and then I took my first real look, my first full look, into his face, into his eyes—which were still tobacco-leaf brown even in the faint light from the lamps by the tracks. I wasn't prepared for what I'd find there; they were the most unguarded, welcoming eyes I'd ever seen, and his whole countenance seemed alive with delight, as if he felt as much wonder as I did. And what I found myself thinking was, *Here you are at last.*

Not that it was all that simple. I was headed north for two weeks, then back to New York, he back to Boston. I had a sort of semi-boyfriend floating out there in the distance to be dealt with somehow, and I'd just gotten to Manhattan and what, exactly, did this glorious night with this stranger mean?

Thus it was a while before we saw each other again, after a breakfast of blueberry pancakes in the hotel restaurant and a long talk standing beside the open trunk of my car. It became clear, in the next few months, that my intuition, looking that first time into Wally's eyes, wasn't one to forget, and in a few weeks I was in Boston to see him, and he was in New York. I ended things with the sort-of boyfriend. Wally and I talked on the phone every day, wrote letters, waited for the weekends. Every weekend, back and forth between cities, and then, knowing each other all of three passionate months, we made a decision. He had a more established life in Boston than I had in Manhattan, a job and a world of friends, so why didn't we try it there together?

Thinking of this today, it's hard to imagine making such a choice after three months. What did I know? I was sure of profound pleasure in his body, delight in his playfulness and good spirits, acres of common ground in taste and sensibility and humor—but did I know him well enough to make this leap? I was certain of the dizzying force of that first night's intuition, a sense of emotional certainty for which I was willing to toss caution and reason out the window.

A very little while later, it was myself I felt like tossing. The day I'd arrived from New York, ready to start a new life, Wally and I were to sign a lease on an apartment, a beautiful place in the South End, on Waltham Street, shot with sunlight, its little balcony looking down onto a courtyard garden. We could afford it; we had a date with the landlord; we were—I thought—ready. On the steps of the building Wally said we had to sit down and talk; he couldn't go through with it; living together felt premature, too much of a commitment. I felt as if the stairs under me were crumbling; the world took on that peculiar exactitude of appearance it gets when we hear terrible news, so much so that I can remember to this day the nervous filigree of the fire escape across the street, the cracks in the steps' cement balustrade which I must have kept looking at, fighting back tears, while he talked.

Of course, from any reasonable perspective, he was right, or rather the position he took was one that conventional wisdom would uphold. But I had no use, at that moment, for wise precaution; if wisdom interfered with love, to hell with wisdom. I had given myself over to love.

I had also given up my job and my apartment.

And so I moved into the first-floor studio in Miss K.'s tumble down palazzo on Beacon Street.

A dozen years later, in the vestibule, outside that old transomed door, I feel the whole weight of the past above my head, floor after unoccupied floor of history, mine, others', the house's own huge inventory of residents and years. Wally lived upstairs in a larger studio, on the third floor, behind those gloriously carpentered shutters; same building, separate apartments. In truth we couldn't afford it, and spent virtually all our time in his place anyway, in that room up the sweep of these stairs, which is for me one of memory's most laden locations, site of longing, pleasure, and despair. That room seems to me almost outside of time; up there it's always evening, quiet above the city's din and motion, a lit cube of memory hung in the immensity and safety of the night. A Cavafian room, it has become ancient, dense with meanings, erotic with the residue of passion the space has come to contain. Up there, in darkness and candlelight, firelight, and the warm parchment radiance of the shade, we burnished that room with the motions of bodies which no longer exist: every cell of my body replaced nearly twice over now, every cell of Wally's body replaced and then burned to ashes. Does that room exist, except in my memory? Well, something does; there is a space there, in the physical world, but that same space has been plucked out of time, become emblem and artifact. It is, in memory, something I have *made*, like a poem or a vase. Now it lasts. In the room that remains there, in the building on Beacon Street, the plaster ceiling caved in—luckily, when we weren't home, since hundreds of pounds of plaster fell right into the center of the room, right into the sleigh bed where we—sometimes—slept. (It hurts me now, to think of that bed, of the wood imbued with us, lonely without us, abandoned. Cavafy says of the furniture of one of his remembered rooms: "They must still be around somewhere, those old things." What poignance that simple line has! Chairs and bed and wardrobe and mirror: the things that reflect lovers, that come to embody their moment.) I don't imagine, in those declining days, that ceiling was ever fixed; those three big windows full of the rainy light of Back Bay in early spring probably still give onto a room piled with plaster fragments, a ruin.

Of the countless things I remember about that room, most of them nocturnal, radiant, passionate in either joy or misery, there is one diurnal memory of such force and beauty I want to recount it here. It was Christmas, the first one we had together, and we'd decked a small live tree bought from a little city lot on Charles Street in front of the toney grocery, with paper snow, lots of it, so that it resembled something from the forests of New Hampshire or Vermont—not a thing on the thick green branches but heaped and gleaming white.

The weather that December, though, was anything but northern, and Christmas Day itself was brilliant and weirdly balmy. Roasting (for once; the boiler was broken down more often than not), we pried open the windows which had been shut since October, and a warm wind redolent of fresh mud, cleaner than any city air down in the street below, came pouring in, filling our lungs with pleasure. But when the wind suddenly gusted, whipping off the river into the room, our tree's tiny flakes all rose into the air at once, swirling around the room in the mildest of blizzards. We were englobed, inside the shook heart of a paperweight. Our room, which already felt outside the rush and pour of things, seemed still further set aside in space and time. In memory that snow spins still; our laughter and our wonder in the storm's interior, lovers suddenly stunned into recognizing how small what's divided and troubled them has been, how lovely their singular, flake-streaked moment is.

My companion—my Virgil, guiding me into this under-world?—doesn't offer to take me upstairs, which is fine, somehow. I want to leave, to pull myself away. I tell him I feel as if I'm dreaming, as if I have stepped outside of time, into the house of the past. And he leans over toward me, conspiratorial, and says, "Well, just don't you plan to come sweeping down those stairs in a big crinoline, honey, because we've got enough ghosts in here already."

With that I thank him and am out the door, onto Beacon Street. I'm walking toward Berkeley and Clarendon, looking at the pouring traffic and the Emerson kids on the sidewalk and the shoppers on the way home from wherever—a world of radiant particulars, in bright late winter light seen through tears. I have never felt so implicated in a *story*. Until today, I have never felt what I've heard other men I know say, that they don't understand why they're alive, when so many are gone. I am alive walking down this street in the early March sun and all the men I knew in that house, that stacked repository of time and memory, are dead. Wally and Bobby, David and Doug, others I never even knew. I am here today, in 1994, walking a city street indifferent with its own hurrying life, and I am filled with the presence and weight of their stories. What am I to do with them?

A Shore Walk

⌒

Early May, a foggy Sunday. It's rained all morning and the sky is contemplating further action, which is lucky for us—the two retrievers and I—because it means that the bicycle trail into the dunes, and the marsh along the shore, and the shore itself will be deserted today, when the town's beginning to fill up with visitors, so we can wander and roam without disturbing anyone or being disturbed by them.

Today we follow the trail only a little ways before a grove of scrubby pines and verdigrised lichens calls me off the path and up onto the sandy slopes. The dogs are always pleased to leave the macadam; they prefer unpaved paths, though they walk in the open dunes with a different kind of poised energy, a different sort of containment, because they are unsure where we're going next. They both explore and keep close watch on where I am going, since they can anticipate the direction of only a bit of the coming walk.

This landscape yields particularly intense contradictions. Sheer expanses of sand alternate with low thickets of bearberry (*Uva-ursi*, beautiful name) and shrub. Bleached sand walls of North African proportions loom over hummocks of wild roses. In the deeper pockets between dunes are forests of pine—from tiny brave stunted things, a few cones tenaciously clinging, to cool and shady groves where, in the most sheltered places, the trees have made for themselves a community, the earth between them paved with rusty needles, mosses, and—a month or so from now—lady slippers. Now they're only gray-green shoots, but here in the sun are newly leafing rugosas, the bronzy, barbaric-looking claw of beach pea unfurling, and the bee-pestered wedding lace of beach plum.

Now an especially dense grove glows below us, lush in the shreds of the fog, luminous. The needles seem to have a new light about them, a more evident pulse, the life-energy in them quickened. I am drawn down the steep dune side along a little path—deer trail? human?—through the bayberries. The dogs see where we're headed and hurry to be there first.

This grove feels set apart, its quiet underlined. The distant waves blur here into a kind of low continuous shush, an aspiration. Why is it that places removed from human habitation bring us so swiftly into ourselves? I walk into this village of durable pines—tall ones for this sand terrain, which seems the very definition of "infertile"—and I am immediately thinking of how abstracted I've been feeling, how far from myself. Not depressed—I have been operating in the world competently enough, though I'm not trying to do much but get by these days—but distracted. Not focused on what I am experiencing, not quite present with myself.

The state of mind above which my distraction floats like fog is suddenly perfectly clear, though the right word for it is less immediately available. *Grief* is too sharp and immediate; maybe it's the high pitch of the vowel sound, or the monosyllabic impact of the word, as quick a jab as *knife* or *cut*.

Sadness is too ephemeral, somehow; it sounds like something that comes and goes, a response to an immediate cause which will pass in a little while as another cause arises to generate a different feeling.

Mourning isn't bad, but there's something a little archaic about it. I think of widows keening, striking themselves, clutching at handfuls of dust—dark-swathed years, a closeting of self away from the world, turned inward toward an interior dark.

This sounds, for one thing, like more of a removal than the late twentieth century will quite permit. *Mourning* suggests that nothing else can enter into the mourner's attention. It doesn't suggest the weird interpenetration of ongoingness and endings, of this spring's sprouting life and my continuing sorrow.

Sorrow feels right, for now. Sorrow seems large and inhabitable, an interior season whose vaulted sky's a suitable match for the gray and white tumult arched over these headlands. A sorrow is not to be gotten over or moved through in quite the way that sadness is, yet sorrow is also not as frozen and monochromatic, to my mind, as mourning. Sadness exists inside my sorrow, but it's not as large as sorrow's realm; it comes and goes without really touching the overarching whole. This sorrow is capacious; there's room inside it for the everyday, for going about the workaday stuff of life. And for loveliness, for whatever we're to be given by the daily walk.

And we are always given something, it seems, since these walks provide exactly the balance which the dogs (and I) seem to prefer—enough of the familiar, so we don't have to think about it too much, and enough of novelty, so that something to occupy our attention is always appearing, something we haven't thought enough about yet. Sometimes, of course, what satisfies the dogs' needs is not what engages my attention, but a good deal of the time we seem to agree on what is interesting. Motion, strangeness, novelty of scent, the presence of an unfamiliar creature, open space in which to range freely—to these both our species respond. Beauty, of course, does not appear on the dog's register of values, as far as I know, though a number of other qualities we could consider abstract, such as affection, loyalty, tenacity, curiosity, cunning, exasperation, patience, and longing certainly do. Dogs have a moral sense, but I am not sure they have an aesthetic one.

Loveliness, even in these months of living in sorrow, compels me. Once Wally and I met an elderly man who had lost his wife to Alzheimer's; he was not a widower, yet, but the woman that he'd loved was, in essence, gone. She'd studied piano, he told us, with a pupil of—Paderewski, was it?—and taught generations of children herself. She lived now in the town nursing home, adjacent to the cemetery. Her needs were such that he could not care for her. Her sense of memory and meaning, and then of language, had dissolved into a hopelessly confused, continuous present, a nightmare fog of not-knowing. He stayed on, in their ancient house, giving tours, which was how we met him. For a couple of dollars, he'd bring you into his low-slung, chimney-anchored house, a perfect full Cape, circa 1745, its twelve-over-twelve windows opening onto exquisitely plain little rooms. Because he'd grown tired, over the years, of repeating the tour, he'd play a tape he'd made explaining the history of the house. But he'd not lost his love for narration, either, so he'd sit poised beside the reel-to-reel and, after a bit of recorded rap, he'd shut off the machine and tell us about himself, and his wife, and their forty years together inhabiting this comfortable museum. We sat side by side on the sofa, enthralled. The history of the house had become, it seemed, inextricable from his history. When it was time to go, the tape completed, our curiosity about every room satisfied, I complimented him on the beauty of the house, what a rich and evocative surrounding he'd found and made for himself.

"Yes," he said, "but as the poet said—Rossetti, it was—you know Rossetti?"

"Dante Gabriel?"

He nodded. "He said, 'Beauty without the beloved is like a sword through the heart.'" I felt then as if he saw into our story, its coming unraveling.

But his experience hasn't been mine, exactly. There is something about the glories of the world which makes me feel, in some way I'm hard-pressed to articulate, closer to Wally. The heart's pierced, maybe, but that penetration's a connection to what is larger than us, more ongoing. Perhaps, in encountering beauty alone, with my two unimpressed companions, I reconnect to what Wally and I used to experience together, which contains something of us still.

So yesterday, when I watched a finback whale feeding off Race Point where the sea-bottom declines steeply from the beach, so that the whales can come near enough to shore for one not only to see them, but sometimes to hear the soft wet *puhhh* of their exhalations, I was happy not only for myself but somehow also happy for Wally. Because he is in a place without limit now, of a piece with animal energies, capable of swimming to the bottom of the sea and hurtling himself toward air and sunlight again? Do the dead dissolve their individuality back into the world? That does not sound to me like such a bad ending to come to, whether we are conscious of the return of our energies or no. But perhaps it is even better than that, the afterlife; imagine that purest portion of self, the soul which lies beneath the incidental furniture and circumstance of personality, able to participate in all the world.

I don't *know* anything different about death than I ever have, but I feel differently. I inhabit this difference in feeling—or does it live in me?—at the same time as I'm sorrowing. The possibility of consolation, of joy even, does not dispel the sorrow. Sorrow is the cathedral, the immense architecture; in its interior there's room for almost everything: for desire, for flashes of happiness, for making plans for the future. And for watching all those evidences of ongoing life crumble in the flash of remembering, in the recurring wave of fresh grief.

But I *do* feel differently. What is this difference?

It still makes me draw a sharp breath, still almost stops my heart to think of that precise moment, when I could feel Wally going, not just each breath descending less deeply into his chest, but a kind of aura of transformation, a quality in the energy around him. After the last breath—no struggle, no grasping at life, the easiest of leave-takings—I swear I had the clearest image of Wally leaping free, as if he'd been so ready to go, as if some space had opened in the wall behind his head, and that he'd simply leapt out through that space. Which was not a space at all in the literal sense, but rather a possibility, a shift in the quality of being from the ordinary life of the room.

The room—the whole house—took on a different tenor; there was a kind of heat and light to it, a humming intensity. My house held within in it the kind of resonance that a cello or a violin creates, that rich sound that seems to move so deeply into us, and to linger there, though there wasn't any sound. I could feel that depth, that vibration, and not because I was mad with grief; I wasn't, not yet. I knew that after that moment, from it, a universe of pain and of loss would open out, but I also knew that this hour was not that time.

This was the hour of passing, and it was clear to me, as certain as I've ever been of anything, that Wally had been lifted, transfigured, and freed in that moment, which had a kind of reality above the ordinary terms of sorrow or grief or madness. What *I* felt or experienced, the fact that *I* was going to be alone now, the outer trappings of loss (strange as it sounds, even the body seemed a trapping) weren't of the essence in that hour.

The essence was the holiness of what had taken place in the room. Later that night I wouldn't be able to go back in there, to his hospital bed and my single iron bed pushed up against it, but in the morning when I walked in I felt the whole space still vibrating, like the aftertone of a struck tuning fork, still resonating. I can return to that tone, even now; I hear it—no, feel it—reverberant somewhere beneath the surface of the world.

In my mind, in the reasoning, arguing, reading part of me which teaches classes and reviews books and conducts daily life, I can doubt this entirely. And in my heart I can sentimentalize Wally's death, because, of course, I want him to live forever. Of course I want to be with him again in some way other than the way I am with him now, in my meditations and reveries and associations, even though no version of heaven ever presented to me has been very convincing.

And I can attempt to rationalize my perceptions about death away by thinking that it's just that human beings crave reality, and that going straightforwardly toward Wally's death together, with only the barest denial those last months to keep us sane, had about it a genuineness which we thirst for, and bears with it a kind of satisfaction. Don't we long for the genuine, even as we flee it?

But still—there is some firm place in me which knows that what happened to Wally, whatever it was, whatever it is that death is as it transliterates us, moving us out of this life into what we can't know, is *kind*.

I shock myself, writing that. I know that many deaths are anything but gentle. I know people suffer terribly; I know how blessed we were that the particular brand of afflictions which the virus made Wally's flesh heir to were easy ones, in a way. They killed him without endless prolonged miseries, without blindness or months of delirium. I know many die abandoned, unseen, their stories unheard, their dignity violated, their human worth ignored.

I suspect that the ease of Wally's death, the rightness of it, the loving recognition which surrounded him, all made it possible for me to see clearly, to witness what other circumstances might obscure. I *know*, as surely as I know anything, that he's all right now.

And yet.

And yet he's gone, an absence so forceful it is itself a daily, hourly presence.

My experience of being with Wally, in the hour of his leaping out of the world, brought me to another sort of perception, but I can't *stay* in that place, can't sustain that way of seeing. The experience of knowing, somehow, that he's all right, lifted in some kind process that turns at the heart of the world, gives way, as it must, to the plain aching fact that he's gone.

And doubt. And the fact that we can't understand, that it's our condition to not know. Is that our work in the world, to learn to dwell in such not-knowing? You can adopt any belief system you want about ultimate things, the nature of our sojourn here and afterward, but doesn't doubt always stand at the ready, prepared to undo the articles of faith? Perhaps so that meaning cannot be given to us, defined for us—at least not in any real way.

We need our doubt so as not to settle for easy answers. (*Need*, I say, as if we had the option to get rid of it!) Not-knowing pushes us to struggle after meaning for ourselves; if earthly existence does have purpose, I would be willing to bet that is part of it. But only part. Doubt's lesson seems to be that whatever we conclude must be provisional, open to revision, subject to correction by the forces of change. Leave room, doubt says, for the unknowable, for what it will never quite be your share to see. The one thing we can say with great certainty about human perception is that it is *partial*. And perhaps that is why we are, of necessity, creatures of doubt.

Stanley Kunitz says somewhere that if poetry teaches us anything, it is that we can believe two completely contradictory things at once. And so I can believe that death is utter, unbearable rupture, just as I know that death is kind.

Doubt, the magician, pulls the white tablecloth out from underneath the china, disrupting everything. But once the cloth is pulled away, what has been built atop is still there. I can have the rug pulled out from under me at any time and am still willing to go back to believing.

Just as I will, inevitably, go back to doubt.

Today, when we come down from the undulant dunes to the shore, there's further evidence to consider. The beach is an arena of mortality, corpses washing in and out, the consequences of predation or pollution or exposure—or just the plain propensity of life to end—everywhere visible.

The dogs relax on the shore, sure of where we're headed. One likes to stay within a few dozen feet of me, sniffing every fragment of otherness the beach has to offer; the other loves to range, and these wide horizontals give him the double pleasure of being able to run far into the distances and keep an eye on me at the same time. (In this way he's an emblem of my spirit: he wants to cleave and he wants to fly.) During this time we have little contact with each other, overtly; we are three students of reality involved in our work, each with his own approach to the problems of epistemology.

Neither dog has much interest in what catches me first. A— flotilla? little armada?—of jellyfish have met their destiny along the line of the estuary where bay and marsh meet. They are scattered far and wide, maybe a couple of dozen of them, and they range in diameter from the size of a doll's saucer to that of a dinner plate. The smallest are simply disks of transparent jelly, gelatinous plasma in which nothing is differentiated. In the ones which are a little larger, something begins to develop in the center, a rayed shading, yellowish or russet, like the petal-ringed faces of the great armload of sunflowers Lynda brought for Wally one day, blossoms that glowed beside his bed with the hot light of an August garden.

A little bigger still, the width now of a dessert plate, and there's a fringe of red threads around the rim, only a few in the smaller ones and then, as they grow larger, a bloody sci-fi halo of tangled whips.

And here is the prize, a grand— mother? papa? (They seem at once too primeval and too sophisticatedly other to be gendered.) Of all these beached starships, this one's arrived at the greatest level of complexity. Around the central, yellow sun with its bold rays are ringed smaller suns, out toward the edge, which sports an oxblood fringe like some obscure piece of Victorian bric-a-brac. It's a glorious and peculiar disk, and I can only imagine how much more complicated and intricate it must have been in the water, animated, pulsing, and distending. A dream flower, blossom of a surrealist garden.

Why have they washed ashore?

Kind death? I can't even imagine their lives. These are the flattened flowers of otherness; imagine—*try*—their subjectivity. I try often to pour myself into the dogs' way of being in the world. I like trying to set myself aside, getting as close as I can (admittedly, not very, but exhilarating anyway) to a world seen through those chestnut eyes, apprehended through the nose, delicate instrument unraveling scent's histories and narratives. But these jellyfish I can't get close to at all, though I can trace in the remains all around me the way this aspic organizes itself from next to nothing, a clear little squib, into this complicated, architectonic event: some kind of flattened art glass paperweight, a vaguely unfriendly example of Art Nouveau? Out of their element, they are evaporating, vanishing.

Walking in the marsh, standing on this shore, what do I stand on but the vast accumulated evidence of death? What do I confront, day after day, but death and death?

For weeks now I have been watching the skeleton of a dolphin, beached in the marsh, further out than we're walking today. I encountered it first when it was a full-fleshed black and white beauty, a small dolphin, recently dead, I think, since the gulls had only just begun to attack. The high contrast of its two colors made it crisp and sleek as a race car. It had come to rest in that arced position of leaping dolphins—the flying forms on Minoan walls. Even in repose it seemed to move.

On each succeeding visit, there was less to see, and more; the flesh gone, the skin becoming leather wrapped around a yard of bone, then gradually the pure configuration of bone itself exposed.

Dolphins have a rib cage not entirely unlike ours, beneath which the long spine narrows and curves into the odd, rubbery fan of the tail, which remained intact while other soft parts of the body vanished. Oddest of all was the skull, something like a bird's but broad and solid. In the shrinking of the fish's form its ancestral relationship to flying creatures seemed to become clearer and clearer, as if what I were seeing were simply the remains of a bird who'd lost its wings.

I loved that broad, strange head, and I thought about taking it home with me, to keep in a cabinet where I have shells and seagulls' skulls, and abandoned nests, and an elaborate whorled fungus from a Vermont birch tree—a sort of Victorian naturalist's vitrine, though in no scientific order, no pattern except an aesthetic one.

But when I touched it, the skull by this time attached to the spine by only a little bit of the dark leather the skin had become, I had the clearest sense that the bones belonged where they were, intact, or rather that it was not my business to scatter them. There was a dignity and completeness about the skeleton, and about its dissolution; it seemed to want exactly what was becoming of it, a return to the ground of being which the marsh is, rich solution in which old and new life are held in the suspension from which possibility arises. I left the bones together, and make a little pilgrimage to them every week, usually to find them moved a bit, arranged in a new configuration. They are visited, I imagine, by gulls, coyotes, raccoons, foxes, other walkers, but so far they've been allowed to dissolve in the sun and wind and rain. At each visit there is a little less of the particularity of the dolphin about them, a little more of the elemental. How firmly and clearly they are coming to resemble the other elements of the marsh.

Kind death? How can we know?

From this walk I bring home one thing: a little lavender bottle—maybe a medicine bottle, something that held once a tincture or essential oil. It's a mystery; purpled, no doubt, because the lead in the glass has turned in the sun, but completely unscathed by the sand, as transparent as the flesh (does that term apply?) of the jellyfish. Out here Coke and beer bottles suffer a sea change, ground in a week into something lovely, coming to resemble the element they join (and were made of) like my unlucky dolphin. So why has this old bottle survived so clear you can see the bubbles in the glass, the seams where the molten stuff was pressed into a metal mold?

My jellyfish, my dolphin skull, and the one object I can actually keep, my lavender bottle: souvenirs in a cabinet of memory, to be saved, arranged like the contents of a Cornell box. Questions, inside the larger mystery of sorrow, which contains us and our daily transit, and is large enough indeed to contain the whole shifting tidal theater where I make small constructions, my metaphors, my defenses. Against which I play out theories, doubts, certainties bright as high tide in sunlight, which shift just as that brightness does, in fog or rain.

One last mystery: on one of the little ponds, this morning, I saw wind riffling the first of the waterlily leaves. They haven't all emerged yet, but new circles tattoo the water, here and there, a coppery red. When the wind lifted their edges, each would reveal a little shadowy spot, a dot of black which seemed to flash on the water, and so across the whole surface of the pond there was what could only be described as the inverse of sparkling; a scintillant blackness. Shining blackly, black but rippling, lyrical: the sheen and radiance of death-in-life.

Is that my work, to point to the world and say, See how darkly it sparkles?

House Finches

⌒

Spring has opened its big green hands.

Yesterday I noticed that there was actually shade, beautiful greenish shade, under the box-alder tree beside my kitchen. The shadow of leaves appeared against the white clapboards of my neighbor's garage; how long since I've seen the shadow of leaves, one of those things that vanish all winter, though we seldom notice that they've gone until their reemergence. The first buds of the three-foot crabapple I planted three summers ago have opened.

But the new season's surest evidence is the presence of two house finches, little rose-throated gray birds who've begun to nest in a climbing rose that scrambles up the wall beside my bedroom window. All morning they perched on the points of the fence pickets, threads of straw and grass hanging from their beaks, before they'd dart out of view. Going out to the garden, later, to take the dogs out for a noontime walk in the woods, there was a hurried rustle and then two arcs so quick as to be almost unseeable out of the thickening green of the rose's tumble of briers. There, half-made, was a fragile cup of ocher, its form apparent even though it wasn't yet solidly built, light still shining through the bowl which would, in time, support the eggs.

House finches: I love the warmth and domesticity of the

name, and their habit of nesting up against walls, in any sort of
shelter or pocket that will protect them. The first ones came
from China, fifty years ago, brought to New York City as pets;
freed, they established themselves in the East across a territory
that grows wider over the years. I've known them before, and
probably that's part of why they seem to me the real heralds of
spring, their appearance that announcement of the new season
which is the one to be believed, the one to be celebrated.

The other pair I knew was in Vermont, back when whatever
shadows darkened our horizon were the ordinary ones—jobs,
money, how to make the best of our lives—those things that
are momentous, but come to seem luxurious considerations
when illness fills up the stage of a life, or two lives. In those
days we lived in a ramshackle thirteen-room Victorian house in
Montpelier. I'd gotten a grant from the Massachusetts Artists
Foundation, just before we left Boston to come north for a
teaching job for me. The generous foundation gave me a check
for $7,500, a princely sum for us, and we decided to use it as a
down payment for a house, since property in the north was
cheap then. Even at the low prices of 1985, what we looked at
was far beyond our means; we were despondent and about to
give up when our realtor drove us past the flat-roofed, down-
at-the-heels New England version of an Italian villa, its hand-
some form abused by a sea of mustard paint trimmed in choco-
late brown. Yellow and brown, for some reason, is a traditional
combination in Vermont's working-class neighborhoods. There
was a for sale sign on the rickety picket fence, which had been
forced to wear the same shade of chocolate.

"That?" the realtor said when we asked. "Oh, you don't
want to see that house. That ought to be torn down." Which
was really all we needed to hear, contrary creatures, scav-
engers, aficionados of barn sales and other people's attics that
we were. And it did turn out to be like a barn sale, really—
except that we bought the barn, for twenty-nine thousand dol-
lars. It had no insulation, an antique wood-fired furnace that
consumed whole cords of timber in a wink, and period plumb-

ing of unquestionable authenticity. Whether the flat roof was a concession to poverty or the Italianate fashion I never knew, but in the course of one Vermont winter the absolute madness of the idea became clear. Snowfall after snowfall meant shoveling the roof, and as soon as there was a bit of a thaw ice dams pushed at the spongy old roofing material until the melting water began to drip, and then to cascade, into our bedroom.

But that was all down the road. First the sellers, Clayton and Rita, taught us the intricacies of the furnace, the mysteries of a kerosene-burning stove. Rita worked in a clothespin factory and made all Clayton's meals; he gathered mushrooms and cut firewood, though I never saw him do anything but sit at the kitchen table and smoke. They sized us up in five minutes, and seemed perfectly happy to accept us as a couple, especially once they'd figured out that Rita could talk to Wally about where to shop while Clayton told me about maintenance, shoveling, plumbing—men's work. He'd even make jokes about the fussy concerns of wives, winking at me and nodding in Rita and Wally's direction.

Once Clayton and Rita vacated for their new house, we found ourselves alone in thirteen rooms of linoleum concealing wide-plank floors, cheap lumberyard paneling covering up layer upon layer of wallpaper roses. The house had long been inhabited in the manner of poor Vermonters who made do, got by, put a patch on what broke. It had been a long time since that house had gotten any serious attention; had it *ever* gotten serious attention? But it didn't matter a bit how much work confronted us, or that the renovation would turn out, eventually, to be unfinishable work—what mattered was it was ours, a great rambling dream of a house, eccentric, temperamental, rife with character, capable of being profoundly loved. And we were thrilled; the house was ours to rescue, to uncover, to inhabit, to play with, a piece of the world on which to make our mark.

For the five years we lived there—in which time my hands, or Wally's, must have touched every surface of that house, inside and out, as we painted and plastered and stripped and cursed, built and caulked and wept—every penny we could make went into the house. Mustard and chocolate gave way to a creamy colonial yellow, white trim, and blue shutters; the town paper suddenly carried an article about "the rising tide of gentrification." In a while it had a rainproof roof shielding new insulation, new chimney linings, a huge soapstone woodstove big enough to defeat—almost—the bitter Januaries of the snow queen. (Bobby or Lynda, visiting, used to wrap up in layers and layers; he in sweaters, she in kimonos and tunics and a plethora of scarves.)

And we bought a new pair of storm doors, beautiful ones, which brings me back to the finches. The house had a narrow double front door, still sporting its figured brass hardware, patterns half-obscured now with a hundred years of paint— handsome doors, but not very practical ones, since it was impossible to effectively block their drafty cracks and seams. For a while we sealed them off with plastic, six months of the year, and then it seemed time—the rest of the house was at least *that* much ready—to use the front door as it was meant to be used. At a salvage company I found just the right thing— for the proverbial arm and leg, but it was grant money, and it was for our *house*. Oh rationalization that justified many an expense we couldn't afford, many an hour spent in the hard folding chairs of auctions, many a Saturday rooting in some collapsing barn! Just the right thing was a pair of oak doors, multipaned; they were french doors, really, but with the right varnish and framing they made the most splendid storm doors imaginable. It was the storm door raised to the level of art, and so the entryway of the house took on its proper dignity, a happy transition from the outer world to the inner one. At Christmas they were best, decked out and inviting.

It's true the invitation was mostly to ourselves, and for a few good friends at the college where I taught, since we fit into our little Vermont town none too well; we were the only out gay male couple in the whole place, and though we were thor-

oughly accepted by the town's liberal community (that over-
layer of exiles which make Vermont culture tolerable) we were
strange new creatures to the ur-layer of native Vermonters
who made up the town's human bedrock. And who, signifi-
cantly, made up most of our neighborhood. Our house wasn't
cheap just because the floors sagged; it took us a while to learn
what people meant by that insistent talk about *location*.

But we had a world for ourselves there, and one very real
advantage to living with a window designer was that he could
make *anything* look good—the right arrangement, a little fuss-
ing with the details: splendor! The high ceilings accommodated
a huge tree at Christmas, thus making use of the ornaments
Wally had been squirreling away for a lifetime, souvenirs of
other people's childhoods collected at a decade of yard sales:
Bohemian glass beads strung into crystalline snowflakes, great
garlands of shimmering glass, an under-tree world of ancient
toys. The big granite cellar was perfect for the universe of dis-
play props Wally used for store windows. For me, a realm of
gardens, borders of perennials out front (against the now prop-
erly white picket fence, every new picket of it cut with my own
hands) and herbs and vegetables out back.

And doors to deck. One Christmas we made boxwood
wreaths from cuttings I took from the ruins of a formal rose
garden at the college; one hung on each of the gleaming oak
doors. They looked so classic, and lasted so long, that by early
spring they were still hanging there, plain without their rib-
bons and trim, cheerful and promising—qualities which
Vermonters need desperately, suicidally, in February and
March.

This is where the house finches come in. I noticed that every
time I opened the door there'd be a buzz of winged activity,
something hurrying through the branches of the wide old lilac.
And every time we'd come home, a parallel commotion. Soon
we saw what the fuss was about, which was the house these
two new colonizers had made for themselves, a woven bowl of
grasses and straw nestled into one of the wreaths, built against

the glass. At eye level! We stopped using the front door right away, and rigged a system of reflective plastic film inside to allow us to watch, quietly, from the front hallway, our tenants about their work. Their long work, it turned out, weeks of sitting, the male coming and going, leaving and returning with food, and then, miracles! A cluster of mouths and necks and awkward featherless gray about-to-be-wings writhing in the nest, a cup of pure and insistent hunger.

Once they'd all gone on, the nest having served its purpose, we considered saving it—but it was too well used a thing, too stained and too shit-in. It made us happy to have been host, for our house to be home, even briefly, to some other life, some welcome and mysterious pulse of energy from the outer world. Where would the new finches go? The bird book said they fed in the wild, individually, in summer, then formed great flocks in fall. I liked to imagine a cloud of them, a storm of gray and rose.

I didn't think of the house finches again until this new pair showed up in the roses, spring incarnate, pulses of desire and intention. How little they'd weigh, if you could hold one, and how utterly intent they are on their purpose, possessed by their own green and burgeoning industry: to build, to nest, to rear. *We further the world, small as we are, little handfuls of feather and heartbeat; we make it go on.*

My friend Chris said that after his wife died, in winter, spring was painful to him, all the world but her—and him— renewing itself. I don't find that spring hurts. I am aware that my interior season is winter, the republic of bare branches, the austere structure at the heart of things. And yet I take pleasure in my garden, even if my heart's not in it in the way it has been other years. In Vermont I gardened with a vengeance, that fire a part of my own imperative to make a safe home, to surround myself with a place to stand. And raise, unlike the birds, not young, but ourselves. And splendid lilies, monkshood and delphinium, campanula and strawflowers and love-in-a-mist.

When we came to Provincetown, I loved my much smaller

garden, a little cottage plot—infinitely more manageable, and small gardens actually are more likely to open onto revelation than large ones; in the intricacy of a contained space the world opens, the way it does in a Cornell box. On the Cape the sea warms the air a bit in winters, and cools in it summers, so that the climate partakes of the marine, of English weather. Thus roses thrive, lavish and luxuriant sprawlers, and if the sandy soil is infertile it also makes for fabulous drainage. I've gardened joyfully here.

But this year, no rush to buy seeds, no pushing at the limits imposed by frost or cool wet nights. I am in no hurry, am no jubilant participant, although I am glad for spring to unfold.

And, I think, this greening does thaw at the edges, at least, of my own cold season. Joy sneaks in: listening to music, riding my bicycle, I catch myself feeling, in a way that's as old as I am but suddenly seems unfamiliar, *light*. I have felt so heavy so long. At first I felt odd—as if I shouldn't be feeling this lightness, that familiar little catch of pleasure in the heart which is inexplicable, though a lovely passage of notes or the splendidly turned petal of a tulip has triggered it. It comes back to me as if from a great distance, this old delight in the world. It's my buoyancy, part of what keeps me alive—and I realize suddenly I can't remember when I felt it last. It's a sort of feeling that doesn't want to be long examined; happy, suddenly, with the concomitant experience of a sonata and the motion of the shadows of leaves, I just want to breathe in that lightness, after it's been so long lost.

Something about this new sunlight and warmth begins to dispel something darker and colder in me. I have the desire to be filled with sunlight, to soak my skin in as much of it as I can drink up, after the long interior darkness of this past season, the indoor vigil, in this harshest and darkest of winters, outside and in.

So this afternoon I lay on a high hill, a dune at the top (and it seemed the heart) of the world, surrounded by blooming beach plums, the glazed new leaves of poison ivy. I lay against the warm body of the hill, a child, and there was some generous and laving quality about the sunlight that allowed me to let go, to let all of tension and grief and chill sink out of me, into the sand, which was old enough and warm enough to hold it all. A few inches down the sand's still cool and moist, this time of year, but it's been busy drinking in the sun as well, and its surface glows and invites like human skin.

In the night it rained, and the wind blew hard, dislodging some canes of the climbing rose from the anchors which pin them to the walls. I think the finches' nest has been jostled; it seems more exposed, and maybe squeezed a bit, not quite so shapely. The birds are nowhere around; have they given up on this site already, subject to their implacable imperative, and moved on?

What a fragile thing a house is, though it doesn't seem so. All the energy we poured into the house in Vermont couldn't complete it; it was so big, and so needy, that I used to dream, even after five years, of part of the house falling away, the sloping floors gone their way at last, tumbling in the direction they'd always pined for. Or I'd dream of whole rooms I hadn't even discovered yet—rooms which, of course, needed immediate and serious attention. By the time I was just getting to some project I'd long postponed, I'd find that something done years before needed doing *again*. There was barely time to enjoy that particularly homosexual pleasure, decor; there was too much work to be done. Paint peels, plaster cracks, and gardens, of course, are the most ephemeral constructions of all.

What disappears faster than a garden without a gardener?

I learned just how fast and entire the loss of a garden is when we left Vermont. The back, private part of the garden was the last thing I studied, just before we left; I stood up on the deck above that geometry of paths and raised beds and looked down into the heart of it. It was a kind of externalization of something essential in me—is that what all gardens are?—and it had anchored me, mirrored me back, held me in place. I like the psalmist's phrase: a dwelling place; I didn't understand how intensely that garden had become a dwelling place for my spirit until I left it. Wally found me there, holding onto the railing we'd built ourselves, its turned spindles the salvage of some Victorian porch from a little town down the road. I *wanted* to go, and at the same time I knew I was taking leave, that moment, of some irreplaceable part of the history of my heart.

Not that I regret that decision, or have ever done so. We stayed in Vermont a year after Wally tested positive, reeling with the news at first and then beginning our accommodation to what Wallace Stevens called "the pressure of reality." The more reality pushes against us, Stevens said, the more the imagination is compelled to press back. He was referring to making poems, but it's also true that our imaginations went to work on a more pragmatic level. How was this news to fit into our lives? That mortal sword that hangs over all our heads hanging now a little lower, how were we to live? Wally was fine, then, physically, but his T-cell counts (vague marker that they are) weren't impressive ones, and we couldn't help but imagine versions of the future. In Vermont we felt as if our reality was exactly that—*ours*, not a shared sense of the world but an isolating otherness. My sense of what lay ahead, should we continue to stay there, was of a narrowing darkness and solitude, an increasing struggle against increasingly difficult demands. And how, someday, was I going to get in six cords of wood by myself?

A pair of friends, Chris and Brigid, offered to buy our house. It was easier to relinquish it to them—this would be their first house, too, and they brought to the prospect of owning it great eagerness, and a palpable love for the place, difficulties and all, which was what pleased me most. This wasn't entirely an easy house to love, ungainly and oddly laid out and, for all our five years' efforts, presenting inexhaustible prospects for the next energetic dwellers.

And so we let it go. As well as the grief I felt, abandoning my garden, and the groundedness it stood for, there was a real joy, an energizing quality in moving ahead. We were taking charge of the future, or at least a part of it. The test results had seemed to take the future away from us; letting go of our old life, pouring our energies into getting ourselves to a new place, was a way of wresting a bit of that control back. We all put up with less appealing aspects of the present for the sake of a future we anticipate later on. An HIV diagnosis calls the wisdom of such deferral into question. What were the pleasures we wanted now? How did we want to use our time together?

That autumn of our move, 1990, was one long golden extension of summer. We rented a house on the beach, in Provincetown, as far out toward the very tip of Cape Cod as it is possible to live. And because that autumn and winter were one of the mildest in memory, we felt we'd been given a radiant sort of gift, a season out of time, which seems to me now something suspended in amber: Wally and Arden on the beach, wrestling or resting, while I am inside the house, my desk up against the window which looks directly out past them toward Long Point Light, our promontory's last, haunted outpost. Wally and Arden wading, further and further out, into the long mercurial wash of low tides, the tidal flats shimmering around these two smallest figures, tiny evidence of my love held in the silver expanse of the afternoon.

It was summer again before I saw the old garden in its new incarnation—for an old garden, without its gardener, isn't the same entity at all, but a new event in the world. I hadn't realized how much the garden reflected my own obsessive propensities to shape it, how much that shape had to do with some ideal garden held in my head, toward which the raw material of the real space would be trimmed, trained, and cajoled. Chris and Brigid, bless their hearts, were not gardeners—or was it that *their* garden was aligned toward some other ideal?

Though they took pleasure in the effort, it was clear that they weren't sure which things were noxious weeds, to be banished, which the perennials I'd introduced and then given years of assistance to. The garden, seen from the street, seemed newly a jungle, an over-the-top efflorescence, consequence of my own overplanting gone mad. I had a visceral, physical response; I wanted to let myself in the gate and *weed*.

That response was, of course, about my not really having let the garden go. But the garden that was mine, I soon realized, was the interior one, the memory; the external garden had already become something else. What I saw as a particularly invasive, enormous weed might be, to the template of beauty which the new gardeners brought to their creation, the model of lush growth, a welcome wildness. Whatever, it was theirs now.

Until Brigid died, the following winter, in an accident on Route 2, the icy two-lane road she and I used to drive to work every morning. When Wally and I had put the house into Chris's and Brigid's hands, it was with a sense of their ongoingness, of the future ahead of them; it was clear they wanted to fill the big space with friends, animals, and, later, children. I was sidestepping a vision of my own future: lonely Vermont winter closing in, Wally sick and needing all the care I can give, no help, the dark little town around us, all the chimneys on its steep hills billowing white smoke and steam into icy and unforgiving air, our street going narrower and darker. Did I think we were sidestepping death, too? Perhaps our leaving when we did made Wally's life a little longer, I don't know. Certainly it made the last years brighter ones; I don't know how we'd have gotten through them without all the help and good company we found.

But I never thought it was Chris who would be widowed in the big house—a place for one person to get lost in, caught in the echoes of his own voice—instead of me. Sometimes I'd catch myself imagining death was determined to sweep someone away from that house, and that we'd somehow leapt out of the way, but that Brigid hadn't been able to.

The following summer the garden became something else entirely, and any sense of regret or nostalgia I had about it was subsumed into a kind of wonder at how the orders we make vanish so quickly, subsumed. The whole house seemed to go into a kind of accelerated decline; paint peeling, fence pickets snapped, the cream-yellow of the clapboards (a Shaker sort of color, it had seemed to me when we chose it) dirtied with the soot of tired oil furnaces struggling to keep up. The building seemed to express the psychic life it held, as if it were grief's outer skin.

Chris lived there for a while, then rented out the house, but he eventually found the payments impossible, the burden of the place overwhelming—and so it went back to the bank, to his sorrow and relief. I haven't seen it now for a long time. I understand that some friends took various perennials from the garden, which is just a shining idea, now. Which, in a way, is what it always was, an idea given not flesh but leaf.

We did not rescue the house, as we'd thought we were doing, those years ago. Oh, we did for a while make it not merely habitable but lovely, maybe more so than it had ever been; even when it was brand new I suspect it was built to be workmen's housing, and I doubt that love had been lavished upon its details. But the gleam of a loved house lasts only as long as he who loves it can keep polishing, keep occupying. What we did was to make for ourselves, for a while, a dwelling place, a deeply occupied zone in which to encounter and to recapitulate all our dwellings, a house deep enough, ours enough, to dream into. And then time swept us away, and in time took the house itself.

Did it? Perhaps now, repossessed, the place will be cheap enough again for somebody to come along flush and foolish with the sense of possibility, indifferent to the politics of location, with enough hubris to see some shining thing this sow's ear can become this time. Apartments? Offices, or the flat indignity of a parking lot?

The birds are flitting about in the box alder; in their hurry to nest, have they found another site? The need must push at them, requiring that they try again—a more protected place, this time. Though isn't it plain that no place is protected?

I enjoy the garden, this spring, but I don't feel that impera-
tive to shape, perhaps because I see how quickly it blows away,
how swiftly occupancy changes. I remember Wally talking, one
afternoon in December, at a time when his speech or his ideas
weren't always clear. I was rubbing his feet, which ached with
cramps as they turned inward to point toward one another, his
legs seeming to wither in front of us. Massage would ease the
pains better than anything else, and so I was always at his feet,
sometimes for a long time, a peaceful, steadying time to talk. "I
wonder how many people," he said, "had their feet rubbed in
this house?" I understood he was talking about how many peo-
ple had been sick here, really, in our room, how many had died
here, in this house's two hundred years. We knew that for most
of this century one family lived here, and raised eleven chil-
dren, enough people to generate generations of intensity, reso-
nant moments and gestures of the sort that reverberate in a
house. Before them, there aren't any records, but since maybe
1790 people have been holding this house, and being held by it.
I felt that Wally was experiencing himself, that moment, as
part of that history; he was joining a community. As we did, in
fact, when we bought this place, and set to work on it—just in
time, as it turned out, to make a home around us for the
onslaught. We had just enough time to do the essential things,
to make the house feel like ours. This house is actually small
enough for me to finish—someday—the projects we started. I
love to be here in storms, when the low-slung roof sheds water,
and I can feel the gravity of the big beams holding the roof
down, as they always have, as perhaps they did when they
were part of some ship. We became part of the life of the
house, one which seems to stand, to go on. When I was rub-
bing Wally's aching feet, did the dead of this house come and
stand around him?

At seven this morning—a clear and resonant day, an aura of
freshness and possibility around everything—there was a com-
motion in the roses: the birds, back at work. The nest looks

larger, as if they've gotten an early start today on reinforcing it, trying to build something capable of withstanding the wind. I've been out to look at it, from a distance I disciplined myself to maintain. They've anchored it with soil in the bottom, the action of wise engineers.

Contagious persistence: the will to inhabit, to make, out of whatever is offered, a dwelling place.

Dancing

〜∾

It's a warm afternoon and I've walked to town, with no real purpose in mind other than being out, among people, in the newly strengthening sun. I've wandered into the record shop, browsing, and found myself wanting a CD it hadn't occurred to me to buy, a compilation of Donovan's greatest hits. I loved Donovan when I was a teenager, his fey exoticism and what seemed to me the foreign sophistication of his picture on the back of *Mellow Yellow* in his pale yellow suit—from Carnaby Street? And the sandalwood-and-patchouli glow of *A Gift from a Flower to a Garden*, the double album from the days when he'd practiced transcendental meditation and decked himself in peacock feathers and gypsy clothes. That was when everyone was making double albums, as if all that expansiveness wouldn't fit on a single disk. I hadn't heard his songs in years, and reading the list of titles I had a sort of hankering for them.

Home, I put the new CD on. I'm tidying up the house, going through a pile of mail, and sorting out bills and books. And then Donovan—who sounds almost unbelievably *young* to me, not fey or worldly now at all, but boyish, untainted by sorrow or the corrosive powers of time—is singing a song I remember on the radio when I was in high school, a sort of stoned Zen calypso called "There Is a Mountain." I'd bought the forty-five then, and thought the lyrics profound:

> *First there is a mountain*
> *Then there is no mountain*
> *Then there is*

I've been moving a little to the music while I worked, stepping around the kitchen in synch with the rhythm, fussing with the pillows on the couch, and then I realize I am actually dancing. It feels wonderful, though I can feel how stiff my muscles are, how rigidly I've been holding myself. When was the last time I danced?

Mostly I've been moving cautiously, numbly, steeled because I know, at any moment, I may be ambushed by overwhelming grief. You never know when it's coming, the word or gesture or bit of memory that dissolves you entirely, makes it impossible, for a while, to go on. It happens every day at first, then not for a day or two, then there's a week when grief washes in every morning, every afternoon. It comes like a seizure, and will not be denied.

This is the first time I've been surprised by pleasure, the body's simple delight at being, after all this, here, still here.

Though I'm watching myself do it, and suddenly feeling self-aware almost makes me stop, I don't quite. Grief will be back, of course, any moment now. But I also know how lovely and light this music is, how sealed off in its innocence, and how happy my body is, these few minutes, to dance.

A Visit with Bill

Each room along this fluorescent hospital corridor has about it an aura of abandonment. These doors seem as if they should be labeled not with patients' names but with inscriptions: Shame, Suffering, Neglect, Nobody-Cares-Where-I-Am. These rooms are either starkly brilliant or entirely without light, and the men who live in them—all men here—have in common the absence of context: no personal effects, no clothes, pictures, no flowers, nothing that says, *This is who I was.* I use the past tense deliberately, since these men are already far along in the process of being erased. This is the AIDS ward of the Ione Shattuck Chronic Care Hospital, a state-run facility for people needing long-term care, a place with the reputation—and feeling—of the end of the road. Half the men here are gay, half IV drug users. There's a quality in the air that bus terminals have, and the waiting rooms of free clinics and welfare offices, a sense that there's no place else to go. It's the ultimate disconnection; our things, our family, our friends, our attachments to life are what expose and externalize identity. Without them, we become these narrowed and diminished faces. How small the body looks like this, with nothing to extend its limits, stripped of intimacy, bathed in the moon-wash of institutional light.

My friend Bill has been here for twenty-three weeks, not because of his lesions, but because of devastating and continuous diarrhea caused by cryptosporidium, an intractable intestinal parasite. Wally had it too, though never to this extent. Nothing cures it, but Wally's infection was controlled by an antibiotic. For Bill, drug after drug has done nothing, so he's dehydrated, malnourished, and requires intravenous feeding, though the plastic tube inserted into his chest as a porthole for nourishment and drugs keeps getting infected and causing more problems. His insurance can't pay for this kind of stay in a regular hospital, where in fact they really don't want him anyway. This is a kind of maintenance care; this place, the less expensive alternative, seems some precinct of hell. Though the faces of the people behind the nursing station are kind and tired; it's almost time for the shift change and they look as if they've fought a long day's battle without much success or help. It's not their fault the place is desolate; they can't remake the inferno. In some of their faces you can see that they would like to.

I've come with Phil, Bill's lover. We've been to a reading in Cambridge together, and we've stopped by to deliver some yogurt and a good night kiss from Phil. I haven't seen either of them for months, though we've talked on the phone, and Phil and I have decided to take some time tonight and tomorrow to catch up face-to-face. We're going to lunch at a museum, letting him relax into a different role for a few hours. I'm bracing myself for I don't know what as we move down the corridor. This was, in a way, what I dreaded for Wally—his life wrenched out of our hands, into this institutional world where he'd be at their mercy, subject to invasion, unprotectable. My chest tightens as we come toward the end of the hall.

I wait at Bill's door while Phil goes in first; it's nearly ten-thirty and he expects Bill to be sound asleep. But in a moment he's back, brightened. Bill is up and wants to see me, and Phil takes me by the hand and draws me in behind him.

The room's a revelation. In memory it seems to me that Bill has draped a scarf across the shade of a bedside lamp, as Blanche DuBois would have, to warm the light to something rosy and flattering. Perhaps I'm inventing that; it *feels* like a room whose glow is filtered through figured silk, anyway. The walls are covered with paintings from Bill's house, the windowsill thick with flowers and leafy plants, the whole room redolent of warmth and human habitation, an aura—in opposition to the severity of every floodlit room we passed to arrive here—of civility. This might be Bill's little studio apartment, in the intimate upper floor of some city brownstone; room just for bed, tiny refrigerator, and the non-negotiable requirements of the civil life: flowers, paintings, music.

And here, in splendor, lies Bill. I realize, seeing him, the apprehension I've been carrying about not knowing how he'll look; he's the first really sick person I've seen since Wally died. But seeing his face I'm flooded, suddenly, with relief, with appreciation. Not because he looks well—always a boyish man, he's become a large child, extremely thin, his head shaved, his lesions darkened against his pale skin, his eyes enormous—but because he is what people are, sometimes, very late in their lives: so fully himself, himself all the way to the edges, the way Rilke described roses as "flush with their own being."

Bill is beautiful to me in the way that Wally was, not in any ornamental sense of the word, but in the way that all things which are absolutely authentic are beautiful. Is there a luminous threshold where the self becomes irreducible, stripped to the point where all that's left to see is pure soul, the essence of character? Here, in unfailing self-ness, is no room or energy for anything inessential, for anything less than what counts.

Bill is unmistakably himself now, gracious host even here, charming, playful, somehow plaintive and fetching at once. He's flat on his back, head propped on a small legion of favorite pillows; across his feet is draped a mint-green chenille bathrobe piped, like a birthday cake, with tendrils, scrolls, and blossoms of more chenille in frosting colors: orchid, lavender, tangerine.

The robe is something Lucy Ricardo might have worn for mornings in Connecticut, the sort of garment which almost invariably carries with it a narrative. Bill discovered it in a Provincetown shop devoted to the pleasures of the bath.

There it hung, a magnetic glory charged with the subterranean powers of gender; *I am someone's mother*, it seemed to say, *in 1957*. Both its over-the-top femininity and lavish price meant, of course, he'd leave it there. Wouldn't he? It was a whim, an indulgence, though a potent—potentially dangerous?—attraction. But he found he couldn't forget it; it began to occupy a new space in his imagination, or rather to draw to itself the energy and associations of a lifetime's imaginings. To go back, to buy it, meant to embrace something profoundly, lushly nelly.

(Odd how the words for this sort of thing have about them a quality of Victoriana: nelly, sissy, fairy, fey. There's something about them of girlishness preserved under glass, a curious kind of delicate, past-prime virginity—as though to give in to that aspect of ourselves is to become someone's lavender-scented auntie, a specter of rosewater and pressed flowers and scraps of lace. Sometimes it seems to me like the last taboo for gay men, one of the most deeply internalized prohibitions, to allow oneself that swooning, gorgeous silliness; in 1995, weirdly enough, it's more okay to be a queer than it is to be a sissy.)

The robe—first coveted, then accepted, then treasured—pools across Bill's knees, its splendid piping the colors of a dissolving petit-four. Old disco lyrics come into my head, unbidden: *Someone left the cake out in the rain* ... The fact that I've never known him well—I've been more a friend of Phil's—melts away as we begin to speak; it's impossible now *not* to know him. The more we talk the more I begin to feel I'm moving inside of some profound connection, the only one there's likely to be between us. But enough. It's the edge of that kind of intimacy I felt with Wally, the aura that surrounded his leave-taking drawing me in, closer and closer into his company, like moving with another person into a very small, warm circle of lamplight, which includes and defines you both. One clear, true instance of *really* knowing each other, which is becoming indelible even as we speak.

I can feel how large, how essential this moment is as it's happening; that is what I have come to love about being an adult, to the extent that I can claim that title: that one knows more about how good things are, how much they matter, as they're happening, that knowledge isn't necessarily retrospective anymore. When I was younger, I missed so much, failing to be fully present, only recognizing the quality of particular moments and gifts after the fact. Perhaps that's one thing that being "grown-up" is: to realize in the present the magnitude or grace of what we're being offered.

Bill wants to hear, first, about Wally's dying. I sit beside him with my hand resting on his, which moves from his side onto his delicate chest, so that soon my hand is resting just above his heart. Phil sits at the foot of the bed and doesn't say much; our witness, Bill's protector, is letting us have this time. I can tell it feels good to him, to sit quietly, to rest on the side of the bed, listening to someone else talk with Bill, in some interaction which is without threat, which asks nothing of either of them.

I tell Bill everything. About the ease of it, the awe and mystery, and Bill listens carefully, closing his eyes sometimes as if to listen more closely, sometimes opening them wide as if to take more of the story into himself. I try not to leave anything out; I can tell what he wants from me is completeness, any sense I can give of actuality, any guesses this eyewitness to last things may have made. I have feelings, experience, intuition more than I have knowledge in any conventional sense—but isn't that part of what being with dying teaches us, different sorts of knowing?

Then Phil's lying across Bill's feet, resting on the soft green chenille, as though he's fallen asleep there, dreaming. I understand, the way he holds him, what Phil has done. It's him who's made this room what it is, who has protected a space for Bill in which he can continue—so fully, and so fully supported—to be himself. My friend Jean, in whose safe blue bedroom I will fall apart, a month from now, wrote a poem that ends

And me,
I got what I wanted.
I died with my life around me.

Isn't that what any of us would ask for, to be fully *in* our lives as we leave them, to have been ourselves all the way first? This is the gift that Phil's love is giving to Bill. In the absolute endangerment of illness, here is safety. In the face of reduction, identity. In the face of indignity, respect. In the face of erasure, here is intimacy, the sustaining of context which preserves the self.

It's as if Bill floats, sweet boy, talking now about his plans for his funeral—only white flowers, *his* music, but what color lining for his casket?—and the carefully orchestrated party he intends for Phil to throw afterward. He drifts in the space Phil's attention has created, easy there, despite it all, an odd and heartbreaking ease.

I know what the price of this is for Phil—the exhaustion, the continuous focus on another, the postponement of one's own needs, but it's also clear to me how much he *wants* to give this to Bill; it doesn't even seem a choice, exactly, just what there is to be done. Phil can't see himself the depth and magnitude of the gift; he is so far inside it he has no means of measure.

Bill is having the best time, talking away, and suddenly he's starving, and eats two turkey-on-white-bread sandwiches and two little packages of salty pretzels, more than he's put away in weeks. We'll learn, the next day, that he'll throw it all up in the night, but it doesn't matter; he's hungry and happy in the moment. A vital pulse gleams through all his pleasures, his plans, his careful posthumous hosting of his friends.

What I'm seeing is the kindest and sweetest mirror of the last of my life with Wally, and so rather than returning me to difficulty and pain, the visit is somehow restorative, bracingly genuine, consoling. Where could it be clearer, here in the heart of abandonment, what love achieves?

A Black Beaded Dress

This is how it happens: I'm driving back from Boston with Phil, in that happily intimate space the interior of a car is, at night, with a friend, a chance for extended conversation interrupted only by a stop for gas or coffee. When have we ever had a chance to talk like this, not at a party or a reading or in the hurry of a chance encounter on the street?

I'm talking about what it's like for me, with Wally three months gone; Phil's talking about how he imagines it will be for him, how he doesn't want to imagine it but has to, needs to, in order to have some sense of a tenable future. For each of us there's so much in what the other says that we recognize, and what an aid and comfort that simple fact is: somebody else feels or has felt like me. We're entirely encompassed in our conversation when we come upon a detour; the highway's been closed, south of Plymouth, and just beyond the makeshift wooden barriers and orange pylons are the flashing red and blue lights of a squadron of emergency vehicles. The bright, alarming row of them conceal whatever they surround, and I have that brief thought one always has, coming upon an accident, *Is this someone I know?* But we're a long ways from home, and I dismiss the notion, and along the dark wooded detour which takes us away from the smear of disaster we continue our quiet and encompassing conversation.

＊　　　＊　　　＊

In the morning the news comes early, my roommate rushing in from morning coffee, out of breath, shaken, saying someone from town's died, a woman, a poet, someone in the Program: is it my friend Lynda? An accident, in Plymouth. I call the police in town who tell me to call the police there and I do, and they're hesitant to tell me anything until I tell them Lynda's name, tell them I'm a friend, tell them I need to know, and they tell me she's died, in a single-car accident, that she must have died immediately, the tree she'd smashed into pushed through the roof of the old white Saab she'd bought after her last accident, a car she wanted because it would be solid and safe.

In memory, all that morning I'm standing in the kitchen, leaning against the counter because I can't quite stand up; sometimes I'm sitting at the blue table but all the time I am talking, talking on the phone: to friends and students of Lynda's and of mine, to her husband David's answering machine, to her parents, to the people who have to know. I realize that Michael, her roommate, my friend, doesn't know yet—but he's at work, serving breakfast in a restaurant down the block, and I don't want to tell him there. I plan that I'll meet him at the door of the restaurant, when he gets off, so that he can hear this from me, but I don't count on the radio playing in the dining room; Lynda's death is reported on the morning news while Michael's serving someone a plate of eggs. So I'm standing in the kitchen when he comes racing around the corner of the house to the door, stumbling, weeping, dissolved in terror and in pity.

Michael weeping uncontrollably in my arms: terrible mirror of myself, three months ago but also in the days since. I cry almost every day, still, though it subsides a little faster, though I don't go back so much to this raw, stricken place of unbearable new grief. And I can't go there now, not exactly, though Michael can. He's twenty-five and no one close to him has ever died before; he can't stop shaking. But it's not as if I know something more than he does about death, not as if I have some sort of wisdom extracted from experience. I'm stricken and horrified and half-numb, and though I'd like it to be otherwise the truth is that I am full of confusion, because my grief is so inextricable from my fury and my fear, conflicting feelings tumbling together like the slap of wave on wave.

After Lynda died I thought I'd never write about her; I was too full of anger, raw and startled and afraid. Of what? It was fear for myself, I guess; how would I hold on through another death? And how could I face the bitter sense that she'd tossed her own life away, with all her extraordinary gifts, that she's spun out of control in a long skid she could have prevented?

She'd said to a mutual friend, reflecting on her own self-destructive behavior, *Well, at least if I die, think of the beautiful elegies my friends will write for me.* I couldn't bear that; I couldn't abide that romanticizing of harm, that weird combination of self-aggrandizement and willful disregard of the gift of one's own life.

And I was afraid too that to try to write about her was to admit chaos, to describe an emotional complexity that would utterly elude and confound me. I knew what I felt about Wally; it might be a great reservoir of pain, an overpowering sense of loss and of awe, but those feelings were clear, as transparent to me as new tide pouring over the marsh grasses. About Lynda's death I had no such clarity.

The last time I saw her she was drunk. The middle of the day; she'd been to an AA meeting; I was to meet her outside the church and together we'd walk to a restaurant to meet David, who was in town for a few days. She's weaving a little as she emerges from the church basement. She's wearing a little black dress, a ragged black coat and beret, leaning on her ebony cane, and as soon as I see her I know she's not all right. But I try to deny it, and take her arm; I try to say to myself, Well, maybe she's just upset, things have been so hard. Our friendship's been strained and compromised these months; we are being very cautious with one another. I don't trust her, she is trying terribly hard to please me, to make a good impression. She takes my arm and we walk to the restaurant together, the Post Office Café, a greasy but basically likable place that's open all year round, as not many places here are, and there's David at a table waiting for us. His face falls when he looks at her and sees the shape she's in; his look says *Why am I here?* and then almost immediately *What's to be made of this?* which is what the faces of those long used to living with alcoholics almost always say: *How will we get through this one?* Lunch is strained and sad and Lynda's bitchy and out of focus; he's come all this way to see her and she's not only not home but is ugly and sniping. All three of us are just making small talk to try to live through an hour. My friend, whom I've loved for years, my adventurer, wonderful poet, survivor, heroine, role model, flash girl, paragon of style and endurance—well, I find I just don't like her at all.

How can I reclaim her?

It's 1984, more or less, and I am dancing with a woman in a red cocktail dress, a dashing little number with a large, elegant, and somewhat daffy bow tied at the back of its dropped shoulders. We've met at a writers' conference where we're both teaching; she's here with her soon-to-be husband, and we're drawn together into a fast, immediate friendship fired by a complex set of bonds we'll be years in getting to know. She's tiny, fiercely glamorous in a kid-playing-dress-up way; she's angular, her firm nose casting a sharp shadow, her high cheekbones rouged. We tango, we glide, we conquer the dance floor like born show-queens—more interesting, more endearing because neither of us really knows these dances. We know how to make things look right, understand the playful and delicate work appearances are.

What launches and sparks any friendship is a mysterious alchemy, of course; how often friends predict we'll adore so-and-so, and put us together at parties only to find that so-and-so and us chat politely until conversation fizzles like a wet fuse. Who can say what makes two people forge a sudden, surprising link?

Though certainly I can say what deepened it. We shared a sensibility, so much so that I can't help but think of Lynda now as almost a way of seeing, a stance, an aesthetic. (Is that one thing the dead do for us, become a set of codes, an approach to describing the world?) So many things will always speak of Lynda, be redolent of her.

Specifically?

A certain sartorial intersection of glamour and trash, a louche but lovely address at which reside faux leopard any-thing, cloches, art deco jewelry, silk scarves worn as head wraps, tiny black dresses worn with a black leather jacket. Lynda looked wonderful, and she loved looking unlike anyone else; she wanted her unlikeness to be seen and appreciated. Her style, as her body fell apart over time, through back pains and car accident, became more and more the sort she admired, a panache which triumphed over difficulty without exactly concealing it: she adored Frida Kahlo, Marianne Faithfull, Lotte Lenya, women made more beautiful by a certain broken quality about them, by the *acknowledgment* of that quality. Thus she loved drag queens not just for their tawdry glamour but also for the way that their illusion was always ultimately doomed to fail. The artifice of making oneself be whomever one liked always revealed the reality beneath, and therein lay both its failure and a good part of its charm. She was a lover of appearances, of performance, of bravura, of failed but honor-able gestures toward beauty.

Because the world was ruined, wasn't it, and how could its children not be ruined as well?

We loved ruined armor, and Wally and I actually bought her a suit of it, in a way. At an auction, we found a black beaded dress, a tiny slip of transparent chiffon stitched with spirals of black jet beads. The beading was unraveling a bit at the edges, but it was perfect: a sheer black exhalation of sin, jazz, and dis-sipation, something so tiny and fragile, and so daringly tough, that I couldn't imagine anyone else wearing it. Beneath her achieved surface, Lynda's vulnerability was always visible; this is what made her such a wonderful teacher, and such a wonderful friend. It made her empathic, grounded, real. And it allowed us to share a common sense of difference, an odd feeling of being in disguise, of impostorship. Why were people reading our poems, taking workshops to hear *us* talk about poetry? If people knew who we *really* were, we used to joke, they'd never listen to us in workshop!

Because we were both kids who'd been in trouble; we both came from households racked with alcohol or chemicals, and we'd both been down close enough to the pavement to believe we could wind up back in some lowlife dive at any minute. Children of difficulty, we recognized in each other certain marks of damage, certain absences of confidence, certain luscious ambitions to be loved or adored, deep convictions of difference. We felt a sense of both being pushed to the margin and choosing that realm of marginality; felt, in other words *queer*, and our queerness—as poets, as born outsiders—both separated us from the world and energized us. Lynda used to like to say she was a gay man trapped in a woman's body; this perception wasn't so much about sexuality as about a whole approach to reality, a position from which one might understand the vulnerability and porosity of the self, the power of its costuming gestures. I knew there were aspects of me Lynda understood through and through; I know either of us could tell without fail what the other would love.

The art we loved was queer art: Hart Crane and Cavafy, Billie Holiday, Chet Baker, Joseph Cornell, film noir: lush surfaces spread over difficult, edgy material, art marked by the transubstantiation of pain into style. Art full of anguish and pleasure in the racked beauty of the world, the kind of alloy she loved, and understood: the sort of thing we make when we're true to the world's comminglings of gorgeousness and terror.

For ten years Lynda and I would teach together, pull each

other through crises of confidence, read all of each other's poems, cheer each other through readings, edit each other's manuscripts. She mattered to me greatly as a critic but even more as an inspiration: she worked at her art with a singular intensity, and in each new poem she'd raise the stakes as high as she could, putting everything at risk, pouring herself into her coruscating, elegant texts. So that one had to live up to *that*, poems had to matter that much.

During those ten years we'd see each other at the regular writers' conferences where we taught, and visit in between or talk on the phone, and mail would always carry back and forth funny, signifying tokens that each knew the other would love. But despite our closeness there were other edges, the recurrent shadows of drugs and alcohol, which Lynda would try to keep from me, as she tried to conceal the fragility of her sobriety from all her friends. She had a lifetime battle with addictions. Out on the streets at sixteen, she married a Chinese gambler, lived in the Chinatowns of New York and Boston, and launched herself through a long stream of cities in a lurching wild life the recounting of which constituted one of her favorite obsessions and activities. She'd made it through alcohol, heroin, and harrowing hard-luck circumstances that would have left most people in their graves, and wound up in Little Rock, Arkansas, newly sober and determined to write poetry. There she met David, and began a remarkable career as a poet and teacher, hammering out an unmistakable poetic voice, winning prizes for each of the two books she published during her lifetime. Becoming, over the years, a larger, deeper person, with a great range of sympathies, with humor and insight, with a kind of palpable distinctness of being that says *I am entirely myself, and no one's like me.*

But the struggle with addictions didn't end, though she didn't want her friends to see that. I didn't know, at first, about the slips; she'd enlist friends to protect her. A certain quality of charm—manipulative, to a degree?—would convince each friend that no one understood him the way Lynda did. And each friend would be eager to protect her apparent fragility. What little I knew I kept to myself. After she died it turned out that many people had bits and pieces of her story, and we were all holding them back from each other, as if we alone were the keepers of the sad knowledge, and not to admit what we knew was somehow to spare her.

But there'd be weeks when she wasn't available on the phone, and David would be vague about where she was, and times when I'd hear her back had gone out once too often to be quite convincing. Odd bits of disjunction or disinformation. And then one summer, on the last night of the writers' conference, she stood in front of me with a group of celebrating students, a champagne bottle in her hand, her face transformed, glazed, not hers. I was terrified, not least because her face reminded me of my mother's: an alcoholic whose visage was shattered, distorted as if one looked at her *through* alcohol, a film of troubling liquid.

Over the years, increasingly, more slips, things unraveling. But she'd try, always, to keep that part of her life removed from mine—as if she knew how much it would trouble me, knowing the turmoil in my own history, knowing that, incapable of dealing with addiction, I'd run away.

I never saw so clearly how she'd worked to protect me as I did on our last happy night together, the last time she seemed to me entirely herself. We'd come to New York, the autumn before Wally died; I'd been nominated for a literary prize, and I needed someone with me for moral support at the tense ceremonies and hoopla that accompanied the event, an Oscar-type celebration where the awards were announced. There was no question of Wally traveling by then; he couldn't walk, and barely understood when I explained the details of the proceedings, though his pride in me was evident, his insistence that I should win. (I tried to explain that I wouldn't, that for a young poet to be nominated was prize enough, but he wasn't interested in the subtleties.) So my date and I arrived at the Plaza; I helped her from the taxi in my tux and shiny patent leather shoes, and she was never more splendid: the black beaded dress resplendent, all its loose traceries of jet stitched back onto the voile, rhinestones on her black cloche, an ebony cane. She was radiant, playful, funny, enthralled with the weirdness of the night, simultaneously laughing at and delighting in its glamour. We were bad kids together, impostors; what were *we* doing here, in this gilt ballroom stuffed with enough black wool and satin to wrap the hotel itself, enough champagne to fill the fountains in the Park?

That night, in the drawing room comedy an event which takes itself so grandly and seriously inevitably is (these are *writers*, after all, in these formal disguises), we seemed to have entered a Manhattan of another era, a penthoused realm of suite and ballroom, glimmer and sheen. Who'd have thought Lynda would be dead in five months? Who'd have thought, seeing her that night, that she'd survived an awful year?

Everything had seemed to push her toward a terrible edge. A trip to Poland, with her mother, had awakened a deep sense of ancestry, as the devastation her family had suffered during the Holocaust emerged—a ruination she seemed to take into herself, identifying with the suffering, the encamped, the gassed. She'd come back filled with a sense of historical burden, one that wasn't in the least abstract or universal but loomingly, frighteningly personal. Her friend Emily—they met in jail, when Lynda, at seventeen, was performing the court-assigned community service of reciting the lyrics to James Brown's "King Heroin" to her fellow delinquents—was struggling with AIDS, and Lynda couldn't help but look at her and wonder how, and why, she'd escaped. Wasn't there something she could do to help Emily and her child? Wally, whom Lynda loved, had begun his long decline. She'd fought her way toward cheerfulness, standing by his bed with her arms full of the sunflowers she'd brought him, and later fallen apart in the kitchen, out of earshot.

And then, in Chicago, her car was hit head-on by a taxi, the front end crushed, the bones of both her feet broken. Never particularly strong—her health compromised by years of living marginally—the recovery was terrible, and partial, though she spent months in bed, though there was more than one operation. David used to carry her, once she could get out a bit, up and down the four flights of stairs leading to their lakeshore apartment.

When she was walking, out in the world again after months of physical therapy, she took a job in Boston for a semester. It wasn't a happy choice: she was still physically frail from the accident's aftermath and addicted to painkillers. Boston had been a difficult city for her, the location—dreamy and often nightmarish now, in memory—of many of her hardest years, the old days of using and getting by from deal to deal. The details of that fall would only emerge for me later: how she'd been hospitalized, nearly dying from an overdose of the painkillers she'd taken, how a friend coming to collect some clothes for her in the hospital had found her closet full of bottles.

And yet, that night, in the middle of that season of dissolution, she was entirely present, in focus, strong, sober. How did she do it? Was her show of strength a gift to me?

In December, she came for a visit; the home health aides who were in the house to help care for Wally insisted she was stoned, but I couldn't see it. Perhaps I didn't want to, or perhaps it was simply that my attention was so focused on Wally, in those late dark hours, that I couldn't see her. Though I could feel that something was off, that her visit was really more about her than about us, as if there was something she needed from us that I couldn't give. How could I give to anyone, when every bit of me was centered around that hospital bed in what used to be our living room? Every bit of my psyche was involved with surrounding that man as he drifted toward being a child, toward a simple radiant awareness, toward being no one.

Lynda decided she'd come to Provincetown in the winter, when her teaching gig was up. In part she wanted to take time to write; in part I believe she was avoiding going home, since she was using and didn't want to confront David and the evidence of her domestic life. And in part she wanted to be near Wally and me, wanted to help us, and didn't understand she wasn't in any shape to help anyone. She told me a dream she'd had; in it, she was living in a cottage on the beach, and out on the shore, hunkering around near the wharves and piers, was a huge, hungry rat, bigger than a dog, red-eyed, malevolent. *The rat's my addiction*, she said, *I'm coming to Provincetown to finally confront the rat.*

Moments after Wally died, Lynda called; I think she knew. I heard her voice on the answering machine in the kitchen, but I didn't go to it then, lost as I was in the unbelievable hour Wally had filled with himself and then with his absence. She called again from Cambridge the next morning, and after I told her she said she'd drive down later in the day. She arrived, late in the afternoon, drunk.

I sat on the bed, in the ringing ache and resonance of that room, the room I'd only just been able to enter again, all its evidence of him—glasses, toothbrush, little wooden angel hanging from a thread above his pillow—precious and unbearable.

And my friend could not see or feel what was happening, could not be with me in the actuality I could barely be in myself, because she was drunk. We talked for a few minutes and then I couldn't stop the anger, the rising choke of it, and I said, *You need to leave, you have to go now, I can't be with you now.* Anger not only that she was unavailable when I most needed help, but that I had to move from that depth of shock and fear and loss into this other feeling, that my energies had to be pulled this way *now*, of all times, when I had no resources to protect myself.

Though I *did* protect myself; did, out of some raw instinct toward self-preservation, push my friend away.

Is this what death always does, push us toward a kind of brink of reality, so we have to stand face to face with ourselves, all our histories up front, simultaneous, newly intensified?

Lynda's drinking brought back fear and anger at seeing some-
one I love obscured by booze, and my own desire to run away.
Suddenly I had, again, to determine boundaries, create limits
in order not to be overwhelmed.

(Other old issues resurface, too: talking to my father on the
phone forces me to look at our distance, the unreality of my life
to him, and I feel invisible, unseen. I'm aware again of how the
central fact of my life isn't one which church or state cares to
recognize; who *sees* what has happened to us?)

Just as I always tried to protect Lynda, I want to spare her
still, and her husband, and her family, but I want also the
actual dimensions of my friend's illness, which seemed to
deepen its hold, in the weeks after Wally's death. Suffice to say
I'd hear about the pills and prescriptions, about things slipping
out of her control, about her going to meetings drunk or high,
weeping about Wally in the street.

I couldn't see her at all, at first, and so our next meeting was
at the memorial service, a week after Wally died. She seemed a
fragile surface constructed above an abyss, held together by
wires, fragmented, as if her energies were split apart, some
fracture setting the self at odds with the self.

Later, we meet for lunch, but it seems strained, all the old
spontaneity gone. She works so hard to convince me she's tak-
ing care of herself that it doesn't ring true; she doesn't want to
be sober, she wants to *seem* okay. So there's an unreality about
our talk, and I don't think she actually hears me. We have that
sort of AA conversation in which we each report on our condi-
tion, state our problems, but it never feels like a real exchange;
it feels as though Lynda's holding on by the skin of her teeth,
desperate to convince herself or me she's going to be all right.
It rankles me, then, that I never really get to tell her the story
of Wally's death, of how it felt; she never really seems to listen.

What can I do? I'm powerless, everyone's powerless in the
face of her addiction. I encourage a friend in recovery to try to
intervene. I try to think how I can see her at all, when I feel
completely porous, when I think there's so little of me and that

so fragile. She leaves a note in my mailbox, written on the back of an envelope I have still: *Please don't hold my addictions against me.*

I'm worried about her, but I know Lynda's a survivor. She's made it through so much already, lived through such difficulty that, of course, she'll get through this, though I've never seen her spinning so fast, sinking so badly. It's going to pass, I think, she's going to hit some bottom and then pull herself up.

She falls in the shower and cuts her head; Michael gets her to the hospital for stitches, and on the way home she stops at the pharmacy in town which must be one of the few places in America where you can buy both painkillers and beer. Then Michael and my AA friend succeed in getting her to rehab, so I think that'll be the turning point: she'll be back now, in her strength again. But sobriety hasn't really been her choice; she isn't ready. She stays a few days and then she's back as if nothing's happened.

I think, What I've done for years, when my friends fucked themselves up with chemicals, is guard myself, run away. Do I have to hide from her? How can I take care of myself but also behave responsibly toward someone I love? Rena, Wally's old therapist, says, *It sounds like you're afraid of her.* And I am; I am holding myself together precariously, learning to move through the simple routines I've established for myself: walking the dogs, swimming laps at the motel pool, buying food for one. Trying to learn how to stumble through the days without falling, without falling any more than I have to. My head feels like a vacancy; I'm a great broken space which fills alternately with weeping and with nothing. Where is there room for the turbulence of Lynda?

I hear things are starting to turn, beginning to change: she's going to meetings, has a sponsor, is admitting that she's been in bad shape, owning up that things have been out of control.

So I think about what I want to say, and build up courage to say it. I want to meet and talk, I want to say, I love you and I can't stand it when you do this to yourself, I have to keep my distance from you now because I don't have the strength to bear it. Please, go home, go where your support is. I'll be here for you later, I'll be connected with you again as soon as I can. So I call and leave a message on her machine that I want to talk. It's Sunday; I tell her I'll be home that night and then away for a couple of days; if we don't talk tonight, let's talk on Wednesday. She doesn't return my call that night (later I'll hear she was out drinking). Monday I'm going to Boston. Tuesday she goes to Boston, too, to see her shrink, and on the way home drives her car—doing what, eighty? eighty-five?— into a tree just past Exit 4.

Wild arrogance, to imagine there won't be more to feel because you won't be able to feel it. To think no more loss can happen because you can't hold it.

But the dreadful rears up, enormous, uncontainable, too large to apprehend and yet stubbornly insistent upon being real. I say, *I can't, I won't, how can I even begin*, but the fact towers, dominates the world.

A single car accident, at high speed on a wet road. A suicide? I don't think so, not in the sense of a deliberate choice made to end her life, not in the sense of Lynda *deciding* to die, then and there, or planning it. And yet all her last months seemed a careening out of control, as if the steering wheel had started racing in her hand months before, as if she'd turned then into some skid she couldn't pull herself out of. How much did it matter, exactly, what she'd intended just then? Her family said she was sober, at the time of the crash, but did that matter exactly either, since that moment was part of a plummeting fall from sobriety—a condition more brittle and precarious for her than I'd ever known? Suddenly everything about the way she'd been living seemed a kind of flirtation with death, a courting of death. Even the poems, beautifully wrought, full of engagement with life, seemed in retrospect full of negotiations with mortality, as if everything she ever wrote was a rehearsal for a suicide note. But she was going to meetings, she was thinking of going home, she was raising the bright flag of some will to live, even if it was wavering, while she stared into the face of her rat.

But didn't we feel, everyone who knew her, as if she'd killed herself? Everyone said to me something beginning with *If only . . .*

If only I'd been there, reached out in some way. A suicide spreads responsibility everywhere; everyone tries to respond, somehow, to the brutal gesture. In stunned anger, in horror and grief, the wind knocked out of us, we're all reacting all day and evening on the phone. Just when I had stopped this, just when I wasn't telling the story of Wally's death over and over again, I'm back in that electronic network of friends, students, everyone who knew her in some way wanting to connect with everyone else, touch base, tell a story, speculate (*If only . . .*). The phone had become a kind of drug for me in the weeks after Wally died: a source of contact, something to do besides weeping, besides lying in that empty bed, besides walking in the frozen world. Now, again I'm living leaning against the kitchen counter, the phone become a part of my face.

Do I feel anything besides stunned, a numb disbelief that I'm going to another funeral, in a few days, in Newark, that Lynda's vanished?

I feel this rush of compassion for David, who couldn't have known what was coming, at least not the way I knew what was coming for Wally. David is my age exactly but a few days younger; we are both forty and our lives have broken in half, ground to wrack and powder. Compassion that he had no time to prepare, when I had this long time to look at what was coming. Was it slow? Did it race by me? Is there any way to even approach getting ready? I made the arrangements, found the help, discovered what could allow Wally and me to live as best we could, but what preparation could I make in my heart? Is it good, the knowledge I had? What's the difference in our grief, our rages, our bouts of numbness (relief, sometimes, from howling pain)?

I feel this dread of the world, of the impossible processes of loss: my lover and then my best friend gone in the space of two months? The world's a maw, a grinding machine. Who or what's to be eaten next? I go to Rena's, a town away, for dinner, and I become completely obsessed with the candles I've left burning on the mantel, those glass-encased prayer candles Catholics light at altars, the sort that burn for days, supposedly seven, though the exact number always seems to vary. One's been flaming continuously for Wally since he died, some outward token of the flame inside me directed toward him. *The dead can see light*, my friend Mekeel says. I've lit another for Lynda. During dinner I become certain they're going to get too hot, the glass will crack, the hot wax will pour out, perhaps the wick will not be drowned by the liquid wax and keep burning, so that the hot wax will all catch flame, the mantel and the wood floor beginning to burn. I am sure my house must be burning; I find I don't care so much about anything in it except the photographs of Wally and the dogs; the fire is going to take my dogs and they are all I have; there is nothing else for me in the world. I call home and discover that the answering machine works, so it can't have melted, but I still can't rest until I call my neighbors and have them check the house.

I am standing in death's floodplain, I am in the way of a tidal rush of loss. What is reality but a system for carrying people and things away?

But mostly I feel anger, inadmissible anger which is so big that it almost obscures grief, a dark body between me and the edges of the sorrow I can see but not fully feel. I struggle because I don't want to admit it, but I am full of rage. Wally did not have a choice, could not through any powers he might muster have changed a stroke of his history, could not rewrite a word of that last nine months' text of erasure and of disappearance. But Lynda could.

Couldn't she? I know addiction's itself an illness, I know she lived in one long struggle to gain control, to hold herself intact, but how can I help but feel she had a choice? Perhaps not to control the steering wheel, that single night, but to alter the course of the nights and days that led her there, to confront and examine her circumstances in order to live. How vain and self-indulgent self-destructiveness looks in the face of AIDS! The virus in its predatory destruction seems to underline the responsibility of the living; life's an unlikely miracle, an occasion of strangeness and surprise, and isn't it appalling to dismiss it, to discard the gift? Isn't it horrifying, to choose not to live when you *can* choose?

Which is not to say that her pain wasn't real, her struggles the result of deep faultlines that shook her to the very core. My friend must have wrestled so terribly, and who am I to say that her disease was any less relentless than Wally's? Partly my rage is just anger that she's left me, too. And partly my rage is at the world, at God, at the blind bone-breaking ugly design of things.

And somewhere underneath all that is the sense of losing the loveliest companion, a sister, a woman I adored, brilliant and accomplished and bright-spirited, my irreplaceable friend.

In her room in the rented cottage, Michael and I find Lynda's notebook computer still open on the bed, a few letters and a journal covered in marbled paper I'd given her spread on the comforter. Her new manuscript, in its heavy black thesis binder, on the floor beside the night table. Clothes here and there, but only her usual disorder; it's the room of someone who's planning to come back, someone who has no thought of *not* returning to these books and papers. And hung on a coat hanger, from a doorjamb, the beaded dress, gleaming, translucent, already haunted.

Lynda's funeral, in a suburb of Newark, one of a continuous strip of town which is actually many towns, a funeral parlor viewing room where her body's displayed in an open casket. She doesn't look much like herself: an austere black dress, a rosary (would she have been appalled, or like the drama?) in her hand, none of the characteristic jewels. Her chest is much too large. I find myself imagining she'd have been pleased to have been given, at last, breasts. I can't be reverent here; the huge unreality of it, the disjunction between person and event prevents that. And I'm newly a student of how we attend to the body, of our negotiations with the dead. Looking at her makeup, the sorrow of flesh reconstructed and propped in its housing of satin, I am feeling this sense of elemental rightness in the decisions I made about Wally's body. I am glad that I could hold him when he died, and in the long time after, and that he could leave our house wrapped in something I'd made, and go to the flames naked except for that wrapping, without makeup or artifice. I have the sense that Lynda would actually like *more* artifice, just not this kind: she'd like a better outfit, a hat, jewels. Her husband and friends are trying, in this regard: David's put in the coffin her black beret, a pin; people tuck in scraps of poems, flowers, I don't know what. These things will be burned with her, along with the flocked lavender coffin, but I believe Lynda would like to meet the flames in her dazzling finest, as she always did. Before the casket's closed, we place inside it the black beaded dress.

David, of course, hasn't had time to plan any of this, to even think of it, and he's grateful to Lynda's family for taking charge. After a couple of sessions of viewing at the funeral home, there's a service tomorrow, in an inner-city church in Newark. This, I think, is the one detail of the affair she'd have truly approved of; the gray stone church is located in a particularly atomized segment of downtown, surrounded by the rubble of failed urban renewal. The desolation is practically apocalyptic. The sanctuary has been broken into so many times that they seem to have given up on repairing the damage left by vandals; most peculiarly, the corpus on the big crucifix to the right of the altar hangs by one arm.

I'm a pallbearer, along with another gay friend of Lynda's, as well as David and a friend of his, and Lynda's father and brother. At the doorway the priest goes to unfold a white cloth

over the casket, and I find myself thinking, at last here's a rit-
ual she'd have approved of, something in good form. But
when it's unfolded it has a big green appliquéd candle in the
middle, an acidy lime green. It's hideous, and my heart sinks
while I am trying not to be a heartless aesthete. Through the
whole damn service I'm trying not to be an aesthetic snob; I'm
trying to think it matters to her family, to reconcile myself
with the fact that it seems to have not much to do with the
person I knew. But Michael reads one of her poems, and
David another, and her brother delivers a eulogy in which I
can almost recognize her; of course the person our families
know (or claim to) isn't the one friends would recall. I can tell
the ceremony's good for David, and the family seems strongly
present together, holding each other up and David with them,
so I am trying to be generous. But the fact is I hate it: I hate
that my friend who is gone is not recognizable in these ges-
tures, is barely reflected here.

I do not say this to criticize Lynda's family; when it comes to
memorial services, I think gay people have a real advantage
over their straight counterparts. We don't have a big tradition
looming over us; most of us don't have much in the way of a
church we can feel comfortable with, and for an awful lot of us
what the family wishes just isn't at the center of things. And so
ritual occasions, not hidebound by church or tradition, tend to
look a lot like the person they celebrate and mourn. And we
have a hell of a lot of practice, too, these fifteen years of epi-
demic.

I wanted Wally's service to suit him; he'd taken no interest in
it whatsoever, specifying only that he wanted to be cremated,
so it was up to me. Without a funeral, it seemed essential—
both for me and for his family—to have some event soon after
his death that seemed *real*, signifying, grave. We reserved space
in the Unitarian church—complain about it I do, but it's beau-
tiful, and welcoming—and in the space of a week I had cards
printed with a photograph of Wally playing with our cat

Thisbe on them, and his name and dates, and a bit of a poem of Rilke's, in Stephen Mitchell's translation.

> *But because truly being here is so much; because every-*
> *   thing here*
> *apparently needs us, this fleeting world, which in some*
> *   strange way*
> *keeps calling to us. Us, the most fleeting of all.*
> *Once for each thing. Just once; no more. And we too,*
> *just once. And never again. But to have been*
> *this once, completely, even if only once:*
> *to have been at one with the earth, seems beyond*
> *   undoing.*

I'd opened the book and there the lines were, from an elegy I'd always loved; they insisted upon themselves. Later I'd think, do I believe this? Just once? Certainly just once *this* way, this unrepeatable constellation of circumstances, the kaleidoscope shifted this one delicate way. Once, in this body, and gone.

During that week there were obituaries to write and publish, and the minister to meet with, and matters of music and flowers and candles, and programs—and what was going to happen, what would the program say? And food for later. In the worst hour of my life, at my most exhausted and terrified and shellshocked, suddenly I am planning a huge gathering for an unknown number of people, and inviting them all to my house afterward for food and talk. The weirdness of it is the wisdom of it: in the darkest hour, give a party.

Some people plan to speak: Wally's brothers Mark and Jim, Rena, our friends Richard and Kathryn. And then there'll be a time for anyone who wants to to get up—and a little singing, a little music. It's a huge project, and it's astonishing how much is contributed by how many people, how seemingly effortlessly all this work flows together. Effortless to me, perhaps, because I am floating along on the goodwill and work of so many friends who are showing up and cleaning the house, shopping, cooking, taking care of the details. I'm half aware of being grateful that I can make lists, can think about the things I have to do to be ready for Saturday, can worry about the parts of the whole. I can spend an inordinate amount of time buying candles, getting exactly the right shape and color and number. Feeling keeps leaking through, spilling out, washing me away a dozen times a day, two dozen. But I have this to come back to, to grasp onto, this world of tasks.

And when it happens it's magic. It's been the snowiest, iciest January in the history of the planet but suddenly the day's sunny, perfect, like April, benevolent sun on the U.U.'s clapboard and steeple. Later Michael will say what he remembers best is the sunlight cascading into the sanctuary through high windows. Because the ice is gone Wally's older relatives can come, can negotiate the steps and walks. The church with its soft gray walls painted in trompe l'oeil columns, its pews with their little medallions carved from whale's teeth, is full of people. As the planned speakers talk—an outpouring for Wally, testament both to him and to us as a couple—I have this extraordinary sense of being *seen*.

This is what this whole day is for, the whole process has been leading to this: that the man who is gone and not-gone, is being held up to the light by all these people who loved him or me or us. And they are regarding what was known as Mark-and-Wally; it is the day when people come together to circle around and to acknowledge what we were. I have never felt such a sense of a love being validated, held to the light. And in this way, strangely, it is a hugely happy day for me. How could I not be buoyed by this sense of what Wally and I had been, how lucky we were to have made what we made? Even though his ashes were in their brass box on the table at the front of the room, surrounded by the perfect candles and flowers and the army of black-and-white pictures of Wally as a kid, blown-up photos his brother Jim had brought, even though the day was a confrontation with the fact of death, there was something joyous about it, something inescapably bright.

After the planned speakers, we sang "Amazing Grace," because everyone knows it, and then the free-for-all speaking started, slowly at first, and then, as such things do, teetering on the edge of anarchy. (Will it be endless? What *will* this person say next?) When the born-again gay Christian biker who'd gone to elementary school with Wally (before he was driven out of town for offering blow jobs in front of the drugstore) began to sing all the verses of "Precious Lord" a cappella, I began to think that things were seriously out of control. But there was at the same time something wonderful about it, in that it resembled Wally's life, resembled our lives together: something to be proud of, something lucky and loving, various, capacious, just screwy enough to be alive.

After Lynda's funeral ended, the coffin was wheeled down the aisle, the hideous green-candled cloth folded again, and we pallbearers lifted the weight of her down the steps, and—a moment which felt like pure horror to me—into the waiting mouth of the hearse. I can see, plainly, David's hand touching the figured surface of the coffin lid, the rose he laid on top, that last touch. And then the doors were closed, and we moved away.

I caught a ride with some friends to the city, and though I was going to the Upper West Side I had them let me off near Times Square, Lynda territory. Those flashing neon come-ons, the dealers' bark and hustle, bright and cheap enticements to touch and look and buy: photographs of flesh, signs and banks of rippling lightbulbs that seem somehow both ephemeral and ancient, as if they'd been forever selling that same tawdry dazzle, working that same spell—tattered, but an enchantment still. Lynda wasn't gone yet; she was walking beside, inside me. The winking, oily world was aflame, everything burnished and troubled by the hurry and harsh loveliness of her transit. People die, but does the slant of light they teach us, their way of looking? It was through Lynda's eyes that I apprehended all those hopeful pitches and lost chances: her arena of transcendence, that hard-edged and lushly human disaster of a neighborhood. For me, that was my friend's real funeral, a walk through Times Square inside my head, looking out, at the beloved world—full of harm and trouble, sparkle and ruin— she was leaving.

Crash

～･

My current chiropractor, a literate, charming lesbian who wears tortoiseshell horn-rims and demonstrates a real sophistication about the delicate mysteries of alignment, does her best, then sighs and suggests a massage and rest. The swollen and throbbing muscles of my sacro-lumbar region (I like it being called a *region*, some part of me as distant and full of mystery as the precincts of the moon) are, clearly, intractable; they are not ready to be adjusted into anything like their proper positions.

And I am miserable. The condition's chronic, but it's been in abeyance — perhaps because I've *had* to be strong, able to pick Wally up, in the days when he could still be lifted to wheelchair or commode. Later, when he was immobile, it just wasn't admissible for *me* to get sick; on some level I think I *ordered* my spine to remain in alignment. The vertebrae obeyed so well, in fact, that I seem to have locked them up altogether, in a rigid stance, prepared for disaster, that's led to a disaster of another sort. Twinges first, which I stupidly ignored and kept on acting as if I had a strength or reserve of energy I didn't possess. But the spine won't be ignored. The twinges continued, a little worse, sudden neuro-flares going off at odd moments. Then, in the car, complete mutiny; reaching my left arm out the window to take cash out of the chrome drawer of the drive-up bank machine, I feel something near my lower vertebrae tear.

It all simply goes out of my hands, things going wrong in ways that I feel I have no capacity to do anything about. There's no strength in my lower back at all, and I feel incapable of supporting myself, as if the muscles just won't hold things where they belong. I slip, dangerously, into a skewed posture, an Expressionist angularity with potentially devastating consequences. To say the back "goes out" is an odd but apt expression, since one feels that its usually unnoticed capabilities have simply *gone* someplace, leaving the body helpless, prone, making it painful to do things such as, say, lift a telephone receiver, or bend over the sink to brush one's teeth. I begin to imagine never being strong or upright again, becoming dependent, compromised. There's nothing for it but bed, ice pack, ibuprofen, reading: nine days thereof, punctuated by hobbling walks to the chiropractor's office and a trip to the masseur. Everything helps a little; nothing helps enough. I'm grateful to my friends for bringing me dinner, walking the dogs, and quickly begin to resent them for being ambulatory, just as I can tell they don't *really* want to hear one more request from me for, say, the Sunday *Times*.

The nine days wear on. I read and read; I spend days living in Elizabeth Bishop's spirited and observant letters even though the book is too heavy for me to hold up and I have to keep shifting around to find different means of supporting it. Elizabeth Bishop has a life of travel and change, Nova Scotia to Brazil; I feel I will never go anywhere again, except, if I am lucky, the kitchen. I start dramatizing things. I read Diane Ackerman's *Natural History of the Senses*, a book I am supposed to review, a huge compendium of arresting facts about the pleasures of smell and touch and etc. Diane Ackerman goes all over the world tasting strange and delicious things; she rhapsodizes about vanilla beans; she puts bats in her hair; she kneels in a grove of eucalyptus and tags migrating monarch butterflies. I think if I am very lucky I may be able to drive to the A&P next week. I begin to hate Diane Ackerman; I hate her pert attitude, her perky enjoyment of all the possibilities for pleasure the world holds out. I hate my life. I begin to enjoy the pitch of my self-pity, even though now I think that self-pity's just a mask for a deeper abjection. I am in pain, up against my limitations. This is the worst my back has ever been.

All spring it's been coming. Right after Wally died I began going to a yoga class; I'd been ready to forget the idea, but a friend more or less forced me to go, saying he wanted someone with me all the time — Wally'd been gone only a few days then — and *he* wanted a break from me, so *please* would I go. The first minutes of the first class we were sitting on our knees on our mats, in the floor-wax and sweeping compound atmosphere of the elementary school cafeteria, with its pink metal tables folded into the walls and its stage masked by a blue velvet curtain. We'd begun doing breathing exercises, listening to our own in- and exhalations, feeling the breath expand in us as we paid attention to it, and the teacher said, "Here you are, in your body. Feel what it's like to be *in* your body." I knew then I was in for it; the tears started to roll down my cheeks. I kept breathing and moving, sometimes calming inside, sometimes crying again. Releasing tension in my arms, especially, which had held and held and held on. Stretching them out above my head, pulling one arm and then the other back behind my neck to feel the muscles opening released another wave of grief.

What had happened to my body — I hadn't known it before, until my attempts at stretching made it obvious — was that I had been braced from my knees up to my solar plexus, like a football player, I imagined, braced for a body blow. I carried myself like someone who expected something to come hurtling right into his stomach, knocking the wind out of him, someone who didn't want to fall down.

The class did release tension. Some nights I fell asleep right there on my mat while everyone around me moved into increasingly elongated, birdlike incarnations of graceful flexibility. Some nights I felt relaxation and a sense of relief. The postures began to provide me with another sort of metaphysical vocabulary—the steadfastness of "the Mountain," for instance, feet firmly anchored on the earth, the spine elongated, pressing up from the crown of the head, body extending from earth to heaven. Sometimes when I wasn't in class, when I needed to feel it, I could call upon the firmness of "the Mountain," and recall in my body that stability and sense of scale. And I loved the noise-making: the forceful expelling of air from the gut into a HA, the loud sighs and exhalations which signaled muscles lengthening and letting go.

The class made me realize I had no idea then—maybe I still don't—what it means to "let go" of a person. How can we, when someone is bonded to us, welded into the mesh of ourselves? The dead live on in our bodies, in the timeless flux of memory, inseparable from us. *You've got to let go* is *the* popular prescription for grief, but what does it mean, and how is it to be done? Whatever has been, we can't undo it; isn't every gesture we've ever made, every one that mattered, part of the stuff of selfhood? Isn't the past the soul's deepest possession? If I were to "let go" of Wally and Lynda, would they die to me again?

But I did learn to perceive tension in my body more clearly, to feel how I "hold on," and to feel a muscle's welcome lengthening and release.

But not enough. No amount of stretching seemed to defuse, finally, the pressure that was mounting in my back. After that unlucky reach out the car window to the ATM, I couldn't even stand up straight. I'd hobble, face to the earth, hunched and clenched, unable to even straighten up enough to look at the sky. I feel more profoundly misaligned than I ever have, literally bent out of shape, my parts in a jumble of unhappy connections.

A week of rest and I am at least walking, slowly. Crunching myself into the position required to ride in a car, much less drive one, is out of the question, so I walk carefully to an appointment with my sweet masseur, Glen, whom I've seen a few times this spring to try to undo some of the winter's icy block of tension and stress. I am making my way up my street when I run into a woman I know slightly, a health care administrator who'd known Wally. She notices my snailish pace—I am holding myself like a delicate construction of glass and string—and I explain.

"You know," she says, "it's *all* emotional."

And I'm furious. It's a thirty-second diagnosis, completely out of context. How does she know what's going on in my body? She seems to deny the physical reality of my problem. She's a representative (off duty, admittedly, but I am in no mood to let her off the hook) of that useless bureaucracy of "providers"—their own bland language, soulless as they sometimes seem to be—who have no call to be claiming expertise with something they don't understand. I'm taken back to the kind of blanket, casual diagnoses Wally's doctors used to make; confronting a symptom they clearly didn't understand, they'd confidently say, "It's the virus." Or, in a phrase which became a kind of bitter joke with us, anything they didn't comprehend and couldn't treat they'd label "viral activity." Wally's life gradually became a stage for larger and larger forms of viral activity, for a kind of terrible possession his "providers" couldn't do the first thing about.

I'll never forget his doctor's single house call, in November, two months before he died. Wally was watching television from his bed; at some point TV had become simply what he could do. First it was a source of distraction. Undemanding electronic company, for many people of my generation, represents a certain sort of childhood comfort, a voice and energy and presence—something paying *attention* to us—that feels, for better or worse, like a part of home. Later I think there was just something comforting in that continual play of light and motion. Wally couldn't tell, by then, if he'd already watched the same show that day; it didn't matter, exactly. He was in the present, with laugh tracks and music and jumping electronic figures, energetic squiggles of light to fill his brain with something else, somewhere else. When Dr. Magnus showed up to see how Wally was doing—since by then getting him into the wheelchair and down the block to the clinic was out of the question—he didn't stay long. He told me later, when I ran into him in the park, where he was out for a walk with his lover taking photographs of icicles, that "Wally seemed more interested in watching TV than in talking to me."

It took me, as it sometimes does, time to get angry; a lag time has to pass in my head before I'll give myself permission to really feel rage. All the doctor needed to do was to press a button on the remote control and switch off the set. If he had, he'd have seen Wally looking at him with the same kind of sweet openness—the self made permeable, expecting nothing, letting everything wash in and out—with which he looked at the screen, when he *did* bother to look at it. By then, I'm not even sure Wally could have switched off the remote control by himself.

Dr. Magnus wanted to be important; he wanted to be the center of Wally's attention. Couldn't he see past his own ego to read the face of a man with wildly increasing neurological damage? He wanted his questions answered, his importance as a "provider" validated—a kind of need I saw in nurses and doctors again and again, as if, as Wally became more ill, they needed to confirm their own importance. A larger man, a more generous man, might not even have needed to turn off the television at all. If he couldn't *do* anything, he could pay attention to the man before him, with his gentle, tender, ruined face lit up in soft artificial colors by the light of the goddamned stupid screen. Why couldn't he see that? His doctor's sense of self-importance only allowed him to see, by then, a man who was indifferent to him.

Even I can tell the difference between brain damage and indifference.

He never saw Wally again.

And so this tossed-off assessment of my condition triggers a profound resentment, an anger which in itself feels like part of the pain I'm in.

Thus raising, of course, the possibility that she's right.

Or partly so—if what's residing in my back is held, pent-up feeling, couldn't that hurt the muscles themselves, too? I imagine the emotional and the physical tumbling together like a pair of acrobats, two halves of a single somersault.

But what would I *do* about this—go home and feel? As if I hadn't spent five months already weeping, desolate, incapacitated, able to function only in my own limited horizon? I'd just *begun* to be able to get out a bit more, traveling a little, doing my professional work. and then my back crippled me as my heart had earlier. And this was because I hadn't *felt* enough?

So I decided to try something else, or rather it was as if something else were offered. As the most useful of Chinese proverbs says, "When you don't know where you're going, go by a way you don't know."

I'd met M. before, socially, and I'd known he did massage work because Bill had been his client since last summer, when Bill's body had blossomed with KS lesions. Bill's easy, bright attitude toward his illness was—shocking word, in this context—contagious; he was perfectly happy to go to the beach and let the sun wash over his body, where every week another pink-purple bruise seemed to develop. He would expose himself in a way that many men with KS would, understandably, find terrifying; there seemed something deeply freeing in his yielding his body to the sun, to scrutiny.

I remember Bill, that July, walking back from a session with M., passing my garden with a dreamy look on his face, and when I asked how he was he answered, "My whole body feels like a penis."

By the time I encountered M., back in town after a while away—a failed affair, a dark season in the East Village—I was doing better, overall, though I still felt fragile and, most frustrating, was unable to sit for any length of time. No writing at my desk, no restaurants, no movies, only the barest minimum of driving. He gave me his card—Mind/Body Massage—and explained that his work was emotional as well as physical, focused on releasing emotion stored in the body.

Days later I was due for another trip to New York. I'd planned to fly, tried to make it as easy on myself as possible; I felt, if I was careful, I was up for it. But the morning before, ironing a shirt, I felt my left hip start to throb, a deep ache, and I knew I'd never handle the plane, carrying even the lightest bag, if I didn't do something.

M. could see me that evening, and said in fact he'd been wondering if I would call. My first session with him—initial encounter of a series which would change and deepen my life, entirely unexpectedly—was a revelation that happened unassumingly enough. I arrived at his cottage, at seven, a tiny place behind a huge emporium of tie dye and bongs and all manner of objects with skulls on them, one of the last remaining headshops (in the world?) which has mutated into something less sweet and optimistic than the way I remember those places. No Donovan there; the prevailing mood is heavy metal. Down a little alley to one side of the building's Boschian murals—Alice gone through the looking glass into the Garden of Earthly Delights—M.'s cottage was a single room dominated by the folding table of his profession.

He himself, in fact, also took me back twenty years—twenty-something, with shoulder-length hair, wire-rims, and a choker of beads, he looked like the men I used to hang out with in 1971, when I was first in college, and then—odd doubling—like my students look now, their retro gestures gleaned from—where? Old album covers? Deadhead tours? The culture reaches back toward a time which feels more innocent, now that it's easier to edit out the past's risky, disturbing edges. M.'s place—polychrome images of Krishna and his beloved Radha, incense burners and wind chimes—made me feel oddly at home.

He explained a little about his technique and study, how he'd begun studying massage in high school, traveled to ashrams and workshops, his own sense of vocation. And then, undressed and half-covered by a sheet in the warm room with its vague smells of incense and unguent, I began to surrender.

Touch, among other things, makes the body real to us; confirmed by another, making contact at the boundaries of our skin, we come back to ourselves, experience ourselves—contained, uncontainable—anew. Some lines of Lynda's, about sex:

> . . . *making love was a way of saying yes,*
> *I am here, these are my borders, hold me down*
> *a little while. Make me real to myself.*

Something about M.'s particular brand of touch—working at the muscles, pulling gently, opening out the closed spaces in the body—makes my muscles feel three-dimensional, awake.

And there's some imperceptible descent, a process I can't quite trace, through which the mind moves from awareness of the pleasure of being touched into a kind of effortless introspection. A paradox, that being stroked all along our edges should move us further inward.

The tension in my arms, beginning to loosen, makes me think how hard I worked, how long, to hold Wally in a space of relative safety, a zone in which it was possible for him to live as long and well as he could. My arms feel so tired, weary of controlling, protecting, lifting. M.'s touching my face, massaging the knots which have appeared on either side of my jaws. "That's rage," he says, though I can't in fact *feel* it. Certainly I can register the clench, but not any emotional correlative.

He encourages me to breathe, to make noises—part of the "release"—if I'm so inclined. The firm and easy series of strokes, gentle but somehow driving, leading the experience forward, is punctuated by permission, injunctions to feel. He mentions how much I've been holding, he says there is so much grief in my body.

He arrives at my hips, my lower back. I am lying on my back now, eyes closed, and he's lifting my legs and rotating the thighs in their sockets, pushing, circling, reversing the circles. He lifts my right leg in the air and pushes it toward the left side, so that my leg is crossed over my body, stretching out the muscles deep in the right hip, stroking the long tendon along the back of my right quadriceps with a firm, long stroke, his thumb pushing deep toward the bone. And I feel everything shift. My face contorts, involuntarily. Without any warning, with knowing first what I feel, I burst into tears. The grief, the knowledge of grief, isn't in my head; the knowing is locked up in my thighs. What my body knows comes welling up, shaking me, deep quaking indrawn breaths and sobs. He keeps touching me, easily; he covers my face with a cloth so that I will not be ashamed. He enjoins me to let it out but I don't need any more coaching. I couldn't stop if I tried; a deep well of the darkest and most brackish water of myself has been tapped, an arterial spring held under tremendous pressure. Except that we think of springs as clear, pure water, and this is the fountain of sheer darkness, interior geyser of bitterness held at such depths it pours forth laying waste, burning everything in its path. How did I ever contain it? These great breathless heaving sobs are mine. I let them rumble and tear loose, rising up out of me into the air. I am literally and metaphorically naked, helpless, entirely vulnerable, and for some reason I feel completely safe, able to give myself over to this pouring out of myself. When we talk about being self-conscious, we're really talking about being aware of others; to be self-conscious is to be afraid of being judged. What I felt was self-possessed, in the old sense of possession: fully entered and inhabited by myself, purely immersed in this body's grief.

And not just the *sorrow* of grief. But the rage of it, too, the salty choking bitterness, the self-pity and incoherence and ferocious negation of it.

The freeing, fierce negation.

The massage ended in peace and stillness; one can weep so much, and then that purging leaves us exhausted, quieted.

Some unidentifiable plant essence, odor of earth and crushed leaves ("Egyptian oil," he later told me it was called) was held under my nose. A prayer to Shiva, god of destruction and dissolution; if the forces of the world dissolve people, dissolve what we love, then they also dissolve tension, pain, difficulty.

My pain—in the suddenly infinite, enormous room—dissolving into this music, some chant on the tape player. Then stillness.

I walked home deeply relaxed, enervated, exhausted. And after throwing a few things in a bag for the morning plane I slept dreamlessly, deeply, given a little hiatus from pain.

Which reappeared in the morning, an ache becoming more pronounced by the time I caught my second airplane of the day, a Boston to La Guardia shuttle, a pillow behind my sacrum, shifting as much as possible in my seat belt to keep the muscles loose. A taxi to my friend Jean's apartment on 110th and Broadway—empty, since she's married an Irish painter and spends half of each year there, though the space she's inhabited is full of her calm radiant depths, her quiet—and then straight to bed, into a sleep from which I wake, early in the afternoon, to the strange sensation of having all of New York City around me, and no stamina to participate in any of its huge, indifferent, multiplicitous life.

What *could* I do? What felt right, that steamy May afternoon, was an easy walk. The cathedral, St. John the Divine, right around the corner, is a place I love, even more so because it remains unfinished, great theater of aspiration, lifetimes till it'll be done. In fact the new plans for it continue to become stranger, more surprising: a design for a sort of greenhouse, high above the transept, will someday have the walker or worshiper below looking up through the great stone vault into *trees*.

Sacred spaces have enormous power, even when one doesn't subscribe to the way their builders or users construe the holy. There's something undeniably affecting about ritual actions performed in places that have been set apart and consecrated.

Once, when Wally was ill, I lit a candle for him at an altar in a mission outside of Tucson, where Latinos and the Tohono O'odham people (who'd built the church, under the yoke of Spanish Jesuits, early in the 1700s) came to pray to a wooden effigy of St. Francis Xavier, pinning onto his pretty dresses and petticoats little metal *milagros*, images of whatever in their lives needed healing, from body parts to tractors.

I am not, anymore, a Christian, but I am lifted and opened by any space with prayer inside it. I didn't believe that my candle lit to Francisco Xavier was going to make a bit of difference in the progress of Wally's illness, much as I might wish it. But there's something in his spirit and in mine that was benefited, joined to our community of fellow pray-ers. Something in us, in this way, is honored and held up, lit.

I didn't know why I was going, today, to stand in the long cool darkness of St. John's; it had seemed just a destination, a manageable whim. But my body knew, as bodies do, what it wanted. I entered the oddly small door of the huge space — like those spaces in dreams, or like Wonderland, whose immensity opens out from the tiniest passage — and walked without hesitating down the right-hand aisle, halfway down the enormous length of the cathedral, to the altar I hadn't consciously remembered, a national memorial for those who'd died of AIDS, marked by banners and placards, a bank of candles. My heart melted, all at once, and I understood why I was there.

Because the black current that M. had touched wanted, needed, to keep flowing. I'd grown just enough of a skin to function, these last months, but the strength I'd been feeling wasn't, in fact, real. It was a gesture toward going on in the world, toward continuance, but I wasn't ready to continue, I hadn't finished confronting that deep internal sense of desolation. I'd needed to know I could go on, but I'd also been needing to collapse.

Which is what I did, some timeless tear-span of minutes sitting on a little ledge at the base of an immense column of naked gray stone. After a while, I could walk to buy a candle—a light, for Wally, his flame rowed with the others there, a double line of representative flickerings, so few of them really that each might stand in for ten thousand dead.

The candles are held in wrought-iron stands, in metal trays filled with sand to anchor the glassed votives and loose tapers people place there. In the sand, next to a vacant space, was a tiny stick of wick, nearly invisible now, a half inch of flame seeming to lick up out of the sand itself, all that was left of some man or woman's light. I used that flame to light Wally's fresh candle—new, the flame high over the rim of the glass, while others around it burned halfway or nearly to extinction. A little arpeggio of lights, each floating above its liquid level of wax, to represent countless and increasing vanishings. Kneeling in public makes me feel self-conscious, posed, but I got down on the padded rail anyway. Then I forgot my self as the floodgates opened again.

The weeping steadied, in a while, to a different rhythm, a more sustainable breathing, a stillness. People came and went—boyfriends, teenagers, a Hispanic woman who knelt alone at the altar, crossed herself, prayed, smiled at me as she rose. I asked her if she might have a Kleenex; she rummaged in her black patent purse and apologized for finding nothing.

I tried to leave then, but I couldn't seem to walk out of the orbit of the altar, some magnetic pull in those ranks of candles, the unrevealing banners of appliquéd felt. I'd begin to walk away and some little spasm of grief would break free, as if floating loose from below, rising to the surface, choking, blinding. I sat back down on the column base, and in a moment there was a tap at my shoulder: the Hispanic woman, come back with—where had she gotten them?—the kind of paper napkins you get with an ice cream cone. It seemed to me the most genuine of gifts, made to a stranger: the recognition of how grief moves in the body, leaving us unable to breathe, helpless, except for each other.

*　　　　*　　　　*

So began my weekend's retreat in Manhattan. Out Jean's bed-
room window a great wall of windows opened across 110th—
panoply of lives, New York's theater of stacked views, glances
into the unknowability, variety, and immensity of human lives.
When I was a first-grader, my family lived in Memphis,
Tennessee, and my father used to take me to a museum called
the Pink Palace. It was an unfinished mansion some wealthy
man had commissioned to be built of smooth pink granite, one
stone fitted carefully to the next, but the Depression or private
ruin had wiped out his fortune and the unfinished estate
became the property of the state, a museum for children. I can
remember only one of its exhibits, which I loved: a large wall of
little doors, arrayed from floor to ceiling, each with a tiny han-
dle. Some I could reach myself, while my father would have to
lift me to others. I must have worn him out with my desire to
open and then close every single one of them. What was behind
each door was a pane of glass, a window which gave onto a
great—real?—tree, and each aperture revealed some different
aspect of its life: nests, squirrels, spiders, stuffed birds whose
glass eyes looked back with gleaming veracity. There was no
way to ever see the entire tree at once, only the hundreds—
were there?—of alternative perspectives the doors opened. This
great curio cabinet, this museum of viewpoints, serves in my
memory as a metaphor that resonates in many directions. The
past itself seems to me like that tree, unseeable in its entirety,
knowable only in its parts, each viewpoint yielding a different
version of the story about what the whole might be.

What is the world but a tree too huge to see at once, known
only through the shaping character of the particular aperture
through which we see?

Jean's window gave onto a world of windows, that wide
bank of apartments revealing—as lamps were lit, blinds
raised—ways in which people lived. This was the world I could
not go out into, the exterior whirlwind. I could lie in her bed
and look out into its various life, until my attention would float
back to the ruin and collapse which was my own.

*   *   *

Journal entry, June 7, New York.

> *Could it be true, that the more I admit the anger and woundedness — the deep, sealed-off hurt long since turned in on itself — the more I'll be able to move freely and flexibly?*
>
> *Once it was important for me not to become bitter, a kind of survival skill. I didn't want to be burdened, always, by the shadow of a difficult family; there was an energy in me that wanted to move forward, not be locked in contemplation of the past. But I'm forty, and my life's at midpoint (hard to think, now, living in a battlefield, my friends dying at my age or younger, my neighborhood full of men who maybe won't see forty) and I begin to think maybe there is a need for bitterness in adult life. Are we children without it, self-deluded? Is there something in disenchantment which strikes the balance, a darker chord in the self which lends us gravity, depth? A ballast, against the spirit's will to rise?*
>
> *Is the pain in my back the sharp, insistent, undiluted voice of my self-pity — as if my body itself were whining?*

After my hour on M.'s table, during my weekend alone in my friend's apartment on 110th, I could weep for Wally's diminishment, the long bitter years of slow erasure, the losses gradual and little: not being able to go to the movies together, the slow decline of sexual life, not being able to share the events and concerns of my work. And then, headlong and tumbling, all of him falling down a long tunnel of loss, one aspect of self after another. I could cry about all this now in a way I couldn't when he was alive, or in the first months after he died.

Now I could cry for *myself* — for the pain of it, for losing what I *thought* the rest of my life would be like — in a way that I couldn't when he was alive, or even when my grief was stunningly new and I could only weep for him, not for myself. Self-pity, we're taught, is the ugliest of indulgences, the one we're not to give in to, our natures at their weakest. Here is Job, in

Stephen Mitchell's translation (Jean's copy, the book I most need there, in the serenity of the blue bedroom), raging about the destruction of his life:

> *If only I could return*
> *to the days when God was my guardian;*
> *when his fire blazed above me*
> *and guided me through the dark—*
> *to the days when I was in blossom*
> *and God was a hedge around me...*

For "God" substitute "life," "the world," even "time," whatever; what you call the power larger than yourself here doesn't matter. Job is articulating what it's like to be young; his definition of innocence has to do not with age but with the quality of being *untouched*, the sense of invulnerability with which we live until the world comes crashing in to challenge us.

The Book of Job enacts the most human and inevitable of tragedies. Job has love, wealth, solidity, community, certainty. And then his world is scoured, and the only purpose given for his harrowing doesn't seem to even convince the great anonymous poet behind the poem. The poem's a wrestling with a mystery, the ceaseless process of diminishment and loss.

For your lover to die is not to be guided by fire but immolated by it; to lose what you love, as Job loses his children, is to be entirely plunged into darkness, vulnerable, unprotected by any hedge. And we're forced to the ultimate question of self-pity: why me? Why did I suffer? Why did I live to lose? Does this have any meaning at all, or is it merely the grinding down of ourselves, the grand arbitrary motions the spheres enact?

That's what I didn't want to feel: my own sense of smallness, rage, violation, my tiny life—especially against the lives of the hundreds of thousands of people with AIDS who've died or are dying—*my* life disrupted, wreaked havoc upon. Who was I to feel sorry for myself when I didn't even have the disease?

When it wasn't me who'd been crushed on a wet highway?

But if I couldn't allow myself to feel the pity and terror of my own loss, then my body would enact it for me.

Here is Job, adult bitterness incarnate, vessel of anger, eye to eye with the sheer uncompromising face of the dark:

> *Man who is born of woman—*
> *how few and harsh are his days!*
> *Like a flower he blooms and withers;*
> *like a shadow he fades in the dark.*
> *He falls apart like a wineskin,*
> *like a garment chewed by moths.*

This is the unmitigated voice of the survivor who is only able to deal with devastation this way, by hammering out the bleakest view of the human situation. Job's losses are horrific, sweepingly total, and delivered to us in swift passages of prose as if to get that part of the story over with and get on to what matters, which is the sufferer's negotiations with the nature of reality. A paradox: there is no consolation available in Job's vision of the nature of things, and there's something strangely consoling about this clear-eyed and sober assessment of what it means to be a man: "how few and harsh are his days." Perhaps because such a stance doesn't *expect* much. It comes after the long tears and groaning of deep grief, a bit numbed, utterly without self-delusion, beaten into a kind of ashen acknowledgment of our brief and difficult transit here. As if life in the world will be tolerable if we expect nothing of it. Here he speaks, in another passage:

> *Remember: life is a breath;*
> *soon I will vanish from your sight.*
> *The eye that looks will not see me;*
> *you may search, but I will be gone.*
> *Like a cloud fading in the sky,*
> *man dissolves into death.*

He leaves the whole world behind him
and never comes home again.

A characteristically Old Testament vision of human life: a breath caught between two darknesses, a difficulty endurable only through submission to God. Submission to power and law, the acceptance of our lot—an expected stance, and one which Job all at once bracingly, completely belies.

"Therefore," he says, "I refuse to be quiet . . . "

This is the opposite of acceptance. Job sees plainly and unflinchingly the unbearable human lot and says, *No, I will not have it, I do not understand it, it is not just.* Job and his friends need to believe—don't we all need to believe?—the universe is sane, benign in its orders. Job's upright friends—righteous men, good spiritual citizens—would have him accept that he must have sinned somehow, must have done *something* to deserve this. Or at least want him to accept, silently, an incomprehensible will greater than his own.

But Job's humanity lies in his no-saying. *No* easy answer, no humble acceptance, NO—I *rage* against the excoriating process of loss in my life, I will not be silent in the face of it, I refuse to be quiet. I will look at the great black tree of the world through the window of bitterness, the window of misery, I'll put my face to that dark, and I will say what I see. Silence is submission to the implacable order. For Job, silence equals the death of the self.

There is so much I don't want to write. I can feel the interior pressure and turbulence, latent feeling opened and invited in—out?—if I begin to speak directly about illness, dissolution, the end of my heart's desire, the wreck of love's body, the failure of medicine. There is so much there to—I begin to write "dredge up," but it isn't at all like uncovering something from which I have recovered, something far in the past. It's that there's all that grief and anger *right there* and I'd rather not feel it than look at it directly, which isn't really a choice, since if I don't look at it my body will embody it. (What else does *embody* mean?)

To go on is to write out of, as it were, the pain in my back, the crashing within myself that seems multiple in its parts. Feelings I had to back away from, for a while, in order to go on, which now want to be admitted—residual anger and bitterness, old and new. I had been moving forward, in this new and unfamiliar life, as if I had more strength than I did. And so my body insisted on a hiatus, a rupture, a period of reflection.

I have no choice but to open the door to the pain, but if I do so I feel as if I'm going to rage, to cry, endlessly. I want to be in control, I *can't* be in control, I want to let my feelings flow fluidly, I want to stop holding it . . .

M. says, *You don't have to* do *anything. It's that you stop doing what you're doing, you stop holding on* . . .

Depth charges of grief and anger detonating, down inside the muscles, way down in the heart/spine/brain, and the black smoke churning up, the feeling letting loose, wordless, as I think about bringing it to words.

Start at the beginning of this story, angel, help me to bring these words to light so that they don't turn to acid in the dark.

The angel answers: *They are acid already. How else could they be? Let them pour out, scalding, a hot black oil to steam on the street, coruscating bitter fluid. You'd keep that in your body? Up and out, let it go.*

M. again: *The only way to release tension is to feel it.*

But I think, old histories surfacing here, that if I'm angry, bitter, negative, there'll be damage, that it's dangerous to feel so strongly.

More dangerous, says the angel, *not to*.

Now I think it is not Wally who has gone into the underworld, but myself—on a long spiraling journey of peril, of unpredictability, in which I must come to new terms. I must reinterpret my life, or lose myself. Have I already "lost myself"? Certainly I am lost. *I awoke, in the middle of my life, in a dark wood* . . .

Losing one's self: is that it? Is the descent of the surviving into grief and incomprehension a death, too? *I awoke in a dark wood* . . . A descent above all into the unfamiliar, the known world made strange, all signposts gone, one's sense of the predictable future shattered. Everything utterly different, though it looks the same.

In the months after Wally died I felt a kind of spirit with me that sustained me, even though I was miserable; it was strange how I could be in so much pain and feel, at once, somehow close to the heart of life, in a place of no little radiance. And then, the descent, the dying back into the world—*a dark wood*—where we are unguided. Lynda died and whatever shine seemed to leak out of the other world as Wally entered it left me. What my soul requires is this going down into darkness, into the bitterness of salt and chewing at old roots. In my heart I make myself ugly and bitter, I say cruel and harsh things, I spit on hope, I mock the bit of life which is tender beginnings, which is promise, which is hope. I will let myself be ugly, I will have a mouth full of darkness, a heart full of bile, I will be sour and hateful and old. I see the future burning, the oily rags of love going up in the black smoke of the torched body. In another time I would have wandered in the desert, I would have torn my clothing and walked in rags, I'd have smeared my face with dust and clay and refused speech, I would have hurled my body down into the dust and my soul into darkness, into nothing, utter free fall in the world of senselessness. Much as I want to hold on, want to cling to any perception which might be redemptive, any solid point, what is required of me is what I fear the most: relinquishment, free fall, the fluid pour into absolute emptiness. There is no way around the emptiness, the bitter fact, no way to go but *through*.

Part Two

THROUGH

Descent

❧

Wally died of a viral brain infection, PML, which stands for progressive multifocal leukoencephalopathy, a condition in which an ordinarily harmless virus that most of us carry around in our livers is able to migrate, due to the suppression of the immune system, into the brain. There it multiplies unchecked, causing certain areas to become inflamed, unable to function. Typically—to the extent that *anything* is typical, since this is a rare opportunistic infection which affects perhaps two percent of people with AIDS—PML leads to a gradual paralysis, symptoms rather resembling those of someone who's had a stroke. One side of the body is usually affected more than the other. Difficulties with speech and comprehension develop gradually, along with loss of movement and feeling. Leading, at worst, to complete paralysis, which was my deepest nightmare for Wally, the scenario I tried not to let myself imagine, that he might be awake and aware but unable to move or to react.

PML: hard, unyielding acronym. Another constellation of letters, in themselves meaningless, full of negative capability. We could imagine into them further because they were so empty, so devoid, in themselves, of content or suggestion. Like "AIDS" itself; if the disease had a name, a real *word*, would we be able to attach so many cultural meanings to it, freight it so heavily with values and associations?. AZT, DDI, DDC, PML: troubling recombinations of letters. A bad hand drawn at Scrabble, letters which we can figure and refigure and still make nothing. PML literally makes *nothing*; where someone was, where clarity and spirit and intelligence and movement were, erasure. As if the self were written in chalk, then powdered away.

If, in fact, PML was what we had. (I write that "we" unconsciously at first, automatically, as though it were my illness too, I lived with it that closely, it consumed my life that completely. I know I can't know what it's like even to be HIV-positive, but there is a way in which people have illnesses—especially terminal ones—together.) The only way to make a positive diagnosis of PML is a brain biopsy. If that test did yield a positive result, then there was nothing to be done. The single experimental treatment we heard about—holes drilled in the skull, the brain flooded with AZT—sounded like a medieval torture, and Wally could never tolerate that drug anyway. And no one even much believed in it anymore, though it's still the first thing prescribed to the HIV-positive.

So, if it *was* PML that erased Wally's ability to use his legs, there wasn't anything to be done about it. And if it wasn't that, what was it? "Viral activity," that mantra of ignorance, a vain attempt to gain power through description.

Wally's progress, on the one hand, seems simple now, a gradual decline, a weakening and fading, a body increasingly unable to cooperate with the dictates of his will: a will that softened, slowly going out of focus, quieting, easing away. But on the other hand, like Bill, he seemed to become more and more himself, or some original, underlying portion of self, as if he were scoured down to bedrock. What remained, despite the diminishment, was the pure and irreducible stuff of character.

"Who needs the full story of any life?" James Merrill wrote in his memoir, *A Different Person*. And who needs the full story of any death? Scenes imply the whole, delineate it. We're raised on film, and movies leave out the continuous, getting-from-here-to-there tissue of experience that holds the heightened moments of life together. All we need, as an audience, are essential gestures.

But how to identify, looking at one's own life, the signifying moments? Now the years of Wally's illness seem to me an avalanche, but at the time they felt more like a descent so gradual as to often be imperceptible, especially early on, before the course of things became clear. How could we know then what was happening? How distinguish a symptom of changing brain function from depression from a reaction to a drug? Then, in the final year, suddenly there we were: in chaos, in hell, and through what passageway had we arrived? Gentle Dante, to imagine hell as terraced—so that the descending pilgrims might have time to acclimate, to walk a little at the pressure of this new depth, before the ground falls away again.

For many people, there's a clear line of demarcation which marks the crossing from being HIV-positive to having AIDS. That's a telling grammatical distinction, the difference between *being* and *having*, between a condition and a possession. AIDS is a possession one is possessed *by*. Often the signifier of change is the first KS lesion discovered on the sole of the foot, the inside of the thigh. Or the first bout with pneumocystis.

For Wally, nothing was ever so firm and clear; it seemed a kind of gliding downward, his process of change, moving forward by such subtle degrees that, when one day I'd recognize how much he'd changed, or see a new limitation made clear, I'd be shocked. When did all the tiny increments add up to this loss?

At nine o'clock on a weekday morning, late in May of 1989, the public health care worker who'd come to tell us our test results blasted the world apart. I can't say I remember the experience all that clearly, so much did it become a kind of whirlwind. She was poised on the edge of the couch, practiced, friendly in a rather formal way. She told us our results. Me

first, then Wally. I remember going and standing behind him;
he was sitting in a wing chair, I don't remember if he was cry-
ing, but I remember the stunned aura around him, the sense of
an enormous rupture—not a surprise, but nonetheless a horror,
an announcement fundamentally inadmissible, unacceptable.
Shattering, but not a surprise, for had we been thinking of any-
thing else? And though she must have told me my status first
in order to deliver good news, before the blow, I remember
thinking it didn't matter which of us it was, that his news was
mine.

At that time testing was offered by the state, and after a
three-week wait one arranged to meet the caseworker some-
place—often secretively, in parking lots or cafés, to protect the
identities of closeted people, to avoid the brand of difference
and contagion. I think she offered us a few phone numbers—a
clinic in Burlington, the phone number of Vermont CARES,
the fledgling support group forty miles down the road. The
phone numbers and information flapped in the void, little
wings in a great tornado. Where were we then, in air, in limbo,
in a not-knowing more darkened by contingency than anything
we'd ever known?

We drove to Burlington. It was glorious dense green spring
in Vermont but it could have been anywhere; there wasn't any-
thing outside our numbed sphere. Inside the car we held hands
as I drove, talking or not talking, I can't recall. A blur of green
outside, shreds of fog, I think, on the mountains and the almost
impossibly green valleys between them. The palpable wounded
shock inside. We went to the support group office that day,
signed up, took home brochures; I remember crying in a
Szechuan restaurant, Wally's hand shaking as he lifted his
water glass. We were inside a zone of silence; we could talk
and still not violate it, even in a crowded room full of carved
dragons and people chattering over business lunches. Perhaps
we looked as if nothing had changed, so that no one would
know we had entered, that morning, into the rest of our lives,
into the harrowing, forward-pouring *next*.

Though nothing *had* changed but knowledge; our understanding had shifted so radically that the world seemed wildly unfamiliar. If my life were the tree I studied through the windows of my childhood museum, then I'd suddenly been slammed to the floor, my face thrust to a glass I'd never looked through before. We stumbled through the days, raw with the new fact. How long was it before any sense of consoling ordinariness — those brief intervals when things seem normal again — would return? Could this knowing become part of the landscape in which we lived, an aspect of the daily?

We began to seek out medical alternatives. Our decision to test had been influenced by a trip to San Francisco, where the word was that the HIV-positive would live longer if identified, since more and more preventative measures were being discovered. AIDS, the buzz had it, was on the way to becoming a chronic, manageable disease, like diabetes. It seemed perfectly plausible, in 1989, to believe that; my faith in medical technology, in science without limit, wasn't the weak and compromised — vanished? — thing it is today. And then there were all the questions which floated around HIV status: would everyone who had been exposed to the virus eventually get sick? Why, presuming that many men of my generation or older had been exposed around the same time, in the late seventies and early eighties, were some people already dead, while others appeared completely healthy? Did that mean that some people were more naturally resistant than others? What about co-factors? How, when Wally and I had unsafe sex countless times, could I be negative? Did that mean that my blood held in escrow some soon-to-be-tapped promise? Somebody had to be working on this, with the same intensity that was, presumably, being brought to bear on the search for treatments of opportunistic infections. AIDS activism would make sure this was so.

(Today, knowing what I do, would I still want to take that test? I don't know if the preventative treatments actually spared Wally anything; he never had pneumocystis, thank heaven, and perhaps that *was* because of the invisible clouds of aerosol pentamidine he'd breathe through a clear plastic tube, and, later, the big yellow Bactrim tablets which would make nearly everyone who took them ill. Who knows? In response to what he *did* have, the medical profession offered us nothing but a CAT scan and a shrug. However, I know that testing allowed us to make good decisions. No one can really be *ready* for AIDS, but we were able to have our house in order, able to get ourselves to a place of relative safety and support. So I'd do it again, I guess, though I admit there's also a strong part of me that wouldn't want to know.)

We'd been inspired by San Francisco's cutting-edge optimism. "HIV is not a death sentence," ran the next buzz-phrase. Everyone was talking about *living* with AIDS, not dying from it, and there was a new sense that people who were HIV-positive *could* live, and live well. Couldn't we, despite the pressure of our tiny bit of knowledge, our huge field of uncertainty? Communities of people with AIDS in San Francisco and New York were offering the first shreds of hope that the HIV-positives might take charge of their conditions, might view themselves as the keepers of their own health, not helpless, not—a word newly understood as dangerous, insidious—victims.

But we were in central Vermont, a state with—at that time—twenty reported cases of AIDS. There was no activist pressure for advanced health care, drug trials, or services to the sick and their families, and none of the community of concern and support offered on either coast. So our central truth, the fact that dominated our days and nights, felt like ours alone; the world around us ignored it and disconfirmed it at every step. Sometimes I used to look at the clapboard houses rowed along our street, the blue and yellow porches, the russet Victorian bricks of the law office down the block, and be overwhelmed by the sensation that no one there knew what I knew, no one lived as we did. Wally and I were sealed together in some kind of bubble, a private sphere. The impact of the news was underscored by the way in which it isolated us, by the strange way in which our reality, more than ever, didn't match the life around us.

Long phone calls to Project Inform, asking about drugs, T-cell counts, what's new. I wanted to hear *anything*; I remember once the weary man on the other end of the hot line saying to me, "What is it you want to know?" I couldn't answer; I wanted everything from knowledge to comfort, names of drugs to gestures of consolation. The world had split apart, and I wanted anything that could pour into that newly opened gap.

Wally made another hasty, not-well-planned trip to San Francisco. We'd seen, for the first time, ads for clinics there specifically for the HIV-positive, with upbeat names like Positive Action or Positive Choices, tags that suggested empowerment, no passive relinquishment but a firm grasp on possibility. A year before there'd been nothing like these ads, which now loomed large in the gay press, the bold type full of promise. We'd thought of AIDS as a catastrophe that left the sufferer no room for any sort of action, but this new attitude promised at least living longer than we'd come to expect, and weren't there after all so many unknowns? Here, at least, the absence of knowledge might lead to hope.

But Wally's experience at the Whatever Clinic wasn't empowering. The staff felt cold to him, the project mercenary; the expensive consultation led to an unexceptional round of advice: AZT, when his T-cell count warranted it, and vitamins. The doctor didn't demonstrate the sort of optimism the ads connoted. Wally's visit there was really like my calls to Project Inform: what did he want? We each brought to our reaching out a wildly unsorted mixture of needs: for knowledge, for emotional support, for medical and psychological and spiritual help. What we wanted was what no one could offer: clarity, understanding, deliverance.

We tried to tell ourselves that nothing had changed, really. Wally's health was, of course, exactly what it was the day before we gained this new knowledge. He didn't have AIDS, or even what was called, then, ARC. He had, we had, instead, knowledge, a new awareness of potentiality—maybe of certainty? Who knew? He had been given a word, POSITIVE, and, as would be the case later, too, when he was given the "word" AIDS, that act of naming stunned us and sent us reeling. It felt, then, like knowledge we couldn't actually use, though we tried to find ways to act upon it.

We got a dog. We'd been thinking about this for a while, before the test, and somehow it seemed, now, essential. I'd had one dog in my entire life, a collie puppy who'd died in infancy; I'd been so upset my parents had decided to stick to cats. I'm reluctant to reveal here what I *named* that little one, whose life ended on the oval of a braided rug out in the chicken coop of our rented farmhouse, for fear of it looking like mere contrivance. But I swear it's true: I called him Wally. I think I'd gotten the name from "Leave It to Beaver," and there must have been something about that boy with his shining dark hair and his white T-shirts that caught my five-year-old eye. Some things never change.

Wally had a loved, longtime companion of a Dalmatian as a kid. He'd thought now to adopt an older dog, one who wouldn't need a lot of training. We tried cozying up to a couple of the grown-up dogs at the shelter, and endured a serious bout of sympathy for a wild-eyed, frizzy thing who seemed made out of the irreconcilable parts of a dozen breeds, with two different-colored eyes and ears that seemed perpetually to be telling time like clock hands.

But sympathy gave way, in the face of the big black puppy who was already way too big for the cage in which he was confined, down at the bottom of a stack of cages. He lay on his side and looked up at us with eyes of a clear, deep chestnut, tail thumping on the floor. We were his in about thirty seconds. Out of the cage, he was an unsteady ball of rippling black fur, a big domed head, a soft tongue pink and tentative as the foot of a snail. A huge snail, in this case. What was he?

Newfoundland and Lab? Some exotic bird-hunting retriever? He'd been found wandering around on a farm, hooked up with an older stray. He'd been growing so fast that, let out of the cage, he seemed hardly able to master his four uncooperative legs. We couldn't wait to bring him home; he was evidence, he was our common futurity, he was blessed distraction, one thing for us to focus on together that didn't seem to lead in the same direction everything else did.

He came home with us, riding back from the animal shelter on—was it my lap, or Wally's? I seem to be able to feel him, still, that body a fraction the size of what it is today, and to see him also with his face against the collar of Wally's red jacket, eager, tentative, being born right then, in front of us, into the rest of his life.

The doctor Wally was assigned at University Hospital in Burlington turned out to be as knowledgeable as anyone; despite the fact that he practiced in the far and rural north, he valued his status as a specialist, flew off to national and international conferences, and when we referred to anything we read and wondered about he'd always heard something about it already. He was not particularly warm, not emotionally available, but we'd begun to try to sort out our whirlwind of needs; if he could give us expertise, experience, intellectual perspective, then wasn't that plenty? A hard science man, he had no faith or interest in vitamins, herbs, acupuncture. He thought the answer to AIDS would lie in drugs, and the drug of choice at that point was AZT (as it is, appallingly, these years later, when we've seen how poisonous and limited it is). The question was, when to begin. Early intervention, in hopes of shoring up a falling T-cell count? Or was the drug itself toxic, something to be used only when the damage it might do was plainly outweighed by the damages of the unchecked virus?

That summer Wally kept on working, a gesture toward normalcy, a way of maintaining routine. He'd take Arden for long indulgent games of chasing a tennis ball out in the park, and long walks on the railroad tracks; I loved the way the two of them seemed alert to every nuance of the other's moods and wishes.

We allowed ourselves to feel our way toward change. Wally had been taking classes at the college where I taught, an entertainingly eccentric little liberal arts school which occupied the grounds of a fine old sheep farm. The woods and fields around the grand but derelict old manor house were dotted with examples of what the catalog called "organic architecture": student-and-faculty-built concatenations of found windows, salvaged beams, decks and balconies mounted one atop the other, full of little hiding places and tiny round windows of colored glass and plastic which seemed to suggest particularly welcome spots for the occupants to hang out on mescaline or LSD. Out in the woods was a swimming hole, a deep spot in a small river where we used to go skinny-dipping, summers, and where Arden first learned to swim when I was peacefully floating on my back and he decided, with unshakable determination, that I needed to be rescued. The school—one of the few academic institutions in the world which offered tuition rebate to gay couples, so that a teacher's "spouse equivalent" could enroll for free—had boomed in the early seventies, almost died in the eighties, and was gradually finding its way back to a kind of small-scale intensity. With its emphasis on embracing one's own way of seeing things, it offered a squirrelly, lively community for writers and young artistic spirits of sundry unclassifiable sorts. My students sought first of all freedom from their parents, and after that were interested in self-knowledge and God. We had wonderful conversations.

Wally, who'd never been to college, had rather different expectations about what higher education would provide, but he spent a year and a half at Goddard painting, writing, and studying Afro-Cuban dance anyway. He'd had fun, commingled with the frustrations, but the experience hadn't really been compelling enough to hold his attention after the test, and he let the idea of getting a degree go.

By the fall his T-cell count, never all that high, had dropped into a range where Dr. Science felt it was time to commence the antiviral. Within three days, how good a drug AZT was or wasn't became a moot point; entirely immobilized by a clenching, unbearable headache, Wally couldn't get off the couch.

It was the first time he was ever unable to walk Arden, into whose new life he'd poured his attention and energy, his love of play; Arden—absorbing all this affection, and sweet by nature—was becoming the most thoughtful and sensitive of dogs. He sat in the corner of the big, battered couch, confused.

Wally stopped taking the little blue-and-white pills; Science said try it again, to see if he could go "through" the headaches, ride them out to arrive at tolerance. But there wasn't any riding out that pain; both the second and third trials left him helpless on the couch, his gripped, pounding, and unholy head held tightly between his hands, while outside the Vermont autumn unfolded its signal fires of wild-leafed maple and birch.

DDI, the next antiviral, was in drug trials, a part of the process leading toward FDA approval; people who couldn't tolerate AZT and who had appropriately low T-cell counts were admitted to the study. Wally qualified, and soon we were receiving cardboard boxes full of white, foil-lined envelopes about the size of grocery-store sauce mix, the sort one makes into fake hollandaise or onion dip. These came filled with a powder like blank white Kool-Aid which dissolved, eventually, to a colorless cocktail. Nothing visible. (So many of our accommodations and negotiations took place beneath the surface, impossible to see.) Wally seemed to hate everything about the drug: the ritual of opening the envelope, stirring the stuff into water, clanking at the sides of the glass with a spoon. He sat at the kitchen counter twice a day, head in his hand, looking glumly into the glass while the spoon went round and round, the cloudy liquid not becoming clear for a long time. He took it regularly—even though we were full of questions:

better to take an unknown drug or allow the body to do its own work? Which was more deadly, the invisible disease, the invisible treatment? We couldn't see anything happening, but then one isn't *supposed* to see; the idea was that the antiviral held something at bay. Neither of us really believed it was doing anything, but what might happen if he *stopped*?

And then came a bout of neuropathy, the most common side effect; his fingers tingled and went numb. He stopped taking it for a while, the neuropathy receded, and then he resumed mixing up glasses of the vaguely salty liquid. But only halfheartedly. Soon it was hit and miss, an envelope here and there, nothing regular. Boxes of the little foil envelopes of medicine arrived by Federal Express, and we stashed them away in a kitchen cupboard; soon we'd have more and more of them.

Do I remind him and encourage him to take the medicine? I asked myself. Do I trust his doubts or intuitions; do I trust my own? Uncertain, I did nothing most of the time, and then sometimes went on little crusades of advocacy for the snowy, scientific magic in its inscrutable packaging. *You've got to try*, I said, and he did for a while, till the tingling and numbness returned. A flyer arrived which said DDI's toxic to the pancreas, that people have died from mixing the drug with even a little alcohol, a glass or two of—wine, was it? The letter was from the drug manufacturer, a hedge against liability, but it read more like one of those threatening chain letters which promise dire consequences to the recipient who breaks the chain: loss, disaster, death, if you don't do things just right. Admiral Y., of Lisbon, ignored this letter, and three days later . . .

New support groups were starting up, as more HIV-positives and people with AIDS appeared in Vermont. The groups—one for people who were positive, one for their partners and families—met in rooms at the Unitarian church in our town. Because there was nothing else like this in the whole northern half of the state, people drove an hour or more simply to be with people who knew how they felt. Our friends were all empathy, and even graciously acknowledged the limits of what they could understand. They couldn't have done better, and yet we longed to have our reality mirrored back to us by someone in the same situation, simply to know that someone saw the world through a lens like our own.

Especially those who were themselves positive; there were enough of them to form a cohesive group, and Wally began to look forward to the weekly meeting in which six or seven men and one woman sat together and talked their way through each week's topic, comparing notes, laughing, weeping, beginning to air the transfiguring knowledge distorting and remaking their lives.

My support group consisted, usually, of myself and one woman, our friend Robert's mother. Peg had moved to town to be near Robert, who already had some minor infections. Robert himself was in Wally's group, which met upstairs at the same time, so there was an odd sort of feeling when we all entered the building, through the side door, for confidentiality, and then split apart to go our separate ways. Peg and I'd go downstairs, to a little Sunday School room which looked out over a narrow, muddy river cutting through the center of the tiny New England capital; Victorian rowhouses, built as housing for granite workers, hung over the edge, yellow paint peeling from the spindles and eaves of the rickety balconies, half-frozen laundry flapping like poverty's own banners. The room where we met had tiny chairs, for the Sunday School classes. It seemed odd for Peg and I to have a facilitator to ourselves, a lesbian counselor employed by Vermont CARES who conducted herself in a tentatively professional way, cautious, careful about maintaining her distance. This was Peg's and my time, which seemed a luxury, although two people do not make a group and therefore there wasn't the sort of energy or spirited exchange I heard Wally talk about in his group. Sometimes, after we'd each talked about our week and had a bit of exchange, we would wind down and not know what to talk about next. Sometimes while we were meeting I'd hear them upstairs, laughing, and feel a little twinge of jealousy that I wasn't with all those other gay men talking and feeling through their common lot. I *knew* it wasn't my lot, exactly, and that they needed the sense of permission that being with other people in the same boat presumably gives, and yet I still felt left out. Perhaps I needed a group of other lovers, other partners, but there weren't enough of us around—or enough of us willing to be seen in a group, anyway—for that.

Robert had passed his fatalistic attitude about AIDS along to his mother. One evening Peg said to me, "How do you feel, knowing Wally is going to die of AIDS?"

I told her I *didn't* know that he was going to die of AIDS; for all I knew I might go first, or he might live a long life *with* the virus, or there might be a cure or at least a life-prolonging treatment tomorrow. It seemed important to me to maintain that kind of openness, to resist fatalism. In my heart I thought there was a slow erasure of Wally taking place, tremendously slow; the metaphor that came to me was of the outline of his body gradually being filled in with a kind of dark transparency, like ink, slowly spreading to fulfill the outline of him. A darkly spreading, bruise-colored tattoo. He looked like himself, still, but I began to imagine his body filling with an absence. I imagined that when we received his diagnosis we entered into the gates of the underworld, beginning a fatal descent, one very small step at a time. I imagine that the god of hell doesn't come out to meet us in chariots and fire, infernal stallions stomping and champing and foaming; it's that the dark god slowly turns the body of the descendant into himself, making it of a piece with his darkness. In my heart I felt this process as inexorable. We were moving downward, on the charred slopes, and nothing I could do would stop it.

But we were also living in the outer world, as well as in the inner, metaphoric one, and in the outer world, the day-to-day, Wally was not sick. Perhaps a bit less energetic, but was that just depression, worry? There was time in front of us, time to be used well, time to live. And I needed to turn away from that internal sense of descent, to live as if that wasn't what I felt. I was, in my spirit, as much a fatalist as Robert, but I railed against his fatalism and talked about positive expectations, uncertainty, living as if we will live. After all, any of us can die, any time; we know we will, we just don't know when. And if the diagnosis made it likely that Wally would die first, and sooner, then didn't we have to live as fully as we could now, not in some death-haunted stasis?

Robert and I belonged to the same gym. He led bicycle tours for a living, and ran and biked indoors all winter to stay in shape for his demanding summer schedule. He painted rather conventional landscapes in oil, made stained-glass objects to sell at a craft store, and pursued a complex arcana of sexual practices involving leather and bondage. He had multiple body piercings before they become the fashion. He was a brave soul, I think, to use the sauna and shower in a mostly straight central Vermont health club in 1989 with his nipple pierced. One day when I arrived he was already running on the treadmill. He nodded hello and kept running while I climbed on the machine beside him, and while I did my idle warm-up and then gained what little speed I do, I noticed that he kept pushing up the lever to increase the speed of the conveyor belt, so that he was going faster and faster, on and on, pushing the machine to the limit, staring straight ahead, the sweat pouring off him. I didn't think he was ever going to stop. But when he did, eventually, as I was winding down, he told me that morning he found, on his right calf, his first KS lesion. He wore sweatpants, and that day he showered at home.

Researching, he learned that the average person with Kaposi's sarcoma survives eighteen months after diagnosis. He circled on his calendar the approximate date he expected to die. He informed his mother, took care of everything, and started thinking seriously about the traveling he wanted to do while he still could.

Wally was horrified by this almost casual fatalism (which disguised, of course, pain that was anything but casual; it was easier for Bob to present this sort of cool surface, a that's-the-way-the-world-is attitude). This was so much the opposite of Wally's spirit, and seeing someone so plainly, baldly negative helped him to see more clearly the way in which he wanted to live. Bob thought Wally was in denial.

In fact, Wally was wonderful at returning things to something resembling normalcy; he'd go watch TV, or eat a bag of the cheap grocery store cookies he liked, or putter with his photographs or his collection of fashion pictures as if things were all right, and somehow then they *were* almost all right. We each begin to feel, in part because of the support groups, in part because of the benevolent agency of time—which makes almost all things begin to seem familiar—a sort of stability. Highly provisional, that stability, but no one can live in endless uncertainty, in full consciousness of it, especially in the face of a diagnosis which the body does not demonstrate. Day after day, whether we were aware of it or not, we were circling the same questions: how can this knowledge be used? *Can* it be used? The way Bob employed his knowledge seemed wrong-headed to me, or at least not helpful. Later, I'd wonder if his difference from Wally was partly a matter of being further along in the process of the disease; was what seemed then a cynical matter-of-factness actually a gesture toward letting go of his life? Or was it a matter of a difference of temperament, each man refined—the way say, oils or perfumes are refined, reduced to essences—by illness to become more clearly himself?

If Bob, marking the date of his anticipated death in black marker on the calendar, thought the virus an insurmountable force which would, in eighteen months, erase his life, then Wally's brother Jim provided almost an opposite perspective. Jim viewed the virus as entirely in our control; a tie-dyed-in-the-wool new-ager, he saw disease as something entirely subject to the will of the individual, since, as he understands the world, we create our own realities.

Wally came from a family of eight kids, from a southern suburb of Boston. His father—also named Wally—and mother met when they were adolescents, and married as teenagers when Wally's dad, lying about his age, joined the Navy. He became a career sailor, away much of the time while Wally was growing up. "Marriage," the poet David Wojahn has written, "is a pact with someone else's memory." (David was Lynda's husband, and he was, of course, referring to *her* memories.) Wally always loved to talk about his childhood, a realm whose texture and details seemed immediately available to him. Now sometimes I feel as if his memories are mine; when one loses a lover, the pact becomes intensified, in a way: who else will keep these stories? It's as if *I* remember a summer evening, 1957 or 1958, Wally Senior handsome in his uniform, Betty in her bright flowered dress, red lipstick, her hair done, leaning over the bed in a little intimate cloud of cologne—Tabu?—to kiss me good night because they're going out for the evening, dancing. Even now, Wally Senior's embroidered jacket from Korea is hanging in my attic, thin black wool embroidered with a dragon twining around a map of Korea which floats above the silky stitches of his name. It seems so small; neither Wally nor I could ever wear it, but it's hung in the closet of every house we ever lived in.

The family has the distinction of being perfectly balanced in terms of the distribution of sexual orientation; there are two heterosexual daughters and two lesbians, two straight men and—until Wally's death—two gay. Wally and Jimmy, his younger gay brother, used to want Betty to march in the Boston Gay Pride Parade with a sign reading, "MOTHER OF EIGHT, FOUR GAY, FOUR STRAIGHT." She was far too shy, though she loved the joke.

She—and Wally's father, who died in the seventies—must have provided a climate of real acceptance for all their children; she certainly provided such a feeling for their girlfriends, boyfriends, husbands, partners, wives. From the first time I met Betty, my sense was that she loved her children so fiercely that whomever they were, whatever contributed to their happiness, was fine with her. And Wally's father, who I never met, must have been a man with extraordinary capabilities to accept difference, too. I loved the story Wally used to tell about coming out to his parents. Just out of high school, he'd gotten a job at a local McDonald's, and soon found himself—thrillingly— courted by the manager. It wasn't long before they'd moved in together, into an apartment in another South Shore suburb, and Wally had busied himself behaving as a newlywed, late sixties housewife; making café curtains for the kitchen, learning to read cookbooks, figuring out how to spend his days when Mr. Mac was at work or wherever it was he went. One day Wally came home, unexpectedly early, from someplace he'd been on his bicycle, and found Mac in bed with another man. He ran out of the house, jumped back on the bike, and pedaled to his parents' house two towns away. When he saw his father he burst into tears and said, "Mac has someone else!"

So much for coming out. His father put his arms around him and said, "It'll be okay, son." Wally was eighteen or so then, and his openness (as well as the lack of parental thunder) led the way for three of his siblings.

(I wish I'd known Wally's father. In photographs, he shares the same twin white forks in his beard that Wally sported, a dashing blaze that would always motivate Wally to shave off whatever facial hair he grew. At a family reunion once in a legion hall decked in streamers and balloons, where lots of Wally Senior's brothers and sisters had gathered, the old relatives kept staring at Wally. He'd grown out his beard and curled his hair, and every now and then an old man or woman would walk up to us, trembling, as if unsure whether to weep or be glad of the likeness.)

Jim had settled in Boston, moving from the suburbs into the city, as Wally had before him, in search of gay life and a wider world. He studied drawing and painting and graphic arts, and worked as a waiter in a large hotel. Between them a genuine fondness coexisted with a certain level of competition. Their pleasure in seeing one another—which was real—would give way, in a while, to a certain kind of exasperation. Wally viewed Jim as something of a know-it-all, so sure of the rightness of his own opinions as to be sometimes unbearable; I think Jim probably saw Wally as too passive, too easily led, though I find it hard to be certain *what* he felt or thought, finally, since he always seemed a bit of a cipher—not quite available to be known. I think they were closer before I came into Wally's life; we had, like many couples, a sense of completeness together, as we became involved with and satisfied with one another's company. Wally liked who he was with me, and I am not so sure this was true of how he felt about himself with some of his old friends, or with his brother. His relationships changed as we came together, as our life together solidified.

Jim tested positive early, in 1985, during an experimental trial of the test. His health has remained good, and he's maintained a high T-cell count, a condition he attributes to attitude, and a regime of meditation and visualization. He says, in fact, that he is no longer HIV-positive, that he's gotten the virus out of his system. Once we went along with him, to see a healer visiting Boston; he was a Native American man from the Pacific Northwest, and he had made appointments for hands-on healing in the Brookline apartment of a woman who led a small group of psychic healers. They worked with pairs of small metal rods, L-shaped, with the smaller end of the rod held in each fist. Pointed at the subject, the rods would move when various questions were asked. "Does Wally have the HIV virus in his system?" The rods would open, to indicate yes. After the healing session—in which the handsome, raven-haired healer touched Wally, prayed over him, guided him into a kind of combat stance and encouraged him to find the warrior in himself—the rods were pointed at Wally again. They still opened to indicate the presence of the virus, but more weakly so. I want to believe, am willing to give, in fact, considerable credence to the possibility that these people may have access to some energy or ability to approach disease from another perspective. I understand that the world reveals new aspects of itself from new perspectives, so why shouldn't another system of belief show us a new way to see?

The signs weren't good, though. For one thing, the psychic had a profoundly neurotic dog, who tore back and forth across the room, flinging himself against the furniture with increasing and unnerving force. Couldn't she see into his pain? Why didn't the rods help with his obvious anxiety? Furthermore, she expressed considerable concern for me, told me that I desperately needed to love myself more if I was not to become very ill. Then she pointed the wands at me, asked the question, and they promptly indicated that I had AIDS, too. My trust flagged.

(People who don't know are forever sizing me up to try to guess if I have AIDS or not—checking out my weight, whether my cheeks look hollow or not, how tired I look. As Wally became more ill, he actually gained weight as his activity decreased. I grew thinner, from tension, exhaustion, riding my bike, and swimming laps to dispel the stress. People told me I looked too thin. My friend Maggie said I looked worse than Wally; "In a way," she said, "it's you I'm worried about." Bill said, "Well, of course, it's harder on you and Phil; you're the ones who're going to have to live without us." Just this week I ran into a straight couple I know casually, on the street. They asked me how Wally was, and after I told them he'd died, after the expressions of condolence, I could see them both—unconsciously?—checking me out, trying to guess. One of them asked me, "Well, how do you think he got it?" As if I cared, as if it mattered, as if it mattered how *anybody* got it.)

The problem with Jim's perspective is the obverse of its strength; it presumes that we are responsible for our own reality, for our experience. This is seductive, in part because there's such a clear element of truth in it; if we take care of ourselves, we do better. And seductive, too, because Jim, stubborn optimist, insistent on his powers over the virus, is alive; Bob, committed fatalist, is not.

(On a business trip back to Vermont, I walk down Main Street and find a U-Haul in front of Bob's building, and a man I know carrying the frame of Bob's bed down the stairs while someone else lugs a stack of boxes down from the little aerie over the movie theater. I think the worst, but in fact he's moving to another apartment, no longer able to manage the stairs. He'll die not in eighteen months but in two years or so, in that little Vermont town, his mother and sister taking turns caring for him. He and Wally had a last conversation, a month or so before, on the phone, Wally in bed, Bob in his wheelchair, both too tired to talk for long.)

Maybe it would be wonderful if it were as simple as this: take care of yourself, attune yourself to the inner life, rid yourself of negativity, focus on the light, and you'll be fine. But this seems to me, finally, a kind of kindergarten spirituality, a view of the soul written in broad crayon strokes. Oh, meditation and thinking positively and attending to the transcendent can be profoundly helpful, I know that. These practices provide a structure for caring for the self. They help us to live well, even help us deal with those aspects of illness that arise out of tension and stress.

What's good about taking charge of one's life is obvious; the negative side is subtler, harder to see, and has to do with all that the philosophy of self-control excludes. *You are calling the shots,* such thinking argues. *There are no accidents, no unruly rupture breaking apart your life, no brutal interruption. You've chosen this path, this plan. Illness has a purpose.*

But isn't transformation, the spirit's education, most often effected by what is out of our hands, the sweeping forces — time, love, mortality — which shape us? The deepening of the heart, the work of soul-making goes on, I think, as the world hammers us, as we forge ourselves in response to its heats and powers. The whirlwind pours over and through us, above and beyond human purpose; death's deep in the structure of things, and *we* didn't put it there. Just as the Voice which speaks to Job out of the whirlwind points out that we did not father the rain or the dew, or light the evening star.

Don't we require, finally, a place in our thinking for fortune, or destiny, or whatever we choose to call what will happen *to* us, how the avalanche will break over us? Contingency is somewhere near the heart of things; we edit and oversimplify the world if we deny it. How much simpler and smaller the universe would be if we controlled it—*or* if things merely went on their course without us, fatal and arbitrary. We live in the dialogue between what we can influence and what we can do nothing about. Do what you will, realities swim into view like planets. Jim says the world's entirely in my control; Bob says it is completely uncontrollable. Neither feels true, finally, to the ambiguous, shifting, complex field of human life. Sometimes we seem to see the whole; sometimes only details, the welter of incident. Things cohere, things fall apart. We make decisions; things are decided. We choose our parts; we enact scripts written elsewhere. To insist either that we are in charge or that we are helpless seems equally wrongheaded. Both perspectives insist on certainty, because they refuse to grant the unknowable. They offer, like any sort of fundamentalism, certainty, a system of reliable answers. They allow the suspension of painful and confusing ambiguities, and offer us a chance to give up the difficult, frustrating work of living on that dizzying, live edge between affirmation and despair.

My hair's been gradually vanishing for years, my face moving toward the semblance of my father's. In the body, in particular, the firmest exercise of will is humbled by processes out of our hands. I can struggle against the loss of my hair—through prayer and meditation, drugs, or through measures ranging from Dynel to, God forbid, the Hair Club for Men—but my scalp retains its identity; its motion toward baldness is slow but ceaseless. It's probably true that I could speed it up by hard living or stress, perhaps true that I could slow it down with antioxidants or perhaps visualizations, but *control* what happens to my hair? The reality of our relationship to our bodies is a shuttling dialogue; we effect some changes, other changes are visited upon us, and we could no more shape them than we could decide where a meteor will fall.

That arrogance which says *I alone* bear the responsibility for my body, for my fate, can suspend compassion. What are we to do, holding these tenets, when people we love fail to stay healthy? What if we "fail" to be well ourselves; mustn't that then be a moral or spiritual failure? And if we *ask* for what we get, if all our suffering and illnesses are brought upon ourselves—cancer from repressed anger, AIDS from wounded sexuality—then what is the role of compassion? Just last night, at a benefit, a man who's lived with AIDS for more than a decade was applauded by the crowd. He said he owed his life to the love of his partner, and the love of his friends and family; I found myself cringing inside, even though I'm glad the guy who said this is alive and well and feeling loved. But so many men who are dead were deeply loved, too, and finally this statement erases them, denies the validity of their real passions, of what was felt by and for them. We would like to think the dead could have helped it, because if they could, *we* could. But a virus cannot be loved away. Jim isn't alive because of his attitude; Bob isn't dead because of his.

We trivialize pain if we regard it as a preventable condition the spirit need not suffer. If we attempt to edit it out, will it away, regard it as our own creation, then don't we erase some essential part of the spirit's education? Pain is one of our teachers, albeit our darkest and most demanding one.

If I am more tolerant of Bob's fatalism here, it is because he was already ill; I can somehow find in myself more empathy for his position, as he must have felt himself being swept away. I am less tolerant of Jim's position because of the outcome it led to; as Wally grew more ill, he became less and less a presence in Wally's life. I don't want to overstate this; it's not as if they were very close and then Jim suddenly walked away. But he simply wasn't around. He visited us in Provincetown when

Wally was still walking, in the summer of 1992. And then I think we saw him briefly at Christmas, in Rockland, that year; as far as I know, he and Wally never saw each other again. During the nine months Wally was bedridden, entirely incapacitated, we never saw him. Intellectually, I can understand the need to stay away—since, being HIV-positive oneself, seeing one's own brother dying would be not only terrible in itself but a frightening reflection of one's own possible future. I understand it, but I haven't forgiven it. My recalcitrance and crankiness about this is in part because of my distrust of new-age attitudes; I'm horrified by a spirituality which is too transcendent for human contact.

And I am intolerant of Jim, of course, because I also long for that sort of control, which illness and death have taught me I cannot have.

A few nights after I wrote those pages, this is what I dreamed: I had to parachute from an airplane in a strange way, sitting in the kind of plastic chair you'd find in a doctor's waiting room. I was strapped into the chair, pushed out the door, and then fell and fell, it seemed almost endlessly, toward the earth. I can't remember landing, exactly, but where I arrived was a hospital room, and the man in the bed was alternately Wally and Jim. He—either man—was in the last hours of his life. When he died I wept and wept; the dream was full of the enormity of the weeping. In a while I knew I had to tell Wally's mother that one of her sons had died, though by then I wasn't sure which.

I woke then, shaken, not crying now that I was awake but aware of the sobbing that had filled my sleep. I think my dream was about compassion for Jim, about seeing him and Wally in the same bed, the same boat. Just as I think the darker underside of his spirituality is judgment, so my dream points up to me how my own judgment of him has obscured my compassion. If I were him, if I were HIV-positive, what would I have done? It's easy for me to say I'd never disappear from my brother's life, but I don't know that; can any of us know what we'd do under that disfiguring pressure? Judgment is easier than compassion, my dream reminds me; the dream instructs me, falling toward loss, the fall I can't control, though I survive it, to see the ways in which Wally and Jim are of a piece.

We tried to steer a course between fatalism and an unacceptable optimism—between feeling completely out of control and claiming a sort of complete authority neither of us could believe in. What we wanted, desperately, was some way for things to get back to "normal"—absurd as that sounds, in a way, it is also the necessary condition of ongoingness. Somehow we have to make whatever dreadful knowledge we have part of the fabric of every day; we have to find a way to continue our ordinary transactions with the world in the light of new and extraordinary knowledge. Of course nothing could ever be the same again, but how to integrate that pressure day to day, every hour? The sense of "normalcy" is founded in part on denial, on forgetting. So it's difficult to remember, to trace the ways in which we moved toward acting *as if* our lives were normal again. Wally still went to work, spray-painting props and designing displays for shop windows. I tended the garden and wrote, through the summer, and in September went back to teaching. We'd go on as if we were fine, and then crash and go on again. Wally wasn't sick, not just then; there was time in front of us—who knew how much, but suddenly any amount of time seemed a luxury, a gift. What would we do with it?

Refuge

We bought a cabin in the woods—a camp, in Vermont parlance. It wasn't something we'd planned to do, wasn't something that really made sense to do, not in any practical way.

There was, one Sunday, an ad in the newspaper with a photograph of a little house, on six more-or-less acres of woodland; there was something infinitely appealing about the picture, and we thought we were planning a sort of elaborate Sunday drive when we called the realtor and asked where the place was located. We'd just drive by, we said, and take a look, and call again if we wanted to see it. We didn't really *plan* to call again; this was an outing, a lark.

Through Plainfield, through Marshfield, two tiny, down-at-the-heels towns untouched for thirty years, the road wound along the Winooski River, through bottom farmlands, past a perpetual yard sale with tables of Avon bottles and farm tools, jetsam collecting rainwater, past the great hulks of barns whose cupolas and turrets made me think of grand wooden Russian churches with their shingled turrets and onion domes. Then a turn off Route 2, a smaller road through higher and higher farmlands, clusters of little trailers ("MAPLE SYRUP SOLD RIGHT HERE") and into the thick woods of a state forest. A few miles through the tall evergreens and birch, a dirt road intersected the forest road. To the left the road climbed to Owl's Head, a bald dome of rock reached by a winding trail, over which mist would often hang, veiling and transforming, so that the trail became a kind of moody Chinese landscape. To the right, the loggers' road curved further down the mountain's slope to the little camp, and beyond it, a couple of farmhouses which were all that remained of what had once been a logging town, complete with schoolhouse and hotel—gone now, their foundations half-visible in fields of milkweed and cow-vetch, butter-and-eggs and ragged sailors and Queen Anne's lace.

The camp was a shingled gray house, trimmed in burgundy. Built in the twenties, the main room—into which we peered through every window, circling the house in an increasing state of infatuation—centering around a wood-fired cookstove. On a built-in table, covered with old red Formica, someone had left a deck of cards spread beneath the shade of the gas lamp. There was a little kitchen sink and counter, sporting calendars and a few old prints on the bare studs of the walls, from which protruded, every now and then, a coat hook made from the hoof and foreleg of a deer.

All along one side of the house, looking out into the cool depths of the woods, which seemed particularly lush and damp, starred with large stones decked in lichens and lavish clouds of moss, ran a screened-in porch. Its heavy old furniture—armchairs and a sofa a little too broken down for home, slipcovered in a faded flowery stuff—looked like the best place in the world for a summer afternoon's reading. On a table beside the sofa sat a stuffed robin, mothy but still presentable, poised on some long-preserved branch, and a windup record player of uncertain vintage, next to a stack of heavy seventy-eights.

Both of us are so completely smitten that there's almost no need to go in. The realtor lives just down the road a mile or two, on the forest's edge. She's a salty, wonderful woman with an interesting mix of country ways and urbane savvy, who herself used to spend childhood summers in the camp, and clearly she relishes the idea of a gay couple buying it because she *knows* what we'll do with it. The tour of the inside only deepens the fascination—playing with the gaslights, climbing the fold-down stairs up into the sleeping loft, where two built-in log beds and tiny windows with green shutters call up fantasies of boys at summer camp. The fact that the whole place smells vaguely of mouse piss and dampness, of musty upholstery, somehow seems just right, as does every object within—taken individually, they aren't much, but as a whole they somehow represent the history of the house, a heady distillation of summer after summer, years of pleasure, childhood, memory, escape.

There are good reasons not to buy it. Does anybody need a second house thirty miles from home? Especially when home is big and ramshackle, and logically we'd be better off using the money (which is not money, actually, but home equity) on decent plumbing. Isn't it decadent to have two houses, when so many people don't have one? And didn't our uncertain future suggest that acquiring another house wasn't exactly sensible?

But this is about longing, not logic, and it's cheap, and practically effortless, and before we know it we own a camp, a mysterious little dacha on an impossibly narrow six-acre triangle bordered on one side by state forest, on the opposite side by the dirt road, and along the shortest side by a grassy, boggy marsh.

That marsh! Water from Owl's Head wandered down the side of the mountain, in little freshets and mosquitoey swamp-spots through our woods. I loved that—*our* woods. The first thing we did was to make a trail, down from the house, winding through the forest toward the marsh, attempting to discover what our acres contained: an old apple tree, the ruins of a schoolhouse, a practical universe of mushrooms in splendid varieties of russet and cream and toast, almond and ghost-white. Evidence of deer, bear-scratches on the tree trunks, a raccoon who woke us in the night by knocking the bird feeder against a trunk to make the seed fall out. Realms of moss, and pockets of mud, and bugs.

Part of the water from the marsh bubbled from our spring—"ours" because the property came with a lease from the state of Vermont, one renewed year after year, to allow use of particularly cold and clear and fine water from a spring on the shoulder of the mountain, up on state land. A rubber pipe ran downhill from the spring to the camp itself.

Each autumn the rubber pipe had to be lifted out of the spring and drained, to keep the line from freezing and bursting; one of our first tasks was to climb the side of the mountain and put the pipe back into the spring, so that the water would flow back into the house again. Finding the spring was the problem. It wasn't possible to follow the pipe, since over the course of fifty years or so it had become completely covered with fallen leaves, fir needles, moss; here and there it was visible for a few inches (just enough for some passing animal to bite, from time to time, so that we'd hear a hissing hose in the woods and know it was time for repairs) but then it would disappear, hopelessly lost. Someone had painted yellow circles on trees, as trail markers to lead to it, but time and weather had worn them away. Eventually a combination of yellow spots and tracking stream beds led to what seemed an enchanted place: out of a dark and mossy grotto formed by a cluster of stones, water welled up from somewhere so far beneath the mountain we couldn't guess how long it had been traveling upward toward us.

It was necessary to reach into the dark, into the chilly water, to pull the pipe up, take off the plastic wrapper that sealed it for the winter, and fit on the brass cone which filtered out any moss that might find its way in and clog the pipe. Wally refused; I lay on my stomach on a stony bower of moss starred with wet leaves, and reached down into the bottomless world of the spring to find the pipe—like reaching down into time, into the darkness of a fairy place. When we opened the valves back at the camp, the sweet water—which had a kind of subtle presence to its taste, not a flavor exactly but a *quality*, which might have had something to do with our knowing its origins—came thundering and farting and blowing out the tap into the kitchen sink, rattling the house until the air in the half a mile of pipe was gone.

The water that we didn't use trickled along, wandered, sank underground, feeding the moss and the alders and supporting the marsh in dry seasons. The marsh lay in a kind of saddle, a valley between bluish, misted Owl's Head and another mountain considerably further away. A creek wound through the middle, frequently dammed by beaver, who'd flood the road and begin their work on the building of their paradise until the farmer who depended on the road had enough and undid their labors—and probably undid them, too, in some unkind fashion. Over the unhurried stream and the surrounding reeds a kind of haze used to hang, as if the light itself were concentrated there, sunlight become something thickened, palpable. It felt, to me, like the heart of that country, a place where the closed and cool world of the forest opened out into long but intimate distances, where the yellow and green horizontals of the marsh countered the mountains' blue-violet verticals. Red-winged blackbirds threaded the air.

On the other side of the marsh, reached by the tenuous little bridge which ran above the twin culverts, lived a bull. He and a few scrawny chickens seemed to be the only nonhuman tenants of a farm on the skids. Its large barn was twisting dangerously on its foundation, like a set for some rural version of *The Cabinet of Dr. Caligari*, and there were never any people to be seen out-of-doors, though occasionally they would roar down the dirt road in large, antiquated cars. They did not slow down to wave to us.

The bull controlled his side of the marsh, which I would have been happy to leave to him except that there, just across the little bridge where dry land resumed, ran a wonderful road, actually the remains of an old railroad which had hauled away—hard now to believe—practically every tree in the region, late in the nineteenth century. The industry had ceased only because, after the clear-cutting, there was simply nothing left, though the train ran on, carrying lumbermen, till early in this century. The first owner of the camp was, in fact, a woman with a great fondness for lumberjacks; in those days there were no trees between the cabin and the tracks, and the story went that she'd hang out her laundry in the altogether just as the train went by, displaying her charms for the men en route. (She liked her whiskey, too; the woods turn up an inexhaustible supply of mossy bottles.) The railroad tracks and most of the ties are gone now, but the old bed winds on forever, through shady vales, past ferny cliffs of granite and deep, shadowy sloughs favored by moose, toward a number of small lakes. An old man who stopped his astonishingly decrepit army-green pickup on the road in front of the camp to talk to me one day told me a lovely story, about swimming with his Newfoundland dog in one of these ponds. He had been a teenager then, and had taken himself for a long, long hike across some trails we knew and some we did not, to arrive at a pond. Then he'd decided to swim across, and, in his exhaustion, something must have gone wrong. He came to some time later, on a large rock by the shore, the drenched Newfoundland towering over him; he had been rescued by the valiant pet.

Our noble pet seemed to lose his nerve in the presence of the bull; we'd carefully slink around the edge of his territory. Arden, never barking once, wouldn't take his eyes off the bulk of the beast, standing spread-legged in his meadow, until we were well out of range. His caution turned out to be wise. One day, alone at the camp, Arden and I are walking down to look for beaver; the bull is himself out on the little road, near the bridge, and he decides that we have come quite close enough. He begins to walk toward us; I try acting nonchalant, but then decide that the appearance of fearlessness is an inadequate defense. We turn and begin to walk away, but hear behind us, gaining a little, the determined hoof steps of the bull. The bull is tall as me, wide as a small tractor, and horned. We walk faster. The bull walks faster, too, and I begin to think this is serious. I'm unsure if he wants me or Arden or both of us, but by this time we're both panicked and start to run full-tilt, which only seems to pique the bull's interest. He chases us all the way up the road back to the camp, and Arden and I race into the house, and I slam the door behind us, my heart racing as if it's about to burst, Arden panting and pacing. The bull stands in the road in front of the house, pawing the dirt, snorting, triumphant.

If Wally had experienced this, I don't think he'd ever have come back to the camp again. Because, as we soon discovered, it was not really such a pleasure for him to be in the woods. He didn't enjoy the operatic thunderstorms which the mountain was prone to; one June night lightning made a crater in the road the size of a Volkswagen. He felt isolated at night, disturbed by the noises of wildlife and the creak of trees, and the endless little rustlings of mice. Even though we'd found and dispersed the great granary they had made inside the wall of the attic, and even though we'd gone out of our way to keep everything edible covered and sealed, the mice were ineradicable, and Wally couldn't sleep because he was sure they'd run across his arm, or he'd wake up with one sitting beside his head. The scuttle of feet on the floor in the dark didn't bother me in the same way it did him; I don't know if what he felt was a city boy's anxiety about uncharted nature or something else, a displaced unsettledness? Perhaps it was a family trait; when his mother came to visit the camp, for an hour or two in broad daylight on a summer afternoon, she was noticeably anxious and in a hurry to leave. She was, it turned out, worried about bears.

It was a disappointment to me to realize, in a while, that the camp was my passion, not Wally's. Perhaps it was simply that it had seemed to represent, on those first sightings and during those first adventures of occupancy, another life, another set of possibilities—and once we had made it ours, the fact was that the old life continued. Part of the romance of the little house was the promise of safety, of tranquillity, of rest—and somehow it didn't feel that way for Wally. He said he was bothered by the rednecks down the road, the kids who'd drive by too fast and leave a beer bottle tossed into the woods; I think he'd imagined the camp as an escape from the working-class Vermont neighborhood we lived in, but the cultures of Vermont were, inevitably, out here in the woods, too. The root of Wally's disaffection, I imagine, was that he had other work to do. Because the diagnosis wasn't mine, I could stand back further, practice the art of avoidance more successfully—though my passion for the place seems now a mixed gesture, both of avoidance and of reaching toward the future, of escape and of hope. I was playing, in some deeply serious way, with images of home, of inhabitation, of safety, of time. And though Wally would play with me at householding, at fixing up the place, occupying it together, his attention was, finally, elsewhere.

There was one superb summer night though, the tenth of August, the most memorable birthday of my life, my thirty-sixth. Four friends came to dinner; Wally had found antique Japanese paper lanterns at a yard sale, beautiful watery faded colors, and he hung them in the trees around the porch, with a lit candle in each one, so that they glowed and flickered romantically and dangerously. We played a stack of records on the windup phonograph—"In the Gloaming Oh My Darling," "Indian Love Call," bits of Verdi—and drank whiskey and a bottle of sixty-five-year-old port I'd found and saved for an occasion. Its complicated savor of plums and smoke and years made all those terms for the flavors of wines suddenly make sense: woody, fruity, resinous, deep, blooming, subtle, one flavor floating above the next like layers of silk. And it *was* an occasion: I was drunk, radiant, in good friendship, in love with my husband and my little house and my black prince of a puppy just now arriving at an adolescent maturity, calmly watching us eat. My friend Kathryn, who that night brought me a gift of a shrub, a forsythia to bring the cabin a flourish of gold in spring, wrote a little story about that night to read, years later, at Wally's memorial:

> We drive down a long road through the woods. It's summer; we want it to last forever, cool cupping the

day's heat, pine trees, sun and moon together in the sky. We want it to last forever because we're foolish and we think it can't.

There's a little house tucked into the edge of the woods. The door opens and we smell yeast, herbs, wet dog fur, the sweet smell of friends. The sun and moon are both big, one going down, the other rising higher and higher. In the trees around the house, Japanese lanterns, the real kind, lit with candles. Nothing in your life before has prepared you for such happiness. Nothing can shield you from this happiness, which is why no one before has ever dared to give it to you. There is also a faint bad smell in the house of rack and ruin, the legacy of the former owners. Wally wrinkles his nose. His nose and the wrinkling of it and the faint bad smell and the smell of Arden's wet fur and the smell of Mark's basil and sausage-stuffed bread and the smell of the pines and the smell of Lois's cigarette smoke and the smell of the candle wax and all of a sudden we can see the scantily clad body of the woman who used to wander out into the gorse behind the house fifty years ago to excite the loggers, their faces pressed against the windows of the little train taking them back to camp. Chiffon and feathers, can't you just see it, Wally says. His delighted eyes and the lights of the train and the Japanese lanterns and the match flaring and Mark's bright smile and even though it would be so easy to judge the woman or revile the world for sending lust-driven men into her back yard while she dances there in her feathers and chiffon while her house goes to rack and ruin, even through we might pass judgement, being a forward-thinking group composed of a lesbian couple, a gay couple and a heterosexual couple, we don't.

We are here in this house. We are here and the

woman is alive and Mark and Wally have made this happen because they are what makes life happen, yeast and chiffon and the bread in your mouth and the train whistle *now.*

You cannot leave us. Sun and moon in the sky. I don't even know which is which.

Only the weight of grief, which is equal in measure to happiness. We drank port and the world grew dark. It isn't as if we weren't prepared. We are always in that house and here. It isn't as if you didn't prepare us, just that we want to revile the world. The lanterns shining in the trees, Arden snoring on the floor, Mark's arm over your shoulders, can't you just see it?

That autumn and winter the camp was my dream, something out of Chekhov. Arden and I would go at least once a week, even in the deepest snow, and build a fire in the stove in the unbelievably icy uninsulated main room, and walk in the snow, and study the marsh and the mountain. On warmer days we'd stay and I'd write letters, or read in the field guides to trees and fungi I'd bought. One winter day there was a sudden, enormous crash; ice falling from the roof? Too loud, too shockingly reverberant through the woods. A fallen tree? After Arden came out from his hiding place, the shelter of the wicker sofa, we walked down the road toward the marsh, our breath steaming in locomotive clouds. The barn had fallen, all at once, into a huge pick-up-sticks heap of gray boards and beams. The bull stood up the hill from it, entirely unruffled, chewing on a mouthful of straw.

Hunters shot the deer on our weather vane, so slap-happy for blood that a metal deer would do. Someone—a camper? one of the people who lived in those tiny blue trailers down the mountain road?—stole half our woodpile. How much I wanted to protect that little house—perhaps not so much from these superficial sorts of insults as on some deeper level. There was—how to say it—a particular kind of presence about the place, an atmosphere of particular density. It had about it the distilled resonance of home, yes, but also an otherness, a spirited presence, as if it were so fully inhabited by its history that we were simply another part of the continuous dream-life of the house, two more of its passing occupants. One lived in the camp on its terms; it imposed its personality upon you, and even your clothes would come to smell of its aura of gone summers, old oil lamps, whiskey, and mice. There is a space in my memory which the camp occupies which finally has not to do with the building itself, or my own experiences there, but with its spirits, which became mine during that year of ownership; possessed by them, I'm bound to that dreaming house always. It was a model of a refuge. But it was an isolated one, so it could not hold, could not sustain us. The community it offered was with the lonely and perfect woods, and with the past, with childhood and with ghosts.

By spring I was doing painting and repairs on my days off from teaching, and though I said I was doing them for us, doing things I wanted to do, I knew on some level I was fixing up the camp in order to let it go; I couldn't know what sort of change was coming, but so much that had mattered before (my teaching, our houses) now seemed temporary, ephemeral; we were about to be moved along, in the course and current of things. Change was gathering speed, establishing direction.

Refuge (2)

～

Provincetown, 1990. The universe, God, the essence of benevolence gives us the unmatchable autumn of our lives: brilliant days brimming with warm October light that seem never to end. Our little rented cottage on the edge of what Melville called "the great unbounded" feels itself boundless; our attention's turned outward from the tiny bayside rooms to the huge horizontals around us, an expanse of harbor and horizon wide as the world. We swim in the bay late into October, and walk the huge pewtery gleam of the tideflats barefoot into November. It seems a long time since either of us has felt this free or this happy. Illness seems far away, living easy. How did we get here?

It seemed effortless, or at least as if our efforts were richly, invisibly assisted; everything conspired to bring us to a brighter, less freighted life. Lynda and David, spending a sabbatical year on the Cape, invited us down for a visit, in February, the off-est of the off-season, a time of the year I'd never seen Provincetown. Weary of the deep snow of Vermont, as well as its icy emotional weather, we found ourselves smitten with the coastal clutter of boarded shops and clapboard houses along the curve of the bay. Our friends had rented a big old drafty place across the street from the water, a former rooming house stocked with more beds than you could count. When it began to snow and snow, keeping us in town another day, we couldn't have been happier. We ate kale soup just behind the steamed windows of one of the two open cafés. Our angelic waiter (a painter I still know, who'd later come to be a friend) welcomed us, a sort of everyday angel whose task it seemed to bless our meal, our visit, our days in a place that offered a sense of respite. After our dark northern days of adjustment and strength-seeking, this town was like balm.

And so a process of realignment began, so subtle that we almost didn't know it was happening. One day one of us suggested a trip back to Provincetown for spring break, and April found us in a rambling waterfront apartment in the West End. It was a week of brash new sun, crocus unfurling while the whole town emerged to wash windows, sweep walks, and take in the new light. As we did, walking with Lynda at the cranberry bog on the North Pamet Road, way up into the high, heathered dunes over the beach near Head of the Meadow. I remember one day especially, taking Arden to the beach at Race Point, and curling up together with a thermos of coffee in the shoulder of a dune, ignoring the books and paper we'd brought, dreaming there in that early sun which the skin receives with such gratitude that it seems better than all the rays of summer. The social climate of the town—its ready acceptance of us as a couple, its affirmation of our ordinariness—felt also like a drink of sunlight; dealing with HIV had underlined our sense of isolation, underscored the sense of difference northern New England's homogeneous culture kept reminding us of anyway.

During the vacation, I had to leave town for a day, on some literary business. It was almost dark when I returned. At the point where the only road into town is suddenly a band of asphalt between two sand dunes, a thought leapt into my head: *I'm home now.* Home? Where did that come from? Home was three hundred miles away, and we'd be there in a few days. But I couldn't escape this new sense of an arrival, a door in my life opening.

Driving back to Vermont, under ragged patches of cloud raining and hurrying across a sky scrubbed a clean April blue, we drove past the tail end of a rainbow whose ending place was plainly visible; you could actually look *through* the end of the rainbow into the wet grass. Home again, we almost didn't even need to say it out loud: what were we doing here? I'd stayed five years in a job I was wearying of, and neither school nor the display business which Wally had built were priorities to him. We loved our house, I loved my garden, but these didn't seem enough; now we needed community, like-minded company. We needed both support and a place that would leave us alone to work on what was essential, which was trying to understand what was happening to us, feeling our way, finding how to live well. Who knew how much time we'd have? Nothing, nothing erodes one's patience like that question.

Solutions materialized as easily as our rainbow, emblem of promise and futurity. A friend called from Sarah Lawrence College, in New York, and offered me a job as her replacement during a year's leave. Sarah Lawrence is a long way from Provincetown, but because the job involved teaching only on Mondays and Tuesdays, it was perfectly possible to drive down to the college, stay over and teach, then have the rest of the week on the Cape. Though the house was sold in fifteen minutes, there were endless things to do: cleaning out the accumulations of two men absurdly fond of barn sales and auctions and flea markets, deciding what was essential, letting go of one life and reaching uncertainly toward another. But a kind of ease prevailed, a sense that the rightness of what we were doing made a complex set of exchanges and arrangements possible. We seemed to be offered a series of gifts.

Walking Arden one morning by the rotary at the end of our town's arterial street, where civilization ends and the road gives way to a wide, luminous salt marsh, I stopped to read what I'd been walking past for weeks, a neglected historical marker hidden in a bushy clump of junipers. Its verdigrised lettering noted that somewhere near the site, in November of 1620, the Pilgrims made their first landing before going on to Plymouth. This was a considerable shock to me, for one reason: my ancestor, Edward Dotey, was a passenger on that overcrowded, brightly painted boat.

This ancestry is no conventional source of pride. My family has been for generations a ragtag batch of poor Southerners; my mother's father was a subsistence farmer in East Tennessee, lugging what millet he could to the mill every summer and living off the meager income it provided. My father's father was a carpenter who, during the Depression, served time in prison for shooting one of his creditors. Southern to the bone, intermarried with dirt-poor Irish escapees of the potato famine, we found the idea of a noble Yankee ancestor oddly distant; I can understand now why my mother laughed, in the late fifties, when she was invited to join the Memphis chapter of the DAR.

And Edward Dotey himself is a bit of a problem, as near a figure to the archetypal American scoundrel as the first citizens of Plymouth can provide. The facts of his early life are scant, but it appears that the young man from London sold himself into indentured servitude to escape some fate worse than seven years without liberty in a relatively unknown and certainly inhospitable country. Perhaps he was avoiding debtor's prison. Whatever his motivation, the hot-tempered Edward probably was a central figure in the *Mayflower* mutiny, in which the declaration of a group of young men that "when they came ashore, they would use their owne libertie" led to the signing of the Mayflower Compact.

Once settled in Plymouth, he distinguished himself by fighting the first duel on American soil, with one Edward Leister. He went to court and was convicted for "dealing fraudulentlie about a flitch of bacon." Free of his servitude, he proceeded to amass a considerable amount of worldly goods, doubtless by less than admirable means. He filed America's first lawsuit. He seems to have been more or less run out of the colony, ultimately, and died on Cape Cod, in 1655, having fathered nine children. He left behind a wealth of copper pots and iron implements, and a nasty reputation.

In November, our town weekly announced that a reenactment of the first landing, with local people in the role of the heroic voyagers, would take place on the beach where the actual landing seems to have occurred—somewhere, the article read, between the Red Inn and the Provincetown Inn. Without realizing it, I had rented a house in precisely the spot where my ancestor, 370 years before, had probably been among the sixteen armed men who first rode a longboat into shore from the *Mayflower*, carrying their muskets and a bottle of Holland gin, since they lacked fresh water. Over the next few gin-primed days, they reconnoitered, discovered a spring and a plentiful supply of quahogs and mussels, and raided a store of Wampanoag corn in what would later become Truro. The women came ashore, in order to allow the children to run on the beach, under close scrutiny—how exhilarating open space must have been, after their matchbox quarters—and to do laundry, for, as William Bradford informs us, "they had great need." (Provincetown's historical museum offers today a mural of the Pilgrim women boiling and wringing out those severe clothes.)

For months, then, I had been filling my eyes with a landscape that was part of my primogeniture, though I did not know it and though that landscape was now, of course, wildly changed. The Pilgrims encountered a Cape much more heavily wooded than it is today, since house- and boat-building would decimate virgin growth and produce a more barren, sandy landscape. As Provincetown transformed itself from an eighteenth-century fishing village to a nineteenth-century whaling town, and then to a Bohemian resort, property would become increasingly valuable. By late in this century the West End— once a less prestigious, Portuguese neighborhood—would contain the town's priciest waterfront property, and every available bit of developable land would hold a welter of cottages and condos skewed at odd angles, a Cubist jigsaw rising up from the pristine beach where the First Laundry was hung to dry.

The town of Provincetown would like America to know that the Pilgrims landed here first (the Vikings were here, too, leaving a fragment of stone wall beneath what's now a guest house a little nearer to the center of town). But travelers to this far outpost are, in general, drawn here by more recent traditions which have, since sometime around the end of the nineteenth century, made Provincetown first an arts colony and then — consequently? — a zone of tolerance and permission. Interest in uncovering and preserving the historical traditions of gay men and lesbians is recent, so it's difficult to know when Provincetown first became a haven for the "Bohemian" expatriates of Eastern cities. Artists were drawn here by the beauty of the place and by cheap rents, and the influx of new citizenry found congenial hosts among the Portuguese fishing community which had arrived with the growth of whaling. Greenwich Village summered here in the teens and twenties, when a boat from one of the downtown piers traveled directly to this little tendril of land sixty miles out into the Atlantic. By the forties — when Tennessee Williams was finishing *The Glass Menagerie* in a rented shack, posing *à la Grecque* with a mock javelin for a nude photo in the dunes, and frequenting the bar at the Atlantic House, where (among others) Gene Krupa and Billie Holiday performed, Provincetown had established a social milieu so different from that of mainstream New England as to make it feel more like an island than the tip of a peninsula. Until the fifties, it was much easier to get here by boat than to risk a road frequently buried under sand, so perhaps the very isolation of the place allowed it to evolve in its own direction, like those exotic islands where very particular sorts of species flourish. Poets and painters from New York built a community of value here, a culture where work was central and the tensions and competition of the city were held at bay. They generated a heady atmosphere of possibility; "We have been nervy," said my friend Elise Asher, a painter in her seventies, "with freedom and imagination."

In such a climate, of course, queer people have felt at home. How kind this atmosphere seemed to us, and how deeply gratifying to be able to do many of the things that heterosexual couples do without reservation every day: to touch one's lover on the street, for instance, without considering consequences. To shop together for groceries or talk intimately in a café without self-consciousness. I didn't realize, until time in Provincetown allowed me to begin to set such self-awareness aside, how *watched* I'd felt those five years in Vermont, how singled out, not allowed to forget my difference. I was perfectly willing to be out, in that little Northern town, and a part of me enjoyed being a crusader. But no one wants to live like that constantly; it takes an enormous amount of energy to watch oneself, to be watched all the time. Provincetown allowed us alternately to celebrate our difference and to forget it, and both opportunities were welcome.

One day, walking home on the beach from the center of town, we heard sudden footsteps behind us. Glancing over my shoulder, I saw that two men were approaching us very quickly, walking with a kind of deliberation that didn't suggest strolling. I felt myself tighten, tension stiffening my neck and shoulders, my body bracing itself as the speeding footsteps came right up behind us. I turned around swiftly, and there were the two men who'd been bearing down on us, just a few feet away—holding hands. First I laughed. And then I realized how much fear I carried, how much learned apprehension was held in my body, a guardedness my environment no longer warranted. How much of their emotional, intellectual, physical energies are gay people required to sink into such cautions? How much of ourselves do we lose, in our necessary defensiveness?

So I'd returned, an unknowing family envoy after nearly four hundred years, to a point of origin. I read histories of the Plymouth Colony. Wally and I spent Thanksgiving wandering through the replica of the *Mayflower* in Plymouth Harbor; strangely bright in its colors, staffed by actors imitating Puritans and sailors, it remained a replica. We even visited Plymouth Plantation, a sort of "living history" park where the staff spend their days in character in seventeenth-century costume, discussing seventeenth-century matters in their reproduction village and producing, at least in us, a weirdly discomforting effect. Most disquieting of all was the "Indian village" beyond the fences of the Pilgrim settlement, where the descendants of native peoples cooked over open fires and played with a deerskin ball, enduring questions and flashbulbs and looking irremediably sad. I felt no closer to my distant ancestor, gained no firmer sense of who he might have been. I used to walk out, at night, to the breakwater which divides the end of the harbor from the broad moor of the salt marsh. There was nothing to block the wind there, a wind that had picked up speed and vigor and the scent of salt and freedom from its Atlantic crossing. Until it was too cold and raw to stay out any longer, I'd study the stars in their brilliant blazing, the diaphanous swath of the Milky Way, the distant glow of Boston backlighting the clouds on the horizon as if they'd been drawn there in smudgy charcoal. I felt, perhaps for the first time, particularly American, embedded in American history, here at the nation's slender tip. Here our westering impulse, having flooded the continent and turned back, finds itself face to face with the originating Atlantic, November's chill, salt expanses, what Hart Crane called "unfettered leewardings," here at the end of the world.

Time had bent back, doubled upon itself; my search for refuge mirrored the voyage of my ancestor, who sought at least an economic refuge if not the spiritual one of his fellow passengers. This doubling came to stand, for me, for the kind of duality which is this town's particular character.

There is first the sheer matter of elements. The narrowness of the Cape at its last dwindling spur means that we are almost completely surrounded by water; the sun comes up over the bay, and sets over the open sea. Provincetown feels like an island, but we are part of the mainland, albeit tenuously. Any shore is a meeting place of continuous activity, of constant negotiation between earth and water, relations shifting by the hour and season. What is land at noon may be sea at three.

Add to this irresolvable dialogue the enormous expanse of sky, whose business is always and everywhere more visible here, where there is so much more of it than in inland landscapes, and the result is a constant, alchemical process of change. This shape-shifting makes the forms and aspects of things mercurial, inconstant—as if this conjunction of elements, life on the boundary, made things themselves restless. We are a border town between worlds, and one of them is perhaps our last wilderness, that sun-hammered, fog-claimed expanse which remains—at least from here on the shore—unknowable, impenetrable.

We are a sort of border town, too, an Alexandria, in that here a mélange of cultures mingle, interlock, and remain separate at once: straight and gay year-rounders, summer people, tourists mixing in a fascinating spectrum of relationships between gender, orientation and identity, a range of possibilities that makes the world seem a broader place. In this zone what is *expected* is difference, surprise.

A sole example, of the endless ones possible: one warm autumn morning, a group of women gathered at the sidewalk café for brunch, then walked through town with a banner reading "DRAG DYKES." They were lesbians dressed "as women," complete with lipstick and wigs, faux leopard miniskirts and veiled hats. What seemed extraordinary to me were the tourists who were taking their pictures, a group of older visitors fresh off the fall foliage tour bus. The peculiarity of photographing women dressed as women seemed lost on them; one of the "cross-dressers" was patiently explaining to an elderly woman just who they were and what they were up to, though she didn't seem to be getting very far. The ironies of the situation made me say—as I have so many times, even after five years in Provincetown—"Where else?" It's something many of us here ask, affectionately, when the town yet again demonstrates its ability to surprise us.

What would my Pilgrim forefather make of all this? It's too easy to suppose that he would find in the town which has evolved upon his wooded shore a kind of Babylon. He was himself an outsider, an opportunist who found in the Puritans' voyage an opportunity to construct a life with larger boundaries than London must have offered a young man of no means or social standing. Provincetown's pleasure-based economy—we live on the sale of consumables, from silk shirts to grilled tuna to soft ice cream—may well have appalled the Puritans, but then *they* were highly interested in selling the bounty of the New World to an eager market back home. Most of us were reacquainted, each Thanksgiving, with imagery of a sober piety, but it's a quaint historical fiction to suppose them a united group with a certain faith in a particular ideology. They were, in fact, contentious and embattled, both in a threatening England and an even more uncertain America. We have more in common with their tremendous doubts, with their fear in the face of an unknown future, than with whatever certainties they may have claimed.

Storms, on the North Atlantic coast, are Shakespearean.

They move in like vast states of mind, and seem allied with moral forces, conjured by enchanters whose aim is to confound and instruct. One autumn Nor'easter of Hollywood magnitude filled the air with so much wind-blown water that it hardly seemed air at all, but rather as if the atmosphere had become a new sort of medium, making those of us unlucky enough to be out in it quite like fish out of water. In the morning, a wrecked houseboat lay on its side on the beach like a stranded whale.

The houseboat had been the only craft of its sort in the harbor, and for good reason; a simple room constructed atop a boat, square and unhappy on the water, it did not seem a seaworthy craft. Unballasted, its boxy shape made it a plaything for any wind, turning and turning in the slightest breeze. I couldn't imagine anyone living aboard.

Cast up, it was ungainly, elephantine, its green bottom painted with big red lines which resembled ideograms, oddly serene, like a huge Buddhist billboard. The storm tore away part of one wall, as if determined to crack open the unwelcome and unwieldy house.

Just down the shore, a dinghy which belonged to our neighbor, the Italian restaurateur, had also been beached, its cheery red and white centered in a bed of blackened seaweed as if it were the centerpiece of an antipasto. Its green interior (Franco had painted it in imitation of the flag of his mother country) was filled with water, and seemed a sort of marvelous aquarium: above a drift of sand sculpted by ripples, a clutch of sea lettuce floated. Dozens of minnows darted, confused by their sudden containment in this smaller, watery globe. Their world was suddenly green and diminished; they could circumnavigate their entire sea in seconds.

The storm cracked open and upended the containing house, and constructed a new house a hundred yards away, one that contained life more gracefully than the houseboat ever did. House became boat became wreckage, open to tides and fish; boat became the fishes' temporary house. So the world's order is constantly open to revision. The day's lesson was delivered with wit and surprise, as if the sea delighted in nothing more than contradiction and metaphor.

This is the sort of pleasure which makes me want to live here forever. There are few ways to make a decent living here, and urban centers which offer more opportunities are hours away. There is no movie theater, in the off season, and even in season there's no place to buy a computer ribbon. Town government is, to be polite, antediluvian, a complex, inbred system of rivalries and affiliations, Florentine in its complexity. Every season we must endure the deluge of hordes of tourists, and our own attempts to sell them all the T-shirts and lobster dinners they can consume. We exhaust ourselves in the process, and they exhaust us further, and we become increasingly rude and exasperated by the crowds, uneasily so, since we know how much we depend upon them. No one has fun in August. One can wait in line to buy a stamp, and negotiate a maze of pedestrians, bicycles, and cars rivaling Singapore to get from one end of town to the other.

There are substantially good reasons not to live here, and just when they descend on me in force, something—be it the low call of Long Point Light perched at the tip of the harbor like the Pharos of Alexandria, or the sight of a pair of teenage boys comfortably holding hands downtown, perhaps for the first time in their lives, reminds me why it's worth it. We're face to face with a raft of contradictions, both natural and cultural. Here, at land's end, in the superb setting of this landscape, our gems are the rich possibilities of human love, human pleasures, the splendid diversity and sameness of our longings. It is a place worthy of pilgrimage, where the elements arrange, as they conjoin, small tableaux of miracle and reversal.

Accident

～

But as the season turns, darkening into a late but raw winter, so do we. Our golden autumn's gone gray and severe. Our neighborhood, out at the end of town, is empty save for us, the windows of summer houses shuttered tight. The dry canes of the climbing roses rattle, and wind whistles in the wires in the masts of the moored catamarans, a chilly singing. Wally's mood shifts. He'd planned, these months when he wasn't working (no shops which could use his skills would be open till April), to paint and sketch, maybe to continue doing some writing, but what he does is walk, whole days of dog-walking, and when I come home from my two days of teaching each week there's a heaviness and darkness in him, even though I know he's glad to see me. It feels as if his life is a weight he has to lift, to carry, and he doesn't quite seem to have the strength. The days I'm away the weight seems to become heavier; free of the distraction of company, he sinks further into himself, into uncertainty, into depression.

And then one morning early in January Wally's walking Arden, on the way home from the lush wrack and tumble of the salt marsh. They're crossing a lawn which is separated from the road by a tall hedge when Arden spies a rabbit, object of wonder and delight, and bolts unstoppably after it, right through the hedge and into the road. Wally, left on the other side, hears the sickening screech of brakes, and then, worse, the sound of a body being struck, and then a cry—pain, confusion, terror? He runs to the road. The car has stopped, but Arden isn't there; Wally looks up to see him racing away down Commercial Street, toward town, and though Wally runs after him shouting Arden's name till he thinks his heart will burst, the dog can't hear him. There's nothing for him but panic's imperative, nothing but flight.

The driver of the car and his passenger, two kind and concerned men, drive Wally around the neighborhood, stopping to ask people if they've seen a dog. Someone says they thought they saw a black dog racing up Franklin Street—in the direction of the dunes and woods, a refuge, but only if Arden also crossed the town's busiest streets.

No sign of him.

Soon Wally's calling me at my office; only one other time, two years later, will a telephone call be so terrifying. There are great huge silences between words, when he cannot still his sobs enough to continue.

"Babe . . ." Long silence, the intake of Wally's breath. I'm thinking, My God, what's happened?

"Arden . . . got hit . . . by a . . . car."

Slowly, my questions get the rest of the story out. I think it's probably a good sign that Arden could run, and has; at least he was able to, though we're both terrified that he's injured internally, that he's hiding somewhere, in pain, where we can't get to him. And I'm frightened by this wild panic in Wally's voice, which is somehow like nothing I've heard before, more desperate, more empty, as if the bottom has fallen out of the world.

It takes me six hours to get home. During this time, Wally's combed the streets, calling till he's hoarse. No luck. He's also called his friend Bobby, who's driven down from Boston; always wanting to please, to make himself indispensable, Bobby shows up all excited saying he's found Arden, who's waiting out in the car. Wally rushes out, but the dog in the front seat is someone else's black pooch, who was perfectly happy to jump into Bobby's station wagon. Later, Wally will tell me how his knees buckled when he saw that it wasn't our dog. Bobby wasn't a stranger to Arden; what was he thinking? Was he so desperate to help that he'd pick up *any* black dog? Certainly he could behave thoughtlessly, but I think now he must have picked up on that panic in Wally's voice, that nearly unbearable note of pain. I would have done anything to salve that, too, but confronting the wrong dog only made Wally's spirits sink more deeply. Bobby has to go home, just after I return, and I'm glad.

We comb the town again, hoping that a new voice might reach Arden; if he's hiding, panicked or wounded, can I draw him out? We call the police and the radio station and make signs to post all over town: at the A&P, the post office, the café bulletin board. Arden's not a dog who's been out in the world on his own. With Wally or me since he was a puppy, carried home in our laps from the animal shelter, he's bound to us by deep ties, and though he likes exploring, he's never evidenced the least desire to wander around without us. He *is* in relation to us; that's his life.

And though I am frantic with worry for him myself, what I hear in Wally's voice, what shows in his face, is some panic and terror more primal than mine, a pain that seems to go all the way to the root of him. We drive through the parking lot at Herring Cove Beach, a place we often walk, thinking perhaps he might have run there. A town eccentric—a former therapist, I've heard, who's become a vision of Father Christmas in his long white hair and beard, who dresses all in white and walks with a tall walking stick—is crossing the parking lot, and when we pull up beside him Wally rolls down the window and says, "Have you seen my dog?" It's the voice of a terrified little boy, helpless, utterly alone.

Back home, having accomplished nothing, we're looking down into the rough January water of the bay churning against the breakwater stones. "Where is he?" Wally demands, as if I or anyone could answer, "Where is he?"

*   *   *

Our descent seemed a long, imperceptible downward glide, but I can see now there were indeed precipitous drops, moments when we stepped down to a new level, a greater depth.

Arden's accident was such a moment. In Reinaldo Arenas's memoir *Before Night Falls* there's a weird and chilling scene when thunder shatters a glass of water on a bedside table; it is, somehow, the beginning of the speaker's misfortune, the physical manifestation of his illness beginning. A glass shatters and a room goes dark; nothing is ever the same again.

What opened in Wally then was a depth of vulnerability and despair like nothing I'd ever seen in him before. It was about the real loss—was it?—of Arden, of course, but it was more than that, too, Arden and Wally both struck, everything out of his control, everything veering into his life, unstoppable, an event from which he couldn't be rescued. We didn't know where Arden was or how badly he might be hurt—did we know where Wally was, or how much he'd been harmed?

We tried to sleep that night, and did, fitfully. I remember walking the beach at five, a bleary dawn, whistling and calling. Late in the morning, the phone rang. Some neighbors, down for the weekend, had gone to town for breakfast, because it was a warm and sunny morning. Reading the bulletin board in front of the café, they'd recognized Arden's name and description. Then, walking homeward, in front of the bank, Arden appeared, walking—with a rather confused and tentative look, they thought—in the same direction they were going.

"Arden?" they asked. And it seemed his name brought him back from wherever he'd been to the world of connection. He shook his head, as if clearing it, and looked at them uncertainly, and when they said it again he began to wag his tail and step toward them.

He wasn't hurt; the vet's poking and prodding later that day wouldn't reveal a thing. He must have run in sheer terror, and hidden, not knowing where the familiar might be, not knowing how to return to his name.

The men stroked and talked to him until I got there. Wally said he couldn't handle going, he was so afraid it would be another mistake, the wrong black dog, and he couldn't bear it again. So I went alone, and when I stepped out of the car onto the sidewalk Arden came hurrying to me, and leaned all his weight against me, and buried his face in my coat.

Later, when both Wally and I were dealing perhaps most directly with the prospect of his dying (not the literal, actual illness, but the preparatory work, the—what to call it? consideration?—which went on about a year and a half ahead of his death) we both struggled in dreams to come to terms. And the dream that shook me most, night after night, centered on Arden. We were walking in a field, the three of us, near a highway, happy, at ease, and then Arden would catch a scent and bound ahead, wild with it, no calling him back, onto the road. He'd be hit, but in each dream there would be a variation— struck and killed, or run away, his situation unknown. I'd wake up in horror, afraid to sleep because I was afraid the dream would start again. I thought of lines from a poem of James Merrill's:

> *the mere word "animal" a skin*
> *through which its old sense glimmers, of the soul.*

Always exploring ahead of us on our walks—the walks Wally couldn't take anymore—Arden was our future's dark vessel, the part of us that would scout ahead, sniffing out what's to come. He was, in my dream, where we were about to be struck.

Refuge (3)

We bought the first house we saw.

Not, of course, without seeing many others between that first visit and signing the offer to purchase. We looked at condos—tempting, with their new appliances and slick surfaces, after our years of living in a Victorian undergoing uncompletable renovation, but soulless. And we looked at other houses, but nothing else drew us back for a second and third look.

I think it was on that third visit to the little Cape—a very old house whose character had been obscured by Sheetrock and awful paneling and shag carpets—that the realtor gave us a key and let us visit the empty house alone. (Joe the realtor's dead now, like so many men who've figured in our story.) Upstairs, in a neglected bedroom which had escaped the remodeler's touch, we were inspecting some moldings on the wall, a chair rail thick with layers of paint, when an odd detail caught Wally's eye. We moved a bureau and there, half papered over but plainly visible, was a fireplace. Its opening was filled with plaster, but the surround, of old wide beaded boards in eighteenth-century style, was intact. It was then that we fell in love, and the making of home again began to be a project and refuge.

Looking at other early houses—in the distinctive Cape Cod style, a version of the rural English house which would be copied and modified, eventually, all over America—we could see clearly how this one ought to look. We talked to a town historian, searched the libraries for books, traced the deed as far as we could, and threw ourselves into making a plan for how we'd work with the house. The camp had sold, so we had just enough money to buy the new place and make the changes that seemed essential before we moved in; our rental cottage was leased till Memorial Day, so we had months to demolish and strip, to haul away debris and sand and paint. We could hire people to jack up sagging floors, repair the chimney, rebuild the rotting eaves and the crumbling sill in the corner of the kitchen. Like everyone who buys a two-hundred-year-old house, we'd read stories about new homeowners who discover a hidden mural, a beehive oven, or perfect wainscoting hidden behind an unpromising wall. Though we didn't tell the realtor, even before the papers were signed we were sneaking around with crowbars and screwdrivers, poking through the plasterboard and peering under the rugs.

What we found was not, in fact, much. Some lucky Victorian fisherman must have come into enough money to modernize the house, and so the old mantels and paneled walls had gone, to the dump or for kindling. But underneath the carpets and a layer of linoleum and newspaper were wonderful wide-board pine floors, from which we carefully sanded gummy red and green paint made of whale oil, lead, and who knew what else. Under the vinyl paneling and the gypsum were the sturdy and simple bones of a beautiful house: hemlock beams in the low ceilings, intimate little rooms with walls of a soft plaster made of sand and horsehair and oyster shells.

That fireplace which had first won our affections turned out to contain a tiny, Victorian chimney with little round openings for stovepipes. Originally, the house would have had a massive brick spine of chimney at its center, opening onto several hearths, heating the whole building and anchoring it in Atlantic storms. But neighborhood tradition held that the house had been moved, brought here from Truro by being floated across the bay. I heard this from my neighbor, whose family had owned the little Greek Revival house across the street since it was built in 1825, so I took her word for it. The great chimney would have been demolished to allow the house to be moved; it probably simply crumbled, the soft oyster-shell mortar falling apart. Some of its bricks must have been reused, since there were odd curved bricks built into the chimney, blackened in all the wrong places.

Our Victorian chimney was so decrepit that we could simply pluck bricks out of it by hand, a situation which called for immediate attention; Bobby drove down to help for a weekend, and the three of us, starting up on the roof, in bright March sun, took the narrow stack of bricks down from its very tip through two floors, all the way down into the sandy dune on which the house rested, where pale beach grass had been sitting in just the same spot, untouched, how long? A hundred and fifty years?

We were finding new reserves of energy, intent as we were on the making of home, and pleased with this luxury, the opportunity to work on a house we didn't have to live in yet. With the coming of spring, I turned to the new garden; here the old roses I'd wanted in Vermont but couldn't grow because of the cold would thrive. The climate of our coastal zone is astonishingly kind to roses. *We* feel the Atlantic winds as brutally raw and damp, but the roses seem not only not to mind but to be entirely happy. I ordered lush climbers, to deck the clapboards (newly white, replacing a pale but undeniably hideous lavender) in heavily lidded pink blossoms.

And we built a fine picket fence, stopping to take walks together to study local styles of gates and posts, cutting every picket ourselves, adjusting and readjusting the angles to encompass the curve of the front garden in just the right way. There were plenty of things in the house that could have used our attention—the kitchen remained a funky zone of 1960s knotty pine, the bathroom a grim extravaganza of blue Formica—but there was something essential about getting that garden right, achieving the proper spirit for the entry to the house. And we *did* get it right; even that first summer the roses grew huge, twining around the windows with their black shutters, reaching for the roof with their fragrant pink clouds of petals, so that coming home always *was* coming home, an event and celebration.

With April and May also came the reopening of the town, and as the garden was a source of focus and pleasure for me, so work reappeared as a place for Wally to center his energies, a locus of activity and a source of new people and absorptions. He worked in a clothing store, selling at first, enjoying the opportunities to play and to flirt with the gay tourists who were shopping for new bathing suits, bright new clothes to wear on their holiday, and soon he was doing windows again as well. It made him happy, to go to work. Though I could tell it tired him more than it ever had, too, especially when things didn't go well; he was ready only for the couch, at the end of a long day. But wasn't it just ordinary fatigue?

That summer, 1991, seems a chain of images, familiar and loved objects: our green and brown bicycles, old Raleighs for getting around town and on the seashore trails. My garden trowel and spade, stacks of paintbrushes for shop-window props, Wally's handsome bow ties, the leather portfolio in which he'd carry sketches or lunch to work. His new black motorcycle jacket, stiff and fragrant. The mantel newly painted a licheny gray-green in a softly lustrous eggshell finish. Lovely rough antique hardware—hand-forged latches and bolts—and a clutch of raised panel doors bought from Ted, a salvage dealer just down the street. (Ted's dead now, too.) A heavy glass vase full of pink and white cosmos, which bloomed and bloomed. A jar of paste wax, for the old oak dining table, so that when I laid out my mother's blue and white china the reflections of the plates would gleam in the scarred, handsome wood.

It was autumn before there'd be another moment of demarcation, another moment of descent. We hadn't heard from Bobby for months, which was very much out of character. Usually he'd call once a week at least to chat, and come every month or so for a visit. But the last times Wally had called he'd seemed vague or unavailable, and said he had a cold he couldn't shake. Then there wasn't any answer at all.

In October, a mutual friend from Boston appeared at our door, and told us Bobby was in the hospital with pneumocystis, had been there for two or three weeks; Bobby's "lover" hadn't called us or anyone else, wanting to keep as much distance between the disease and himself as he could. We tried to reach Bobby in the hospital, but he'd checked out. No answer at home, so after a number of tries we called his parents, and there he was.

The lover had told him not to come back to the house they shared for eight years. *I can't*, he said, *take care of you*. So Bobby packed a suitcase and went to his parents; he'd told them he had plain old pneumonia, but now he told his mother the truth. She got him to agree not to tell his father, and he'd stay there awhile, under these circumstances of deceit.

If this all seems a tangled skein of bad behavior, such circumstances weren't exactly uncharacteristic of Bobby. Was the dishonesty he'd learned at home what he carried on through his own life? We'd known that he was HIV-positive, because of a previous bout with shingles, but there'd been no discussion of this, really, and no ongoing treatment or medical attention. He'd taken to going to Mass every day, we knew that.

And now he wanted to come for a visit, and it seemed plain that his family would very much like him to do so, too. His sister agreed to drive him halfway down to the Cape; we'd meet him at a rest stop on the highway.

I hardly recognized the man we picked up that afternoon. He'd lost twenty pounds, his hair had thinned, his face grown both craggier and less focused. He seemed confused, sitting in the passenger's seat of his sister's car, wearing a huge red parka to keep warm, a yellow flowered pillowcase on his lap containing his clothes. He'd brought a big brown plaid blanket, too; he was thinking mostly, it seemed, about staying warm.

The next morning, after I'd left very early for work, Wally and Bobby and Arden were walking on the shore of the bay, just half a block from the house, when Bobby suddenly said he felt strange and needed to sit down. Wally led him to an upturned dory and could tell by his eyes something was seriously wrong. He turned for help, and then looked back to see that Bobby had fallen to the ground, in a grand mal seizure, thrashing, his eyes rolling. Wally screamed for help, and indeed it was a very few minutes before the rescue squad was there.

By the time Wally reached me and I'd made it home, Bobby was in the hospital in Hyannis. It seemed impossible, in 1991, that the nurses were reluctant to enter his room; they put on their latex gloves outside the door. (Later, when Bobby began to have dementia, I took him back to the hospital for an MRI. Cold as he always was, he was wearing enough clothes for three men, and there wasn't a body fluid in sight, but I watched the technicians arm themselves with latex charms. I don't begrudge anyone their protection, but paranoia's ugly, as is making your fear obvious.) Nobody in the hospital wanted to tell us anything. Perhaps because they didn't know anything; two days later, the seizure was ascribed to "viral activity" and Bobby released.

To us. He had a prescription for something to prevent seizures. But no antivirals, no preventative medication for pneumonia. No doctor monitoring his case. No insurance. No income. No lover. No home—just his belongings, left in the house he had been booted out of, and a family that didn't seem to know if they wanted him or not. His mother told him not to cry in the house, on her couch; she didn't want those germs around.

Bobby had, of course, set up this situation, or at least played a role in its formation. He hadn't made any plans for his medical needs; he'd stayed with an untrustworthy man, one he *knew* was untrustworthy. He hadn't been truthful, or established a system of support. And we were *assuming*, in fact, that he was being truthful with us, that the lover didn't want him, that his family couldn't contend with the plain, spiraling fact of his illness.

Whatever questions we had, we had a friend to take care of first. In a hurry, we converted our unfinished guest room—used as a storeroom then—into livable space. We covered the bare studs of the walls with fabric, stretching the warming and concealing yardage over them and attaching it with Wally's staple gun. Window dressers are great for making almost anything look better. A futon and frame filled most of the room—which was fine, since Bobby slept most of the day.

And, we soon discovered, ate and complained for the rest. What illness seemed to bring out in him was the soul of one who's felt deprived, who's never really gotten his rightful share, and so must fuss and whine, blame and rail. Of course he felt awful, of course the world didn't make much sense to him, and he must have felt that all he could control was what he ate—or didn't. And yet such understanding has its limits. People can't help it if they act more like themselves when they're ill, for better or for worse—but those who take care of them can't help how they feel, either.

With Bobby I experienced the most intense and peculiar combination of annoyance and pity. Food became the arena of combat. Since Wally was basically useless in the kitchen except for peeling and chopping and opening packages, it was Bobby and I head to head. He wanted mother food, comfort food, meatloaf and mashed potatoes, liver and onions, puddings and custards and vegetables boiled to bland innocuousness. My cooking tends toward salads and grilled chicken and crisp vegetables; I've never made gravy in my life. And I was also cooking for three, and teaching, and taking care of a man who'd just collapsed in my house; learning to cook like June Cleaver didn't exactly seem an option. I did try to please, but the matter of oatmeal just about put me over the edge; Bobby wanted his prepared in a precisely undercooked fashion, with just the right proportions of milk and sugar. He'd remonstrate about my failures in a tone I wouldn't accept from anybody. Though as soon as I'd feel myself flood with anger, I'd look at this ancient, withered forty-five-year-old man, his diminished body failing, and wonder how I could forget what I was dealing with. How could I set my temper aside?

Curiously, I was better at it than Wally was. I think because my friendship with Bobby didn't go anywhere nearly as deep—was in fact, becoming attenuated, was more these days like a kind of discipline of compassion I was practicing. This was a fellow human being who needed help—not particularly a person I liked very much—and in some funny way that made it easier.

Not for Wally. One of the things I loved about him, after all, was that the boundaries between him and anyone or anything he loved weren't very strong ones. Permeable, emotionally available, things entered right into him. I could see his patience wearing thin, his good humor taxed. He looked forward to going to work, and worried what he'd do when the store closed for the season. Upstairs, in bed, we'd talk as quietly as possible about how we'd get through this, about how we might handle the next day. That was one thing I always loved about us, one of any couple's ordinary pleasures: intimate time, after no matter what, to talk through anything and nothing, to find reassurance, sustenance, at least company in the face of whatever. What talk is better than talk in bed?

The annoyance we felt was replaced, all too soon, by something deeper—wonder and fear, because Bobby as we knew him began to disappear, his consciousness slipping to some different plane of perception. He'd say, when I brought him tea, "There's something wrong with this quilt. These boxes won't hold still." Patterns seemed to trouble him, to move and shift, just in the morning at first, and then at any time he was resting. He'd call me into his room to tell me about it. At the breakfast table one morning he seemed agitated, close to desperate. "You guys have got to tell me something," he said. "You've got to tell me the truth now, no matter what, I really need you to tell me."

"Okay," we both said, thinking he had something to ask us about his health, some fear, some question.

"The boxes," he said, "do they ever hold still?"

How could we answer?

Wally couldn't bear it, found it frightening and maddening, but I will admit there was something about his talk that fascinated me—an aesthetic interest, if you will, in perception and language, a professional interest. And cool and detached as it seems, as soon as I found that interest, I was suddenly able to care for Bobby with equanimity. Observing and thinking about how he saw the world gave me a way to be with him, and he must have sensed that he was welcome to talk about his new perceptions. He was, sometimes, heartbreaking. He'd sit on the couch and be unable to tell where his legs were, or how many of them he had. Once he looked at me quite directly and plaintively and said, "All I want is one head." And he became weaker, more disoriented, and spent more of the day in his bed.

As soon as we could, we got Bobby an appointment with Wally's doctor. While he was decidedly not compassionate in his demeanor—he didn't much like the idea of Wally taking on extra stress, trying to take care of someone else—he did get Bobby started on preventative drugs for thrush and pneumonia. If we couldn't do anything else, we could get Bobby connected to services he could use—Medicaid, food stamps, medical help.

Once when I took Bobby to Dr. Magnus's office, in a borrowed wheelchair, the physician seemed to lash out at him with an uncalled-for anger. Bobby wasn't easy to deal with. He was a relative stranger to this clinic, here only because we'd brought him in, and in the vicinity of a nurse or doctor he tended to become at best passive and at worst appallingly weepy, dramatic, and overblown. He was manipulative and needy, but he was a patient, a confused man who could barely stand up, and the doctor brusquely said, "What are you doing here? Why don't you go home? Where is home?" His intention, I imagine, was to protect Wally, but there was something ugly and unnecessary about it. Why did I just swallow it at the time, and glare? I suppose my intention must have been to protect Wally, too, by not offending his doctor, even if I believed him a rude son of a bitch.

Sometimes I think I'd like to be able to maintain a judgment; sometimes empathy slides in when we don't really quite want it to. It'd be easier for me to blame the doctor, to see only his limits and failures. But I can't help but think of all the men he's seen, everyone who's come into his office bright and alive and full of charms and fears, like the rest of us, everyone who's been reduced and diminished by the wages the virus extracts, the fevers and sweats, the losses and limitations, the new debilities wearing away at the self until people are just too tired to want to go on, though they do. How hard it must be, to watch them pour by in that slipstream, and be able to do nothing or next to nothing, to be unable to offer what medicine promises — not a word or a gesture of consolation but a cure.

I think, too, of Dr. Magnus's own lover, a gentle and diligent young man, an artist who wants so much to do his work, who looks as if illness has subtracted from him everything that's not of the essence. He looks burnished, burning with a flame just behind his skin, a flame that seems to be flickering at the edges, glowing steadily but not strong. How terrible, to live to cure, and not be able to offer any such herb or salve to the one you love, to live face to face with that limitation.

And yet, in the face of all we can't do, might not we be led to make the gestures we can?

After Wally died, the young artist came to the memorial service alone, and explained that Dr. Magnus sent his regrets, but he just couldn't bear another memorial.

I couldn't bear it either. Nor do I imagine the artist could bear seeing in the Universalist chapel that day a version of his own future. But it's like when young writers ask my friend Jean how she found the courage to write and to publish her work. "I didn't find the courage," she says. "But I did it anyway."

For Bobby, Dr. Magnus at least provided a prescription for AZT, and for once that drug truly did hold out more than a distant promise, since it had been known to produce dramatic results in patients with dementia.

The first few days, nothing changed. Bobby would report to me his operatic dreams, his hallucinations, which would be narrated, disarmingly, with absolute faith: crystal bottles in his chest, lawn furniture in his brain, distortions of pattern, his obsessions with geometric figures. I'd note down what he said—feeling almost opportunistic myself, but also as if this focus sustained me, occupied my nervous energies, since any poet's a student of perception, of the ways in which individual sensibilities filter and arrange the world. I dreamed one night that I was wondering how I would survive this, how I'd come through these days, and I saw in front of me a stack of books and papers and pens. The message: *You have everything you need.*

Then, one evening, Bobby came into the living room, wanting to watch TV. He still had that kind of swimming vagueness in his face, a lost look, but when a Supremes song began to play he suddenly grabbed the nearest piece of cloth and wrapped it around his head, stood up and began to lip-synch. He could only stand like that, arms out in the air in imitation of Diana Ross, for a few seconds, but he *did* stand, and he did move his lips to the words, and he was, for that moment, the man we knew.

And the next morning when I woke up he was in the

kitchen, banging pots while he made his own goddamned oat-
meal.

And not a moment too soon. Dr. Magnus, seeing the tension in
Wally's face, thought the stress of the past month unhealthy. A
blood count confirmed it. Wally's T-cells had fallen violently,
by over two hundred. Dr. Magnus said, He's got to go, *now*.

And go he did; though I hated the doctor's blunt demeanor, I
knew he was right. We encouraged him to stay in Provincetown,
to find his own place, but it wasn't his familiar arena. His mind
cleared, his energy level rose; he could travel again, and went on
to stay with other friends in Boston, the ones who'd first told us
Bobby was sick. And when they couldn't deal with him any-
more, he went back to his parents for a while, and then to the
YMCA in Cambridge, in Central Square. We thought—most of
us would think—this a bleak prospect, but there seemed some-
thing familiar about the atmosphere for him, a sense of freedom
and autonomy, a world in which he knew how to operate.

The fact of Bobby's living in the Y was hard for Wally to
accept; he'd have liked to intervene, but there was nothing to
do but let go. He'd encourage Bobby to check into housing
programs for PWA's. Bobby went to visit one, he said, and
reported that it was "depressing"—a term hard to countenance
when the user lives in the YMCA! I don't think Bobby wanted
to identify himself as a person with AIDS. He stayed away
from the support services Boston offered, out of a sense of
shame. Or pride? Or the independence that had, in fact, made
it possible for a difficult and marginalized man to build a life
for himself in the city, over the years? The world he occupied
in the few blocks around the Y was a small one—coffee shop,
barber's, corner store—but one he could negotiate, for a time.
One where Wally would visit him. But not yet, not today.

The house was quiet again, but it had not regained the sense
of peace, its atmosphere of safety. Wally looked strained and
weary, a little—transparent, somehow? I've seen that look in
other men, that weightlessness, that quality of being stretched

thin, but not in my lover's face. He's been pushed to some edge. We've entered a new world, in which illness is no distant thing. AIDS, he said, was somewhere out there, present but not close. "I wasn't ready," he said, "for AIDS to come into my house."

Suspense

~

Illness is anticipation; illness surrounds us with the vertiginous, the branching paths of what *could* happen. Our year of spiraling down, the hard stretch from the winter of 1992 until the winter of '93, is the most difficult time for me to describe. Harder even than Wally's death, my life's watershed, toward which all the time before it moved, and all the time after hurries away.

Emily Dickinson, a poet so encyclopedic she can be consulted like an oracle, helps to explain.

> *Suspense — is Hostiler than Death —*
> *Death — tho'soever Broad,*
> *Is just Death, and cannot increase —*
> *Suspense — does not conclude —*
>
> *But perishes — to live anew —*
> *But just anew to die —*
> *Annihilation — plated fresh*
> *With Immortality —*

Death is "just death, and cannot increase"; there is no further, no still-to-come. Death puts an end to the multiplication of possibility. *This* has happened, nothing else. Black as this obliterating balm is, it also has in it, after long illness, an element of relief.

There is no relief in long illness, which suspends us in not-knowing. Every case of AIDS is unique; each person has AIDS in his or her own way. We couldn't know what was coming, we could only hold our breaths as it began, slowly, it seemed then—though so swift now, in retrospect's compression—to make itself known.

A season of fear, after Bobby, though not always fear expressed. Fear contained, lived through and with, "Hostiler than Death." It was the time when Wally was most in pain—psychic distress, the terror of uncertainty, the fear of what opened before him. Physical pains began, too—headaches, especially, gripping sieges that would keep him on the couch for days, dosed on horse-pill-sized ibuprofen, then on codeine. Then he'd feel better suddenly, released from the punishing grip at his temples, but tired, pale, erased.

Perhaps this year's hardest for me to describe because I could hardly bear to look at what was happening, to let myself *see* it. There was so little I could do. Later, I could at least attend to the countless little needs of a man who couldn't walk, but now his difficulties, his growing sense of diminishment, were things neither of us seemed able to do a thing about. We both wavered on the edge of depression. These darkening months, what could I be but his witness? And how could I bear that?

That late winter and spring were the season of Wally's most powerful dreams, which frightened me, with their seeming rehearsal for death, although he'd report them, mornings, with a tone much more like wonder.

In one, at the end of a long tunnel, a great Being stood in the light. The Being himself didn't really have a gender, Wally said, though you had to call him something. He was of human size, but his arms were full of people, men and women, and somehow they were of human size, too. The proportions were all just right. The people said to Wally, "Come with us, we're going dancing."

"And they seemed so glad to be going," he said, "and so glad to have me join them. But I said, 'I'm not ready yet.'"

In another dream, Wally watched his own funeral, which was taking place in a church in Rockland, the town where he grew up. His body was dressed, laid out; from the air above, he watched himself, watched his mother and me, wanting to tell us where he was, but removed from us, still, literally above it all.

Another night he traveled to a distant place where a group of men sat a table playing cards. It was a room between heaven and earth, and when one of the men stood up to greet him, Wally realized it was his father, dead these fifteen years. He was so happy, so reassured to see his father again, but the older man said, "It's not time yet, son. You've got to go back home."

The tone of awe with which Wally'd tell me these dreams was contagious; I couldn't help but feel it, the sense of dread turning into something else—that sense of adventure, that eagerness with which he'd always greeted the world? And yet I wanted him, too, not to accept. Shouldn't he struggle to live?

To write was to court overwhelming feeling. Not to write was to avoid, but to avoid was to survive. Though writing was a way of surviving, too: experience was unbearable, looked at head on, but *not* to look was also unbearable. And so I'd write, when I could, recording what approached like someone in a slow-moving but unstoppable accident, who must look and look away at once.

Though I carried it with me everywhere, ready to use, all that year I'd fill only one small notebook.

February. When I'm at home I'm with W so constantly, we are face to face together in the terrible dynamic of him get-ting weaker, more limited, and it's hard for me to remain

intact, feel like myself. I don't have much of a sense of my
own borders—and that's not so bad (it's an asset, in some
ways, and a given anyway), as long as I do what I need to do
myself—walking alone, writing, sinking down into myself
enough so that I am not always being in relation. But I don't
want to pull back psychically too far, either—it's the right
balance that's so hard.

Wally begins to live on the couch. It's a cot, really, a fold-ing wooden Victorian contraption with beautiful lines, for which Wally'd made pads and pillows long ago. It is surpris-ingly comfortable, if slightly shaky, and long enough to let either of us sprawl our whole long lengths, though it seems ages since I've lain there myself. It is Wally's place in the world—the two living room windows looking out to the gar-den and, over our picket fence, the life of the street. And when the view wearies, he can turn to the big blue-painted cabinet holding the TV.

Arden's beginning to expect less from Wally. He looks to me for trips to the bay or the woods. Wrestling together used to be their joyous, daily occupation. Arden sleeps on the floor by the couch, Wally's hand drifting down over his back, tangling in the black curls.

Spring's coming. I am trying to write a poem which won't come right. In it, I imagine watching a flowering tree, in early spring, trying to see the gradual process through which it bursts into flower, into fever. How does it happen, the hard sheen of the bark opening to admit such transformation? I try to imagine what it would be like to really *see* that moment of change.

And I'm trying to write a poem about Wally on the couch. I try to write it as a villanelle, an obsessive form which repeats whole lines; my watching him, sitting beside him, taking his temperature has about it a quality of ceaseless repetition. One repeated line I try is "an absence the size of you."

"How could I prepare," I ask, "for an absence the size of you?"

"An absence the size of you," I write, "sprawled on the couch . . . "

"The future," I write, "is an absence the size of you."

My poem stalls, fails.

Wally's T-cell count is falling. Dr. Magnus has said all along that Wally can have an AIDS diagnosis written down if he wants. If he does, he's Medicaid-eligible, can be a client of the Provincetown AIDS Support Group, and we can receive a supplementary income through something called the Family Care Program, which will, in effect, pay me a bit each month to care for him at home. And he'll receive disability benefits, and not have to work again—not that he's been working anyway, but he has received unemployment during the winter, which has helped us through these months and will soon run out. (One real advantage to living in Provincetown, for people with AIDS, is that the epidemic has hit so hard here, for so many years, that people have figured out appropriate systems to help those in need; the maze of the available systems of social welfare has long since been threaded through, the options and procedures made clear. Elsewhere, understanding all of this can be a full-time job.)

Helpful benefits, but a very powerful word to accept.

Suddenly there's no decision to be made. His T-cell count falls to below two hundred, just as the CDC officially changes its guidelines. Weird, to think that people someplace draw the boundaries of a disease, define its parameters. Now they have said that having fewer than two hundred T-cells constitutes a firm diagnosis, so Wally officially has AIDS.

We try to say it's just a word. Not even that, an acronym, cipher of letters. And, of course, it's anything but a surprise. And yet it has enormous power; it sits before us like a mountain, a fact too huge to apprehend. And also strangely after the fact, at the same time: what is this that has been erasing him, a little at a time, if not AIDS?

But AIDS of what sort? Other than the minor annoyance of thrush, none of the familiar OI's show themselves: no pneumonia, no lesions, no toxoplasmosis, no cmv retinitis. He's had nothing identifiable but those cottony white patches of fungus in the mouth which a daily dose of some drug prevents. He looks thinner but he's not wasting away. He just seems increasingly tired, less present, more transparent, as though he were stretched taut over some vacancy within. HIV fatigue? his doctors ask. Viral activity?

Sometimes I'm overcome by waves—no, a continuous molten outpour—of anger, though it's never directed at what I'm really in a rage about. In the bank, for instance, some petty annoyance or irritating policy sends me into a fury; I'm flushed, my heart's pounding, I want to pound on the counter. I know the teller can hear my voice shaking with all I'm holding in, though I am also letting out quite enough.

April. Support group. We all had a good week. Andy and Martin have forced pots of bulbs, and they're blooming, and because Martin feels better, they've been to the movies. Saul, blind now, loved feeling the sun on his face, these bright days. Alan held still for his injections, so this time they didn't hurt him. Jerry made a huge pot of vegetable soup, and Henry cleaned his plate, and asked for seconds, and between them they ate it all, then Henry got up out of his wheelchair and helped to wash the dishes. Wally and I, given a week without fever or headaches, went for the longest walk.

Whatever it is comes and goes, a lost week followed by a brighter one, a flourish of energy. The inability to predict is thus a source of terror and a gift.

May. Wally's feelings are so contagious, he's such a restless and unfocused presence in the house, which we'll really have to deal with somehow, this summer. I'm weary of school, but the time I've had going to and from work's also the only time I've had alone. I don't want to get cranky and tense, I want to

stay cool and enjoy our time, but I worry about that being
hard when he's so much at loose ends. The most important
thing for me to do may be to make decisions about how I'm
going to use my time. We can't both fly around madly or
we'll go nuts.

Wally's planned to do windows for the clothing store this
summer, a bit of work out of the house that would give him a
project every couple of weeks, allowing him to work for just a
few hours and rest in between as much as he likes. But the first
time, for the Memorial Day windows, retail preparations for
the season's opening weekend, it's clear what an enormous toll
it takes to sketch a plan and gather the props. I drive him and
them to the store, he works for a few hours and then comes
home to rest, later works a few hours more, and then he's
exhausted for days. He accepts one more offer to do the win-
dows, after this, but then postpones twice, and finally cancels.

In June, Wally goes with a group of men with AIDS to
Watershed, a workshop in ceramics in Maine. I'm happy for
him to have something new away from home, away from me,
with other people; his illness and his depression isolate him.
We talk on the phone every night; he loves the landscape
there, and likes the workshops and the people he's with, but
tires so easily and deeply, feeling weary to the bone. Long
afterward, nearly a year after his death, I'll find a yellow spiral
notebook mixed in among the cookbooks, a little journal he
began there and soon abandoned. How it'll shock me then, the
fact of his handwriting, his voice coming through the plain
clear print:

June 13, 1992. It's very hot outside. I worked a little with
clay and felt nervous. Nervous that I might do the wrong
thing. I know there is no right or wrong. Just do what you
feel. There is a part of me that just wants to break free and
work. Let it out and not be afraid. I feel safe—but I'm still a

little shakey. I'm always thinking, what if? I could turn this around to what if I'm always thinking. It's not so bad to think. Think about what I'm doing here. How I feel about my surroundings. I would love to just go and lie in the grass. Feel it against my body. Chew some grass. I just had a thought of painting myself black and white like a cow. Peaceful, content. No one pushing me. No one telling me to get in the barn. If they did I would run very fast through the fields. Laughing all the while. I would like to do that for a couple of days. Then maybe I would come home. My dog would come and find me. Lying in the grass afraid to go home. He would lick off my cow disguise. Looking down at myself I see me. The peaceful cow. The peaceful man.

I'd thought I wanted some time to myself, but by the end of the first day I don't know what to do with it; I'm out of focus, tense, unable to relax and enter into anything. I ride my bike, work in the garden, try to read, and give it up, ride my bike around the trails again. I feel restless and pointless the whole five days.

On the way home from the workshop, the cardboard box full of things Wally's made rides in the AIDS Support Group's van, down on the step just behind the sliding door, and when the door's opened the box tumbles out and most of his work is smashed. He says he doesn't mind, really, that what's mattered has been the process of entering into the work, into himself. But there's something sad about it still, as he explains to me each broken piece of clay, showing me the way the fragments fit together.

August. I have this feeling that there's a word behind my life I can't quite say, a word that's pulling at everything, a word that's keeping me from writing because it's just too hard to say it. What word?

My friend Jerry walks by and says, How are you? and I say I'm tired and he says yes, he's tired too, because Henry's

*sick. Not that Jerry's working so hard taking care of him,
but just that the knowledge makes him tired. That's what it's
like, the knowledge underneath everything, the rock-ledge of
the knowledge, the soil on top of it so thin nothing grows, or
almost nothing—a few green words, lanky stems, not quite
connecting, not finding strong nourishment or sun.*

We take a little trip to Vermont together. A college for which
I work sometimes has loaned us an empty house on the edge of
a beautiful meadow, a place in which one can walk and walk
and never come to the end. It's decked, August, in Queen
Anne's lace and cow vetch, daisies and turk's-cap lilies. Wally
hasn't been back since we left, and he's excited to see the old
territory again, the world we left, and we're planning to take
Arden back to the old railroad tracks, in search of Shadow, the
pit bull he used to wrestle with when he was a puppy.

We talk on the way about how it'll be to look at a familiar
place from a new, more distant vantage point. But we don't
calculate just how hard on Wally the drive will be. Once we
arrive, the most time he's spent in a car in months, he's entirely
exhausted; we fix a bed for him on the couch, in front of the
TV, and I walk Arden in the endless meadow—brilliant jewel-
weed, butter-and-eggs, drunken humming in the clover—and
bring us sandwiches from the Grand Union, take-out pizza,
pastries and coffee from the new French bakery that opened
after we left town.

*August. Grim day in support group. Martin on the way out,
with hospice care; Alan blind in one eye, Henry not recogniz-
ing people, also very much on the way out. It's so painful to
hear, and makes home feel more grim—and I'm having a
hard time not letting W's recent sickness sink my spirits. I
want to be able to be with him well, but I'm restless and
uncomfortable, I guess just because it's hard for me to face it.
Easier to keep moving, doing things—that way I can stay
up, cheerful, not look at the sadness so much. I want to be*

*cheerful for him, but I also don't want to deny things or act
like my father here—so the best thing I can do is try to be
present, be right there when I'm there.*

On the couch: low-grade fevers, headaches, fatigue. And
then there are times when he feels better, wants to go on a walk
with me and Arden, or on a shopping trip to Hyannis, or out to
lunch. What I can hardly remember now, what I can't call back
up from the strongbox of memory in which I've locked it, is the
gradual process through which such days or hours or moments
of feeling good came to be a *surprise*.

Of course they were the norm, at first. There'd be a bad
spell of a few days, and then it would clear, and we'd have a
good week, maybe weeks. I have hidden in my heart the recog-
nitions, the knowledge that he was surely failing, each month a
little worse.

I knew it, one brilliant day, when I'd ridden my bicycle out
to Herring Cove, and gone for a walk by myself along the
curve of beach, the barrier arc of dunes that keeps the salt
marsh from being swept away. After a long walk, I turned back
toward home. Halfway across the marsh, I saw a man and a
black dog coming over a cleft in the dunes up ahead, and I was
suddenly flooded with delight, thinking Wally had brought
Arden and come to meet me. But I knew, as soon as I thought
it, that Wally couldn't manage it anymore, that he couldn't
have driven himself here, and walked across the sand. And my
heart sank in me, I think I let out a cry, out loud, knowing I'd
never again see the two of them coming down some bright
slope together, running toward me.

How did I know? People with AIDS got sick all the time,
sick unto death, and then before you knew it there they were
pushing a cart around the A&P or exhibiting their paintings or
singing at a benefit. The familiar opportunistic infections
killed, but there were treatments for them, too. Whatever was
happening to Wally didn't follow any pattern anyone seemed to
know, yet it was clear that it was progressive, deepening, that

he was steeping in his illness, taking on its color, the way fabric steeps in dye.

At the end of August, Hurricane Bob swept through Provincetown. We had a few days warning; the tourists cleared out, the hardware and drugstores sold out of flashlights and batteries and radios. We battened every hatch we could find.

The morning of the storm was hushed, expectant. When the wind began to blow, it was as if not only the town but the world had exhaled, all at once. A grand horizontal stream of watery air—airy water?—came tearing down our street, rocking but fortunately not tipping over our big box alder tree. Every leaf in town was shredded, windblown, and mixed with saltwater to form a sticky pesto which would, hours later, cover any exposed surface, turning the white New England clapboards a mossy basil green.

About five in the afternoon the wind simply stopped, and the citizens of Provincetown crept out to survey the damage, a tentative examination, at first, which swiftly became a sort of festive promenade. *Everybody* was out, walking the length of our arterial Commercial Street, exchanging stories, pleased to see one another, responding with wonder to the few real disasters: great trees thrown down, some of them onto the roofs of houses, and the lid of the Surfside Motel (frankly, an eyesore) blown clean away and dumped into Bradford Street. It was the strangest sort of party, and there was something extraordinarily communal about it, and tender; how glad we all were to have survived together, how happy it wasn't worse.

There's a photograph a friend took of Wally and me together that late afternoon, a photograph I never saw until after he died (evidence of the past keeps floating up, new ways to see, new prompts and reminders). We're standing side by side, his left arm linked in my right. I am clean-shaven, and wearing a cotton khaki beret from the army surplus store, a favorite hat; Wally has a little shadow of a beard, and an oversized cotton sweater, one that makes him look boyish, lost in the big warm knit, whose sleeves hang down over his hands. I am smiling; it's a real smile, and yet it also betrays strain, how much I am trying, how hard I am working to see that things move on. On Wally's lips a little faint smile floats, too, but that is not what dominates his face, which looks somewhere away from the camera as if in a kind of reverie. This walk must have been hard for him, much as he wanted to go. But what plays across his face isn't just this moment but all these months. He looks hollowed out, his cheekbones high, as if he is being consumed. It's the face of someone who has known a good deal of pain, yet there is some unmistakable tenderness in it, too, some sort of gentle bemusement that seems, impossibly, to coexist with suffering.

I try to imagine what I'd think if I didn't know these people. How would I read this picture? I'd know they're lovers, from the fit of their bodies but more from a kind of resemblance in these faces, which is not just of the flesh but of the way shared experience, the psychic stuff held in common, shapes and illuminates the face. I'd know they've been down close to the bone in something that taxes all their strength, requires every resource they have. I'd know that, whatever it is, they're in it together. I'd know they aren't done yet.

School starts again at the beginning of September. Nervous about leaving Wally those two days a week, I've been busy making arrangements—our friend Paul to check in on him every day, the freezer full of quick frozen meals he can just thaw out, pans of lasagna in the fridge.

The caseworker from the Family Care Program insists we install a "Lifeline," a machine which serves as a kind of instantaneous way of calling for help. It consists of a red button Wally's supposed to wear around his neck, on a chain.

Pushed, the button sends a signal to a big, ominous-looking box beside the phone, which automatically calls the first on a list of friends and neighbors. If no one answers it phones the second, and so on, and eventually calls an ambulance.

The idea is that Wally might have some sudden crisis, might fall and not be able to reach the phone, though right now that seems to us perfectly remote. His fevers or headaches make him feel listless, washed out, but he's always been capable of making a phone call, or fixing himself a sandwich. He takes Arden down to the bay in the morning, though slowly; he walks the few blocks downtown, some days, to rent a movie. The caseworker's alarm feels excessive; perhaps she's right to be cautious, but we can't help but feel we're being pushed. We make a point of saying that we want to emphasize how well Wally is, that we want to behave in accordance with his capacities, as long we're able. She's not about to budge, and so we reluctantly accept the thing, and learn to joke about it, even though it's a symbol of the loss of autonomy. There's an ad in the newspaper practically every day for a similar product, and it pictures an elderly woman with black lips lying stricken on the rug a few feet from her fancy French phone; the image and its accompanying quote—*I've fallen and I can't get up*—becomes a kind of silly joke for us. Wally threatens that one day I'll come home and find him on the floor in a tweedy suit, and stockings with seams, his lips painted black, his nails clawing after that big red button.

I'm holding myself with increasing tension, steeling, bracing. I'm never alone, at home, so my solitude is in the car, and I find myself weeping there, listening to stupid songs on the radio. I fall apart in between places, and then pull myself together to work, pull myself together at home to run the household, take care of the exhausted, fading man on the couch. What can I do but watch? What can I do but sit next to him, and rub his head when he has a headache, and bring him sweet things to eat?

September. I man I knew—a little—is dead. [Reading this journal now, I realize so many people I've known have died that I don't know who this entry refers to.] All our under-

*standings, all our consolations and considerations feel so
flimsy. Faced with real loss, they're paper, flimsy little cut-
paper flowers. Name them: A Better Place, Universal Mind,
Being—worst, Heaven!*

Wally begins to complain about stairways, high places, not
the work of climbing them but a feeling of uncertainty about
his footing. Especially the stairs at the video store, this one par-
ticular flight that's giving him trouble, because they're open
between each tread, so that you can see between them to the
ground below, and it disorients him so that he fears he's going
to fall.

October. This whole landscape's varnished with death.

He starts a new drug, D4T, another in the same family of
antivirals, the same damnable class of drugs that have done
nothing at all for him so far (unless, of course, what's happen-
ing now would have happened sooner without them, but why
believe that?). Dr. Magnus says there's a good buzz about this
one; people report having lots more energy, a new wave of vital
force. And after a week or two there's a flicker of new strength
in Wally, too, and we wonder if he might in some way be
mending? If what's weakening him is just "viral activity," then
an antiviral ought to help. But soon he's tingling in his fingers
and toes, his hand going numb; this drug's dangerous side
effect is also permanent neuropathy, painful nerve damage to
the extremities. He seems to feel as tired as ever, and his head
hurts even more.

*Dream: Wally and I are rehabbing a huge brick factory we've
bought, gutting lots of it. We climb around on a large, dan-
gerous stairway which is hard to get down, dangerous for
Arden, who keeps getting his leash caught. We break for lunch
(suddenly with a bunch of people) explaining how we'll only*

*heat one room, which will have a ceiling, even though the rest
of the vast space will be open. It is beautiful—like a nine-
teenth century brick facade turned inside out, and extremely
daunting. But I feel certain that together we can make one
warm, enclosed space inside the great ruined structure.*

In January, we go to Florida together. I'm teaching, in a
two-week program for writers held at a resort on the
Panhandle, in the area known as the "Redneck Riviera," a bril-
liant strip of astonishingly white sand and water of a mild
Caribbean blue, and hotels and golf courses chewing up what
must have been a startling, pristine landscape once. In the dec-
orative pool by the resort office, a stunned-looking great blue
heron resides; he must be wondering what's happened to the
world he knew.

It's been touch and go whether Wally will be able to come
along; I'm not sure I've ever really believed it would happen.
But he's feeling mildly perky, as the date arrives, and eager for
a change of scene. The setup is perfect: we have a condo with a
kitchen, a bath on the first floor, and the requisite couch, so if
he has to spend the whole time lying down, at least it will be on
a different couch, watching a different TV.

I teach workshops in the morning, and then come back and
pick up Wally in our rented turquoise Mazda, a few shades
darker than the sea. We eat lunch—sandwiches I pick up at
the Winn Dixie—sitting in the car, watching the pelicans on
the beach. Wally never feels well enough to walk out onto that
white sand, but he likes going for little drives, finding a place
to park and watch a shore so different from our own.

One night I'm to give a poetry reading, and Wally decides to
come, his first social outing during our stay. I drive him to the
building where the reading will be held, and our friends Roger
and Ellen meet him at the door. They haven't seen him for over
a year now, and it's a shock to me to read in their faces *their*
shock at seeing him. Is it *that* clear, how changed he is? Later,

Roger will tell me, he had to excuse himself from the conversation so that he could go into the bathroom and cry.

I have an awful feeling, on the way home, about the toll it takes on Wally to walk through the airport in Atlanta, to make it to the plane to Boston, as if that walk's drawing upon reserves of energy he doesn't have any more—and since there is no reserve, it's *him* that's being drawn upon, disappearing.

My journals repeat, painfully, obsessively; they have one note to strike, helplessness.

> *January. What can I do but stand with my mouth open, no sound emerging? My lips move and I wave my arms making gestures from the other side of the glass, which I cannot penetrate. No articulation possible.*
>
> *No, that isn't true, people can speak out of anything, though the struggle takes years. The problem is, whatever I say about the present feels false—nothing contains it all, or catches the depth of things, or their terrible one-dimensionality.*
>
> *What am I living on? Someone said the other day, "that old irrepressible—impossible—hope." And I thought no, this doesn't feel like hope. But maybe that's what hope is, no shining thing but a kind of sustenance, plain as bread, the ordinary thing that feeds us. How could we confuse this with optimism, when it has nothing to do with expecting things to be better?*
>
> *Hope has to do with continuing, that's all: thin stuff, unprepossessing food which—looked at in this light—seems really neither thin nor plain, but miraculous. What keeps us going? Some native will to live, as much the stuff out of which we're made as blood or bone?*
>
> *But many refuse to live, or continue on but refuse to feel, or try to. How do they lose their will? I can imagine, now, where I couldn't before, this long erosion of faith, this steady drawing from one's strength, until what's left is tenuous, transpar-*

ent. I used to think depression wrong—a failure to see, a rejection of the gifts of one's life, an injustice to the world's bright possibilities. But I understand better than I did before.

W's leaving me—already—though who knows how long, to what degree, when—and nothing I can do can even begin to touch that fact. Already he's starting to make his peace: the dreams, the things he says ("this will be my last trip," on the way home from Florida) seem to say he's preparing himself. I'm terrified of being alone—sometimes I think I won't be anyone without him—and terrified of his suffering, of being unable to be there with what he needs. The whole thing scares me shitless, plain and ugly fact—ugly? Human. Who could be looking at this without fear?

I walk Arden alone, in the chilly, ice-locked woods, on the trails around the ponds. "Here in winter one learns to love austerity," begins a poem I'm working on, "or else not to love."

When I call home from school, Wally's vague and empty-sounding; he seems to have barely enough energy to speak. I'm still going to work a couple of days each week, our friend Paul stopping in every day to visit, run errands, see if there's anything Wally needs. He's saying he's fine, but I can tell he leaves the couch less and less when I'm gone, sleeping there at night, too. He doesn't trust himself to get up, to climb the stairs; he doesn't want me to see how shaky he feels, because he wants me to feel all right about going to work.

When I'm home, I help him up the stairs at night, walking right behind him, to support and guide. The steep and narrow little stairway to our bedroom—in these houses they built stairways like ship's ladders, designed to take up as little space as possible—becomes, this once, an asset: Wally can hold onto the walls, supported by the narrow passageway to bed.

❀   ❀   ❀

We order a new couch, from the Pottery Barn catalog, since Wally more or less lives on the couch now. Since we can't go shopping together, we pore over catalogs and compare sizes and slipcovers—the world of fabric and texture, ongoing things, gestures of occupying, furnishing, inhabiting. Gesture of hope, though he'll never get to use it much. By the time it arrives, in six weeks, the world's changed unalterably.

Accommodation

The call comes one morning at school, as I've known it will. It's a couple of days before spring break. I've spent the night in the pleasantly austere little faculty house, and when I get to my office at ten, balancing a briefcase in one hand and a large cup of coffee in the other, the red light on my answering machine is flashing. I've eyed that light with dread these two years, each time hoping the messages will be students, business, colleagues. The few times the telephone's rung at night in the faculty house I've practically jumped out of my skin, racing down the stairs only to find the call was for someone else, or a wrong number.

But this morning the first voice on the machine is one of the town nurses from Provincetown. Wally has fallen, and couldn't lift himself up again, though eventually he managed to make it to the phone. He couldn't get himself onto the couch, couldn't stand up. They've gotten volunteers from the Support Group to be with him, as the nurse feels he can't be alone. When can I get home?

I post a note on my office door, a graduate student takes over my class; the students I meet on the way to the parking lot know what's up by the look on my face, and they manage a graceful balance of expressing concern and staying out of my way. In half an hour I'm on the highway: Connecticut,

Providence, New Bedford, Hyannis, home. All the way I'm clenched tight, holding the fear at bay, or sinking into it, crying now, before I'm home and have to manage things. Or imagining how, now that the apocalypse is here, I'll do what needs to be done.

The first lesson is that just when we need help, a world of help appears.

Certainly there are aspects of the system of services for people with AIDS that are problematic. I dislike its sometimes coercive tone, the kit of conventional wisdom about how to cope, how to feel, how to live, and the offhand and overly easy way such wisdom is dispensed. What's more annoying than bland consolation? ("Loss is hard," one caseworker used to say to me, until I wanted to slap her for the banality of her utterance, and the intolerable contradiction between her statement and her cheery, "reassuring" affect.) But I can't deny that, when a crisis comes, the system goes into extraordinarily effective high gear.

I'd gotten used to doctors—in Provincetown and in Boston, at the hospital clinic where we'd travel monthly, on trips which became increasingly arduous for Wally—who'd see us every few weeks for short visits which yielded nothing, or next to nothing. If there were no drug to offer, no chemical solution, then there was little exchange. And so it was surprising and wonderful, at first, to experience the difference when one dealt with people on the lower echelon of the health care system. A nurse came to visit at least once a week, and would do so for the remainder of Wally's life, monitoring Wally's vital signs, offering practical, useful kinds of suggestions about the day-to-day.

Even better were the home health aides. The lower one goes in the medical system, it seems, the more humanity, the more hands-on help, the more genuine *care*—perhaps particularly so when a disease is one the doctors and specialists themselves really can't decipher. The gentle and patient people who will come and give a sick person a bath, rub his feet with lotion, or do the laundry and the dishes seem like ministering angels, the level of their involvement immediate, physical, engaged.

We can have this help for a few hours twice a day; what at first seems like too much rapidly seems necessary, as it's fast becoming obvious that Wally's not about to walk again, at least not now. He tries to use a cane, a little while, but it seems hardly any time before that's replaced by the greater support of a walker.

Suddenly a confusion of people pours in and out of the house: a "primary care nurse" who's in charge of Wally's case, and various substitute nurses who appear in his frequent absence, a town nurse, a caseworker, a physical therapist, an occupational therapist—and the home health aides, of whom three or four come, on a rotating schedule which shifts from week to week.

Thus, a self-sufficient couple must suddenly let a host of people into their home. And a control freak must relinquish control. This isn't easy; at first I'm hovering, and I know I'm hovering, trying to make sure the home health aides have everything they need, showing them where things are, where things go. But they must be used to dealing with the discomfort of new clients; they seem, most of them, expert at inobtrusively finding their way in our house, establishing their place, slowly reassuring me, making friends with Wally, getting into the rhythm and tone of the household.

There's one HHA who emerges, right away, as a friend. Darren's forty-five, a veteran of the AIDS wars, so reassuringly down to earth that Wally takes to him immediately, and he to Wally. It's only a matter of days before I'm working in the next room, listening with one ear, as usual, to what's going in the room where Wally is, and they're both laughing, teasing each other and carrying on. And then I know there's someone else involved with Wally whom I can trust.

I begin to get used to not knowing what drawer the forks are in, not being sure where someone's put the folded laundry;

of course I feel invaded and confused, but I also begin to feel how long and hard I've been pushing, carrying us up a steep slope by myself. I haven't asked for much help; it's hard to accept it now, and yet whenever I do it's welcome, salving, not only in the little practical ways but in a kind of spiritual sense: I feel less alone.

There are endless accommodations to make. Stairs are out of the question now, so I move our bedroom downstairs, working like a man possessed, taking apart the big green bed and reassembling it in what used to be the living room. I'm startled myself at what I do alone; bullish with my will to make things all right, I'm an engine of activity. I am not yet willing to ask for *that* much help. I lug mattress and box springs, shoulder the furniture from room to room. The new bedroom's sunny, full of light, and allows Wally to watch the street from bed. It's tight, between the four-poster and the big blue armoire that holds Wally's essential TV, but there's room to move around, and it feels like home, not a sickroom.

Our oak dining table—too big for casual use anyway, made for a party, or dinner for a dozen—is banished into storage, and what was the dining room is cleared out just in time for the arrival of the white seersucker-covered couch we've ordered, which seems superfluous now, now that the big green bed has begun to be the circumference of Wally's world.

> *April. Wally goes down like a brave horse incapable of stand-ing. All the dread breaking loose, terrible sense that we can't handle this disruption, that I don't know what to do. Somehow I must always know what to do.*
>
> *Then a spring break of accommodation—moving down-stairs, having help around in the form of home health aides, visiting nurse, physical therapist—at first it's all too much, like the world's cracked, but gradually we put it back together. It seems like that's the process, our work: we reassemble things, after each collapse, we find a way to make it feel inti-mate again, whole, after the rupture.*

The poems I'm trying to write move very slowly—as if my vision's out of focus, so hard to make anything clear. Is that depression? Or an inevitability, when AIDS is the subject— the unencompassable subject. Though in truth it's not "AIDS" I'm writing about, some phenomenon apart from us, but our love, the crack in our lives, and the going on in spite of the rift, beside it—that's the central thing. All we have.

W seems very brave to me just now. He wants to walk this summer, and so he is doing his exercises. Happy because Darren said a man who'd had a stroke was up and walking independently in three months. It's been a long time since he expressed an ambition to get better—an ambition, as opposed to just a wish.

Ambition which fades, as the realities get clearer. Soon the physical therapist is giving up, quietly; he needn't do exercises, she says, but use his strength to get dressed, lift his legs when he's helped to the bathroom, and so on. Wally says he thinks he's lost strength in the muscles in his legs, and that's why he can't walk, but soon none of us believe his difficulties are about muscles. Something's going on in his nervous system, some-where.

The town nurse's office loans us a chrome and plastic com-mode, a portable toilet we can fit into the corner of the bed-room. I help Wally to stand, and then he pivots, and sits; at first I'm merely there to guide and steady him, but each week he's doing a little less of the work. I bend my knees and lift him with my thighs, trying to be careful with my lower back; it won't do to hurt myself now.

His legs, increasingly, seem lifeless. His feet have started to turn in, toward one another; they seem to cramp often, and he loves to have them rubbed and massaged with lotion. His skin's gone so dry, on the lower half of his body, that his calves are suddenly checkered, like alligator leather, and they drink and drink all the moisturizer we can pour onto them.

The Boston doctor tells a nurse that he thinks perhaps Wally has PML; the nurse tells me, and says the doctor hasn't spoken to us because he isn't sure, the symptoms aren't classic or clear. I learn the etiology of the disease, reading the few vague but terrifying paragraphs I can find about it: paralysis, they say, usually swift-moving, usually becoming complete.

It seems hardly any time before one of the nurses has brought us, on loan, a chrome and vinyl wheelchair. Wally hates it. He says he doesn't need it. I can tell he's embarrassed by it, that it's another emblem of losing control; he says he wouldn't want anyone to see him in it, and that if we went to town people would stare.

We make one awful, difficult trip to Boston, to see the doctor at the Deaconess. Getting Wally down the high, single step at the kitchen door is a major project, and then we wheel out to the car, and Wally works hard to help me transfer him into the front seat, and I fold the wheelchair up in back. In Plymouth, Wally has to pee, and we discover for the first time what an elaborate process it is to get the wheelchair out of the hatchback, get him into it and into the rest-stop men's room stall, onto the toilet, and then back out and into the car again. In Boston we go through the same process, get him up the elevator and into the doctor's office for his fifteen-minute appointment; the doctor eyes the wheelchair sadly, evidence of Wally's lost vitality. "It may just be viral activity," he says.

Back in the car, the wheelchair folded behind us, both of us exhausted, we think maybe we won't come to Boston again.

May. My last trip to school of the year, a great relief to be done with any responsibilities outside of the house, to put all my attention at home. Darren's with Wally overnight.

White herons, in the Bronx River, near twilight.
No wonder the bird is figure for the soul. Here, in a channel of black water, in concrete, beside a swifter river of traffic, this pair: their beautiful and useful necks, serviceable despite

their unlikely, sinuous delicacy. Two white partners, in the
black rush of the water, the color of untouched paper. These
feathered presences shouldn't even be called bodies—so fluid,
heaven's own white linens. Can anything so aerial actually
be flesh?

At home, I spend the weekend building a ramp, of
pressure-treated wood, something like a sloping deck. It has to
be enormously long to make a gentle enough angle to get the
wheelchair up. Even though I make the slope a very gradual
one, when we test it out it still seems a major task to push the
chair up that incline. Though not as major as lifting Wally, not
as scary as trying to neither hurt him nor drop him while car-
rying that solid body, with its uncooperative legs, down the
stairs.

Something else shifts about this time, so gradually that I can't
quite tell just when it began, or when the balance has shifted
entirely. Instead of Wally telling me what and how he feels, I
find myself interpreting, trying to figure out what's going on
with him. Does what's happening in his brain affect his self-
awareness, somehow? It feels as if he's aware of now, com-
pletely, yet can't stand at a distance from himself—not in the
way to which we're accustomed. But it's no specific thing I can
put my finger on, though I begin to understand it's been hap-
pening for months, this shift of consciousness begun so subtly I
could hardly see it happening, deepening till I'm guessing at
what he feels. I'm not sure what he knows, what he under-
stands.

He's himself, of course, unmistakable, and yet changed.

But sharp enough, still, to be frustrated.
I *want*, he says, to go for a walk.
Okay, I'll get the wheelchair ready.
No, I want to go for a *walk*.
I wish you could go for a walk.

I can, I'm going to.

It would be nice if you could go for a walk.

(A vague noise from him then, sigh of frustration, annoyance.)

Later. When you're gone, he says, I'm getting up and going to town.

Me, remembering my days, years ago, as a preschool teacher: *You wish you could go for a walk to town.*

It works, this time; he nods, and lets out an easy little sigh, reconciled. Maybe, he says, later.

Of course I'm afraid that if he really believes this, or gets confused and tries to stand, he'll fall and hurt himself. It happens just once, when I've gone shopping and there's no home health aide there, and somehow the remote control's been left on top of the television, and Wally very much wants to change the channel, so he sits up on the edge of the bed, which he can do without too much grief. And then when he collects himself from the work of sitting up he goes to stand, just enough to reach over and pick up the remote control, but of course he goes down, his legs useless, liquid, so that when I come home in maybe half an hour there he is, on the floor. Though I'm terrified for his poor body and afraid for his dignity and spirits my poor love is laughing, and once I get over the shock of it I say *why* are you laughing, even though the sweetness and clarity of that laugh make me laugh too, and he laughs some more and says, "What else can I do?"

Grace

That "what else can I do" seemed to signal a kind of internal adjustment, an acquiescence. Even, in an odd way, a sense of relief. If taking to bed, this new set of physical limits, meant confinement for Wally, it also in some way seemed to mean safety; he wouldn't have to *try* now to negotiate a world he couldn't manage. And of all the dire courses his disease might have followed—pneumonia, retinitis, KS, dementia—this one was what had occurred, a kind of mysterious failing, a fading from the ground up that no one seemed to know a thing about. Our caseworker had seen one other man with PML; he'd gone so gently, she said, a kind of softening of his awareness mediating his increasing physical weakness.

Rationally, of course, having one sort of illness did not preclude having others, but I believe that for Wally the course of things had somehow become clear, the waiting ended. It wasn't that he could have articulated that. It was simply as if some weight he'd been carrying were lifted; freed of the terrible suspense of uncertainty, he seemed lighter, more serene, ready to laugh.

And a curious thing happened—not just at that moment, I mean, but over the course of that summer, gradually, and by season's end entirely clear: the descent of some form of grace.

Was it PML itself that gave Wally that peace, erasing terror, disabling that sort of acute self-awareness that would make a misery out of watching oneself fail? Was it a kind, compensatory mechanism in the disease, that took his nervous system's ability to control his legs away, but gave him childlike pleasure in return, allowed him to keep his delight in the world?

When we heard, late in the spring, that Bobby had died, in a Catholic chronic care hospital outside of Boston, I was afraid Wally would take it hard. Of course he was too sick, by then, for us to even consider going to the funeral, where I doubted we were welcome anyway; Wally, in his wheelchair, was the undeniable evidence of AIDS, everything the family wanted to deny. But Wally had already said good-bye to his friend, that day in the hospital lobby which already felt like decades ago. He met the news with equanimity, a little period of quiet, and then calm.

Over the months which compromised the rest of his life, there'd be moments of pain, of frustration at his growing limitations—but imagine, confined to bed for nine months, having only little frustrations! Darkness might flare at the edge of things, but this lightness would stay.

It took the form, first, of pleasure. Wally's response to being brought something good to eat, or to a foot rub or a warm sponge bath, would be so enthusiastic and grateful that the people who took care of him found it somehow easy, their work in itself a pleasure. It became a source of wonder to me that a man who could do so little could take such unmitigated pleasure in the world.

A photo from that summer: Wally's sister Susan had come to visit with her two dogs. Both the visitors—a weimaraner and a spotted spaniel—are standing on the bed with Arden, all of them looking excitedly in the direction of the sun pouring in the windows, and Wally's sitting up, propped up on pillows, naked, as he was all that summer since it was so difficult to get him dressed and he didn't much seem to care. A plaid sheet is pulled up to his waist, and he's leaning sideways at the angle he'll more and more assume. He's grinning in utterly absorbed delight at the pack of dogs who've taken over my side of the bed. It's the face of a very happy man.

A certain boyish stubbornness emerges, too—mild, at first, though later he'll tend toward the bullheaded about what he wants or doesn't. For now, there's something undeniably sweet about his wanting, his ways of insisting on his preferences. He decides that it's fine to be seen in town in his wheelchair, and every day or two we make the trip. Preparations—choosing clothes, getting dressed, packing a little bag of supplies, getting into the wheelchair and out of the house—are themselves a major undertaking. Often, moving Wally stimulates his bowels, so we'll be halfway out the door and need to turn back. Getting to the sidewalk café for a lemonade or glass of juice, bumping along the potholed street or ripply sidewalk (one never notices, until pushing a wheelchair or riding in one, just how rough familiar surfaces really are) exhausts him, so that he'll sleep for hours once we're home. He conceives a desire for a pair of Birkenstock sandals, a good idea, since they'll be easy to slip on and off, and some of his shoes present a problem for whoever's helping him to dress. Wheeling to town for the new shoes on a sunny afternoon, we must comprise a scene: a black umbrella's spread over the chair to keep the sun from Wally's face, a blanket's draped across his lap, a straw bag hung on the back of the chair to carry his urinal and his money (he wants to use some specific funds to buy the shoes).

He's tired today, after getting ready, though determined to accomplish this, but when we get to the store where he wants to look there's an impossibly high concrete step out in front, one neither of us ever thought twice about *walking* up, but in the wheelchair it's entirely another matter. We try tilting, much too far backward to be safe, but it's no go. A friendly stranger tries helping me lift the chair, one of us on either side, but the ill-designed single step is so high that we can't clean-and-jerk the two hundred pounds of Wally and chair and accessories. But he will have those shoes, and have them today. A clerk in the shop, happily, is willing to bring all the sandals out to us;

from colors and styles spread on the sidewalk, Wally chooses just the right pair, and wears them home, new tobacco-colored suede shoes whose soles will never even be soiled.

> *Dream: I'm going down to the shore, a crooked and circuitous path, and I have to negotiate my way through dark little ravines, like person-deep cracks in asphalt, to make it out to the water. It's evening on the bay, the surface shimmering, very quiet, a sense of mystery. Arden's come with me—only he's a lighter color, all golden—this is the spirit Arden—and I'm loving him up to say goodbye, because I'm going on a journey, by small boat, where he can't go. It doesn't feel like forever, the separation, but something personal, compelled, arduous.*

I'm terrified, but I can't spend a lot of time looking at my terror. There's so much to do, when I'm with Wally. Attending to his physical needs, keeping him company, maintaining a certain kind of steadiness that's important to us both. The fear comes when I'm alone. Finally, it seems, I have an appropriate use for all the caretaking skills I learned as a kid; now it helps, my ability to act strong and focus on taking care of others no matter how awful *I* feel. I can seem most strong when I'm falling apart inside, but the paradox is that it isn't *just* a matter of seeming. Strength, at the darkest hour, may be just an effective ruse, a strategy by means of which we convince ourselves we can do it.

Wally's new experience is of being carried through this new part of his life, supported by the home health aides, by me; we find ways to make each task possible. As each daily necessity becomes difficult, in its turn, someone suggests a means to make it easier. We find ways together when it seems there aren't any ways.

And with each new indignity or limit—increasing incontinence, for instance, since Wally's more and more frequently missing the opening of his plastic urinal, and winding up with wet sheets—he fusses a little bit, and then seems to accept the new situation with laughter.

Take, for instance, the matter of shit. Inevitably, sometimes Wally just doesn't make it to the portable commode in time. Other times, being moved for some other purpose—changing his sheets, say, or getting into the wheelchair in order to visit the doctor—sets his bowels to rumbling. Shit is a new fact of life, and one I find myself thinking about; powerful, it interrupts every other interaction—no matter *what* else is going on, it stops while we clean up the shit. Like death, excrement is the body's undeniable assertion: *you will deal with me before all else, you will have no other priorities before me.*

Poor Wally feels, I know, mortified at first. He needs someone to wipe him, someone to clean him up; he has to let go of the privacy of the most personal of bodily functions, the most hidden.

I learn, quick, to use a new set of tools: latex gloves, chucks, plastic washbasin, baby wipes. The first time I clean up a huge, particularly odorous mess I feel an involuntary, physical sense of revulsion. I think I'm going to be sick, though I don't want to show how I feel. And then the feeling passes as quickly as it came. It's just Wally here in front of me, needing cleaning up, and he's easy to help.

Still, for him this is a deep admission of incapacity. But only for a little while, since Darren, when it comes to shit, is a wonderful influence. Darren's genius is to make the whole situation funny—making a joke out of whether or not Wally needs a bedpan, about the size of his bowel movements, about the noises he makes. Whenever Wally looks the least uncomfortable, Darren transforms his vexation to laughter. Patient, earthy, he eases Wally (and me) toward acceptance.

(Even now, writing this, I'm helped by thinking of his practicality, his wise focus on what-do-we-do-next. Whereas my tendency is to spin off into some airy interiority, to focus on grief and upon spirit, he brings me back to the plain facts of cleaning up, the daily work of making things better, cleaner, brighter. We're sustained by the daily, held in the world, and because people who do the work Darren does are accustomed to being with the dying, they're used to staying in the present, seeing what there is to be done *now*.)

It's August, and the start of school is looming. I can't *not* work—how else will the mortgage be paid?—but how can I leave for the two days each week I need to spend at the college? Darren's the solution for that, too. He's been looking for an apartment, and our second floor is empty now, since I've moved my study downstairs to the room next to our bedroom, so I can hear Wally if he calls. After some discussion, it's agreed: Darren will live upstairs, and in return for taking care of Wally the nights I'm away, we'll charge him a reduced rent. My impulse is not to charge rent at all, but he insists, saying if we don't charge him he'll feel responsible for everything. We try to keep the boundaries clear, and I breathe a huge sigh of relief. It's still enormously hard to go to work, those first days—is everything all right? how many times a day can I call without being a complete pest? And yet it's a break for me, too, a chance to think, to listen to music in the car, to listen to silence.

I travel to a distant city for a reading. My sponsors have housed me in a fancy hotel, and I have the night to myself, up in my room on the eleventh floor. I go out for a walk, have a little supper, and then back in the room I open the sliding glass doors and step out onto the balcony. Suddenly I find myself utterly terrified by the height, the cars and people and strip of beach below; I can't stop seeing myself plummeting, thinking what it would be like to fall head over heels, tumbling all the way down until the moment of impact with the hotel driveway.

I back into the room, sit down beside the glass-topped desk, with its phone and blotter and stationery. I grip onto the arms of the bergère chair, as if I'm fighting a gravitational pull toward the balcony, the lure of the eleven stories. I break out into a sweat. Is that what I want, to die?

But I have a dying man to take care of, I have a life resting almost entirely on my shoulders.

Or is it that my life already feels like that plummeting free fall?

I can't think of anyone to call and say, *I feel like throwing myself from the hotel window.*

Or, *I feel like I've been falling from a hotel window for months.*

I force myself to bed, and in a while into lucky, obliterating sleep. I have work to do, the next day, which almost blocks out the memory of the balcony view.

And once I'm home, I can place the experience, that terrible pull, in firm brackets. I have so much to do here, now; I have this sweet, needy man, this illuminated face—and in fact when I'm with him I don't think so much about the state of *my* life.

Darren's move into the house goes perfectly smoothly. If asked, a few months before, we'd have said we'd never have been able to deal with all those people coming in and out of the house, all that disruption of our privacy. In the same way, we'd have thought it a burden and a distraction to have a roommate, like having a continual houseguest, but it's not that way at all. And there's an unexpected benefit, for me—another person around who isn't sick, someone else to talk to, someone to confirm or question my perceptions. Company, support. We talk in the kitchen, often, while Wally's asleep. Darren helps me to chart a course, to have a sense of ongoingness. He helps me to feel it isn't me who's dying.

There's only a bit of confusion, which seems in retrospect about displacement, about fear and anger at losing control. Darren has a pair of faded jeans, 501's with rips at the knees and thighs, and they look exactly like a pair of jeans Wally used to have—ones we gave, I think, to the thrift shop. In any case, I can't find them, and Wally's convinced for days that Darren's stolen his pants. He's insistent, troubled. *I tell you*, he says, *he's taking right over.*

＊　　　＊　　　＊

September. At school —just talked to W on the phone and most
of the conversation was about his various minor complaints
about Darren: not taking Arden out, running too much water,
not getting the light switch all the way off, all whining and
exasperation. I couldn't help feeling a flare of anger at him
(we do all this for you and this is how you react!) —as well as
worried because we desperately need Darren around. I don't
know what we'd do if W rejects him now.

And beneath these feelings is sadness —at seeing W get-
ting smaller and meaner —I understand, I guess. It's
inevitable —how could he be in bed all day every day, in the
same room and not get ugly? Doesn't seem able to focus on
reading, not much in the way of energy for conversation to
mediate the boredom —it's just TV, food, me, home health
aides, volunteers. How can he stand any more of any of us?

Wally's legs twist inward, aching feet pointing toward one
another, muscles stiff. The home health aides and I all rub his
feet; he relaxes, with his feet massaged, eases back into his
familiar, lighter moods.

Every other day I drive to the pool and swim furious laps. I
think each week they get faster, harder. I plow at the water,
flail at it. Later, I'll see a picture of myself taken at a reading
and be shocked at how thin I look, close to cadaverous, an
Egon Schiele face out of German Expressionist painting. I'm
not aware of losing so much weight.

Wally, on the other hand, actually gains, and the preparation
of his lavish breakfasts becomes a ritual. He wants bacon,
sausage, eggs—salt and fat in abundance. Of course no one
expects someone with AIDS to have much appetite, so every-
one's delighted and only too happy to make him seconds; some-
times he'll finish all his bacon and ask for more. Various home
health aides become his favorites for the breakfasts they make,
Beau's poached eggs, Nancy's extra-crisp bacon, one week's
favored skill giving way to another's. An elderly client of
Darren's provides constant gifts of sausage and cheese, mail-

order presents which Darren brings home—more salt, more fat. Wally's eating and eating, though in fact Arden is getting a good share of the bacon, too, growing wider and lazier as the weeks go by.

September. How little I've written here—how full these days, or how I've filled them, so hard to be still and let myself think, let myself feel. Of course there is this pressing and demanding reality, but I also keep myself hopping, speeding along, since to slow down is to hurt. And what is writing but sinking into oneself, into the actuality of these waters, these days?

If I could have anything now, besides W's health, I'd ask for a period of rest and quiet and reflection. I'd write and read and let myself, a little at a time, step down into myself—like a stairway down into a dark, intimate kiva— where the work of vigil is taking place, the necessary attending. I imagine there's a little fire burning there, a few steadily glowing embers, and a quiet chant going on, from me, from some singer in me, honoring and accompanying W's soul, which is with him as he is making his passage. It's true, I can see his passage out of the world, or away from it. Not right now, I mean not that he's dying now, but rather that there's a leavetaking in process, a movement toward increasing simplicity, away from complexity, activity, expectation. Almost away from personality? The bout of paranoia, with a childlike quality of being threatened, seems part of that—like a day or two when he couldn't just let go and float on the energies of other people, which are bearing him up—but had to doubt them, struggle. So much better when he can trust and float. There's enough love around him to carry him now—I want to keep telling him that. And I want to maintain a kind of good spirit for him—he doesn't need my grief or anger, too. But how to do that without bottling up, putting it away someplace, so that it will manifest in disconnection or depression?

Attention—the work of paying attention.

*   *   *

Wally has bouts of diarrhea of a particular intensity and virulence—not painful, luckily, but persistent and messy, four times a day, six times a day. A good thing, now, we've developed this easygoing attitude about excrement. Dr. Magnus diagnoses cryptosporidiosis, an intestinal parasite which can be devastating, since there's no cure for it. The hazard is dehydration, and malnutrition from the inability to absorb food. We're grateful Wally has this cushion of extra weight, and an appetite. He starts a new antibiotic, one that might at least control the parasite if not kill it.

Wally develops new food cravings. He's dying for pretzels, the little thin-stick kind, and I'm always buying him another bag, and sweeping up spilled ones like pickup sticks. And he longs for salt bagels, which I bring home from a bakery in Connecticut on my way home from school. They're studded with big crystals of kosher salt, and no one else can abide them, but Wally would eat them all day if we could keep them in the house. Overnight, the sea air turns them into a slick mess of salty dough, so we have one day a week of feasting on salt bagels, then they're gone till I go to school again.

The antibiotic's one drug that actually does what's hoped, controlling things so that a bout of diarrhea or two a day is all we deal with. Wally certainly isn't wasting; we all notice he's harder to move, but it's hard to say how much of that is his weight, how much the increasing deadness of his legs and thighs. It begins to feel to me that his center of gravity, the lower back, the pelvis, is increasingly inert.

But he's a round-faced little Buddha—radiant, newly short-haired since our friend Glen's come over and cut his hair, setting up a temporary salon in the kitchen with all his hairdresser equipment, a ritual tonsure. And there's something very Siddhartha-like about his sweet acceptance, too, the way he's here breathing in the present, smiling on this green raft of a bed with his companion dog and cat floating with him. One of our cats, Portia, spends nearly all her life in a trance, dreaming in a corner somewhere, but Thisbe, the lithe, owl-faced tortoiseshell cat we've had ever since we first moved to Vermont, seems never to leave Wally's side now; she's always curled on the pillow or down near his feet. The world may be flood and unpredictability, a dangerous rush toward heaven only knows what, but the bed's a safe vessel, the three of them stretched out or curled, sleeping or blinking in the sunlight. Lynda calls and asks, "How's the Buddha?"

Rena comes once a week to sit beside or in the bed and listen and talk. Their sessions seem intimate, domestic. I go out and ride my bike or run errands while she's there, but sometimes I come back early and there are Wally and Rena, each with one hand stroking Arden or Thisbe, the four of them serene in the conversation's deep, quiet round.

> *October. Hard to think this little book is the journal of nearly two years—so much darkness and sorrow, joy, too. But not today—today I watched Darren wheeling W backwards to go to the doctor, they were backing toward the gate, W's face growing smaller ... Not a good day today, so tired, though the last couple of days have been really fine ones, and Monday we had an amazingly clear, energetic talk, like a conversation we might have had a year ago.*

Wally craves Hot Tamales, a cinnamon candy which comes in a cardboard box decorated with cacti and serapes. I buy them at the A&P, in those big boxes candy comes in at the movies, half a dozen boxes at a time. He gets on a roll, eating them one after another, and then slows down to savor one at a time.

Then he remembers bubble gum. We buy it by the box, and he keeps adding a fresh piece to what he's already chewing, until it all seems too much work to chew and I have to ask him if he'd like to stop—he looks weary, chewing so much gum.

Then he gets a hankering for licorice, the English kind, multicolored, striped, fancy little pieces of candy which resemble

tiny pillbox hats or art deco buildings, little Guggenheim muse-
ums or Miami Beach hotels. They're beautiful. I find them and
Hot Tamales in the sheets, down in the crack between the bed
frame and the mattress, under the white metal drawers by
Wally's bed, the nightstand that's become a repository of
equipment: thermometer, bedpan, toilet paper, wipes, urinal,
moisturizer, drugs, Chinese herbs, remote control.

The Chinese herbs come from our acupuncturist, Samantha.
We're trying acupuncture at the suggestion of our friend Billy,
who feels he's really been helped, that his energy level and
overall health have improved.

Samantha comes to the house once a week, and treats us
both: tiny stainless needles to boost Wally's immune system,
calm his spirit, and clear his head. I get my spirit-calming
points, at the very top of the ears, done too, as well as other
points to boost my energy level and strengthen my lower back.
I've started taking an herbal formula, too, for energy and
strength, since I've been feeling twinges, the muscles near the
base of my spine starting to ache and complain.

Acupuncture always makes me feel terrifically relaxed; a
twenty-minute session is like an hour's nap. Wally claims it
does nothing for him, but during his treatment he always falls
asleep, and usually stays in a deep, peaceful nap for a couple of
hours.

Samantha's a great believer in herbs, and she's started Wally
on a formula, too, big green tablets containing ginseng,
assorted exotic fungi, and some animal products we'd rather
not think much about. The pills smell greenly brackish, and
Wally would put up with them more gracefully were it not that
he's supposed to take six or eight of the great big things after
each meal. He already takes a raft of prescriptions whose
names run together into a Latinate litany that would occupy
half this page, so more pills aren't exactly welcome. I think he
just does it for me, till one day he's fussing, after I've made him
lunch, about swallowing anything else. I say, Oh, you can do it.

And he sighs and says, Okay, if I have to. But as he's swallow-
ing the fragrant tablets (what *does* that scent evoke? spoiled
hay? a stagnant pond?) one seems to get stuck in his throat,
and then he's quickly swallowing some water to wash it down,
then choking on the water.

Then he looks right at me and vomits vigorously, a startling
turn of events. As I've learned to do, I start to make a joke of
it, saying something about Linda Blair in *The Exorcist*, and soon
Wally's laughing till the tears run down his face, and it takes
him a long time to stop laughing long enough to say he'll never
swallow another Chinese herb. And he never does.

Our big green four-poster goes back upstairs, to make room
for a hospital bed; the hope is it'll be easier for Wally to sit up,
easier for us all to help him. We're changing the sheets all the
time now, and because it's become very difficult for him even
to shift his weight a little bit in the bed, much less to sit up, it's
hard for us and for him—hard to eat, to look out the window,
to be washed and changed.

He moves onto the couch—the first and only time he graces
our new one—while I disassemble our bed and clean the room.
The medical supply company sends a sweet kid who sets up
the new bed, shows me how to work the buttons and crank.
It's semi-electric, which means the head and feet raise and
lower by the push of a button, so the patient can control it
himself. (Medicaid would prefer to pay for the hand-cranked
model, something appropriate to, say, a Victorian orphanage.)

The bedroom looks serene now, orderly, but awfully empty
with just the single new institutional bed in it. Arden, fright-
ened by the noise and movement of the thing, won't go near it.
Wally sleeps that night with just Thisbe; I'm in the next room
on the couch. The next morning, his anger is strenuous, and
he's more passionate with refusal than I've seen him in months;
this will *not* do.

I say, let's give it a try.

He says, No, I won't have it, no.

Just for a week?

Silence.

Let's see if we can't make it better, and then in a week, if you still don't like it, back it goes.

He's grumpy about it, but he agrees: one week. I bring down an iron single bed we've had upstairs, for a guest bed, and push it up against the hospital bed's chrome rails. Two single beds together make quite a gigantic bed, it turns out; there's barely room enough to walk around the perimeter of the room. But there's room for all of us *in* the bed, and Wally discovers, by the next day, that he *likes* going up and down. It's far from perfect—he keeps sliding down, when the head of the bed is raised, and when he does he looks like a little boy lost in his parents' bed—but it helps.

New sheets—patterned in scrollwork and flowers, as far from hospital white as we can get—soften things, and help it feel like home. By now, I know this pattern of accommodation: from the disruptive, cold edges of the new fact, toward the familiar. To make something familiar is to make it bearable. Is that why so many gay men have a tradition of redecorating, of knowing how to make anything look good? Since difficult lives require, in order to make them livable, style?

Wally's legs point more severely inward, seem to want to cross over one another. They're slender, the muscles soft, atrophied. All his body from the waist down seems more inert, so that it's really impossible for him to use his portable toilet anymore (so hard to transfer him onto its seat, so hard for him to sit up) or for him to be helped onto the padded bench in the shower. It's a strain, to try to lift him, and makes me afraid for him, too, the way his legs seem to drift off to the left, his head to the right. It's harder and harder to straighten out his neck; stiffness is setting in. I rub the muscles to help them relax, but it seems to move back into that angle.

One night when I'm sound asleep there's an *enormous* crash. I sit straight up in bed and look around and see that Wally's gone.

In my groggy, startled confusion I can't think what's happened, but when I jump up there he is, on the floor beside his bed. His legs have drifted, as they do, off to the left, and he's been unable to stop himself from simply sliding onto the floor. He's not, thank God, hurt—is, of course, laughing, but this time I can't laugh with him. I can't lift him. Darren's out for the night, and here I am with this helpless, inert man on the floor, and I can't do a thing but get a pillow under his head. I think what to do, and come up with nothing. We talk about it. Wally, bless his heart, says it's not so bad, being on the floor till morning.

In a while, slowly, we get him more-or-less sitting up, then rest like that for a while, me propping his back so he'll stay upright. Then, his arms around my neck, my legs bent, I try to lift, but his weight nearly strangles me. We try again in a minute, his arms locked around my shoulders. And while he says *Oh, oh* and I see blinding white light that seems to begin at the base of my spine I haul him straight up off the floor and onto the edge of the bed, and he falls back into it, and I fall next to him.

> *W's voice smaller on the other end of the phone—this connection, tender—his narration recognizing just one room and the slice of neighborhood held in his view.*

I am so grateful he's not in the hospital. I'm so angry there's nothing for his doctors to do, and yet I'm glad too that they can't hurt him, that he's here, at home, in a room that feels like us, full of animals and his own food and his own music and his own TV.

> *November. You've seen waves breaking, at the end of their long travelling—it's as if he were breaking inward, foaming into himself, a tide turning back toward its origin.*

I look at him sometimes, just taking in his face, the way he smiles back at me, the way he takes in my attention, unquestioning, loving. The way he says, as he always has, *Now what* . . . a sign that means, What are we doing next? Where do we go from here?

Wally's primary nurse, Paolo, means well, but he's not a subtle man. There are things about him I don't like: he wants to be very important to his patients, but he doesn't really know them, though he thinks he does. He isn't really paying attention. But Wally adores him, and flirts with him outrageously, admiring the tuft of hair that pokes up at his collar, his thick mustache. All fall, when he's felt well enough (and, in fact, he always seems to summon some energy from *somewhere* when he knows that Paolo's coming), Wally has subtly teased him, turning his serious remarks to jokes, subverting the conversation by turning it to sex in a way that I find hilarious and charming. Paolo only gets the grossest of the innuendo; I love to watch Wally lead him, play with him, and occasionally come forward with startlingly direct questions. Wally is particularly enamored with Paolo's tattoo, an image of Pegasus, the horse's wings just unfolding across Paolo's biceps, his hooves visible, warm days, beneath his T-shirt sleeve. Wally likes to find ways to get Paolo to bend over him, so that the patient can look closely at the nurse's tattoo.

It makes me think, now, of a man I'd meet six months after Wally's death, when I visited a writing workshop in New York for men with AIDS. He had watched his own lover die, had come close to death himself, and in the space of a year had endured the deaths of most of his friends. He and I were talking, during a break, about the persistence of desire, about still wanting, no matter what. He said, "It was my dick that kept me alive."

Is lust a form of hope?

In the last months of Wally's life, he seemed to experience a reflowering of desire. It was a curious thing, a kind of sex-in-the-head, to borrow D. H. Lawrence's phrase. Wally's body, he'd lament (though only for a moment, before he'd go back to the characteristic smile and laughter), was long past cooperating. The last time he and I'd had sex was over a year before, in the autumn of '92. Even then, though his body accepted mine against him, I could tell it was something that was over for him. Hard to say, now, whether his impotence was a matter of depression or tension, or whether an early effect of PML was to sever the connections between genitals and brain. Even the thought of sex seemed to vanish for a while, to go underground.

I'd long since taken to quick, congenial encounters to relieve the pressure—the sort of erotic adventures that Wally and I used to enjoy together, when the need for sexual variety had presented itself, as it usually does, for gay couples who stay together for years. Well, I suppose such needs present themselves to *all* couples, but gay men have different traditions for negotiating these waters. We'd learned over time to relax about sex, and to know the difference between our commitment to each other and casual, playful sex outside the relationship.

The current of Wally's erotic life had slowed, been dammed.

But in those last months, desire made itself *quite* visible once again—the underground stream rising, as it were, from a trickle to a roar.

My friend Richard—a poet and novelist in town for the year, on leave from the university where he teaches—would come once a week to sit with Wally for an hour or two, usually while I was away at school, an opportunity for different company and chat. Wally loved these visits, because Richard was a fountain of gossip, good stuff, the specifics about various men and what they liked to do and with whom. Richard's been through this before, and he understands being with the ill in a way that only experience teaches; he knows how people at the furthest extremes of life crave the daily, the little news, the everyday meat of the world. (Sometimes my friends would apologize to me for talking about their problems, saying that what occupied them seemed trivial next to what I was experiencing. But I *wanted* to hear the sound of everyday talk, the chatter and questioning and considerations of ongoingness. I was *living* in the essential.)

So Richard understood that Wally wanted to hear all about his friends, and Wally would ask questions, and also ask about people passing by on the street whom they could see from the bedroom window. In this way, Wally found out about Daniel and Jack, handsome men in the neighborhood who were friends of Richard's.

These two became important elements of Wally's fantasy life, a set of uncensored longings and imaginings which tumbled out all during the day. Expressions of lust might be followed by a kind of sweet sigh which seemed the mark of a schoolgirl crush. "Do you think," he'd say, "he could like a man with useless legs?"

Sometimes I'd feel a little threatened, weirdly displaced, but only for a moment; looking at this compromised, inexhaustibly sweet man, who could be upset? What he was saying wasn't about us, but about a kind of nostalgia for all his life, for desire, the ties by which the body threads us to the world. The one time I lost my temper, in all that long last year, had to do with flirtation. I had been racing around making arrangements to be out of town for a couple of days; I'd won a literary award which was to be presented in Los Angeles, and I was going to the ceremony. Wally had been thinking about his earrings, which he'd taken out a year before, for a CAT scan, and never replaced. And he was thinking specifically of Paolo, due that day for a visit. A half an hour before I had to catch a plane, he announced that he wanted his earrings in, wanted *me* to put them in.

I'm doing last minute things, trying to make sure Darren has everything he needs, that the home health aide and volunteer schedule is set. I'm a little nervous, and already dressed, and I've never liked putting in earrings, and they've been out so long I'm afraid the holes have closed, and the last thing I want to do is deal with blood and alcohol.

Wally says, Oh just shut up and put in my earrings.

And I find myself furious. Without even thinking about it I'm saying, Will you please just think about my needs for once, what you need always comes first . . .

As if he could help it, as if what I needed could have much of any reality for him, as if he could see past the bed, the room, the round of his visitors, the little opera of wishing. Before I even get the words out of my mouth I'm ashamed, and though it's nine o'clock in the morning I feel tired and sad.

Darren takes care of things, inserting the earrings, getting me into the taxi to the airport. I call from Boston, and Wally and I have the sweetest talk.

Flirtations continue to occupy his daydreams. Darren helps him write a note, to Daniel, inviting him over for a visit. Richard, I'm sure, explains the context of the out-of-the-blue note. Sometimes I feel embarrassed at this outbreak of lust, my lover's unapologetic interest in practically everybody. Sometimes it makes me sadder, this autumnal flowering of love for bodies, the longing for beauty. And other times I see it in perspective, a way that a man who's always loved the world continues to do so. One day Richard and Wally are watching MTV, and there's a particularly awful video whose intention, like lots of late adolescent heavy metal imagery, is to romance death, to borrow the intensity or charge of the conventional imagery of darkness and mortality. In this particular video, a distraught woman is walking around a cemetery in a shredded black dress, singing.

At Wally's memorial service, Richard will tell the story about how Wally eyed the woman on the screen and said, "Girl, take off that graveyard gown."

Which was, in part, what his little flirtations were: a refusal to mourn.

In November, I give a poetry reading at an arts center in our neighborhood, an evening with a special sort of shine to it because I've been nominated for a literary prize and the evening feels like a celebration. Wally very much wants to come, though he's also nervous to be in a group, in a public setting. He sits at the end of the aisle, in his shiny wheelchair, next to Darren, and he hears just one poem before he wets his pants and needs to leave, but it doesn't matter. The important thing has happened: he's come to see me, he's been a part of things.

Just after Thanksgiving is Wally's birthday, and I plan a surprise party. I'm afraid it would be too much to have everyone come at once, that he wouldn't be able to enjoy it. So I invite his family to come first, earlier in the day, and then friends to drop in during several hours in the afternoon. Wally loves the attention, seeing his mother and some of his brothers and sisters, and even gets up in his wheelchair to sit in the living room for twenty minutes before he feels he has to go back to bed. We crank up the hospital bed and he receives friends and home health aides who drop in, even Daniel and Jack, who bring him presents which delight him no end. Our friend Polly brings a beautiful little painting she's done of Arden with a ball, and Wally especially appreciates the way she's included Arden's genitals in the picture. By seven in the evening, his bed and bedside table full of candy and cards and little presents, he's exhausted, and happy. We're lying quietly in bed when suddenly he realizes it was a *surprise* party; he hadn't thought to be surprised. There's something infinitely affecting in his after-the-fact surprise, his gratitude. He's had such a good time today we decide we'll have a Christmas party.

But in the two weeks between that bright day and the party we've planned much changes.

Some changes are for the better. School ends for me, the poetry workshop I've been teaching brought to a close, not a moment too soon — I'm needed at home, and ready to be there.

And there is a whole new presence in the house. We'd made the decision to adopt a cocker spaniel about to become an orphan of the epidemic, but his owners decided at the last minute they couldn't go through with it. Wally has been imagining a new dog that would, unlike the dignified Arden, lick his face. He's imagined the cocker spaniel, small presence, might sleep close to him. Disappointed, Wally sent me to the shelter, and I fell in love with a youngish golden retriever, Beau. The first time I met him he seemed awfully docile, thoughtful; later I learned he was recovering from anesthesia at the time. On my second visit, we went out to the run together and he leaned his golden weight against me, trusting. He wasn't exactly small, but he *did* lick, and there was something in the way he let his body relax against me that banished all doubt: this dog was for us.

Beau arrives the day before the planned party, a fireball of energy. The pads of his feet are soft and pink; this dog's been penned indoors, as underexercised as he's been underfed. You can see every one of his ribs; his chest is sharp and narrow. He's wild for play, food, attention. Dealing with him, the startled and intrigued Arden, the bemused home health aides who're trying to keep Beau from devouring Wally's breakfast, and Wally himself, I think, What have I done?

Even Rena, with her great capacity for acceptance, will later tell me she thinks I may have lost my mind; it isn't, rationally, a good time to adopt a dog.

It's true, Beau's a handful, but there's something about his brightness and eagerness that's welcome, fresh—golden. And the problems he presents are ones I can deal with, too; confused and undertrained as he is, he'll learn, he'll begin to understand. Most of what's troubling in my life right now I can't do a thing about.

And when he's tired, Beau heads right for the open space in the middle of the bed, and before falling asleep (he seems afraid he'll miss something, holding his tobacco-colored eyes open absolutely as long as he can stand to) he licks Wally's face with a long purple-spotted tongue, source of laughter and delight.

*   *   *

But other changes aren't happy ones. Wally hasn't been want-
ing to get out of bed. The morning of the party, he'd like to
take a shower. I'm skeptical, but the home health aide who's
there is stronger than I am, and he cheerfully decides to try it.

The results are disastrous; placed on the toilet, Wally can't
remain sitting up. The room's so narrow that the aide can't
really get the wheelchair close to the toilet, and it winds up tak-
ing both of us to lift Wally back into the chair, and then back to
bed, and by then he's exhausted and in pain, saying his waist
hurts—pulled muscles, I'd guess, or aching ones, jarred by
movement.

Getting up even for a few minutes for the party is impossi-
ble. People come into the room to see him, but Wally can't
really connect with anyone today, and wants to sleep. In the
living room, one eye on him and one on the guests, I have the
odd sensation of entertaining while, in the next room, Wally's
barely there. A strained, difficult afternoon, and I can't wait for
people to leave.

Incontinent all the time now, Wally's hooked to a catheter. It
looks really unpleasant, when Paolo inserts the tube, but it
doesn't seem to hurt. I have to pee, he says every fifteen min-
utes. You *are* peeing, I say. He's used to it in no time, though it
causes an infection which he must take more antibiotics to
treat.

Strain and more strain, but his humor sparkles out of
nowhere, just when I least expect it. Darren, getting ready to
go out, walks into the bedroom one day, rubbing moisturizer
into his face. Wally looks at the tube, looks at him, and says,
"It's going to take more than that."

Another time, I stand by the side of the bed while two eager
retrievers leap up from the comforter where they've been sleep-
ing until I said the word *walk*. Excited, bumping into each other
and me, they practically knock me over. Wally, entirely dead-

pan, says, "I don't know, they're a lot of work for an old lady."

"You bitch," I say, but he is too weak to answer.

Someone in the nursing community complains about Darren living with us—a violation, he thinks, of professional boundaries, even though we'd asked for approval first from the powers-that-be, even though we'd agreed that Darren wouldn't be scheduled as Wally's home health aide anymore, he'd just be involved with us as roommate and friend. After meetings and phone calls galore, Darren's fired for his "lack of boundaries." This seems to mean he has too much compassion.

But what's a difficult circumstance for him becomes, for us, a gift. He gets a part-time job selling lottery tickets in a convenience store, to earn a living, but there never even seems to be a question as to what he'll do next, which is to help Wally and me through. And so I have a place to turn with questions, someone to talk to, someone who's seen all this before.

> *December. That face. If it were possible for a face to shrug, it would look like this. A "that's-just-me-what-can-I-do" face, one I've seen W make for years, but which has fallen away. I don't even realize he's stopped making that face till suddenly it's back. Now it means here I am, helpless, immobile, my mind slipping, but what can I do, what can any of us do about it?*

I tell Lynda that I'm starting to feel I can't remember what Wally was like before he was sick; it seems so long now that I can't visualize the old face, hear the old voice. So she gives me a beautiful Italian photograph album, bound in marbleized paper, and I begin to go through our old pictures and make an album, reaching all the way back to right after we met. With a Polaroid someone gave us ages ago which we've hardly ever used I start making new pictures, too, putting the best of them into the elegant book with those old-fashioned photo corners.

The book's a record and testament; I don't realize, then, how important it will be in a month, how people coming to the house the week before Wally's service will focus on it, use it as a departure point for stories, memories.

Wally begins to have trouble finding the words he wants. We're lying in bed talking about something and he says, "Oh, I'm going to mush my mouse." Then he looks puzzled. "Mush my mouse? Oh, what's happening to me!" Though it's said more in amusement than in frustration, more in wonder than in fear.

More and more, he seems to me like someone who's had a stroke—the trouble with language, his head leaning, one side of his mouth turning downward.

Our friends Michael and Thelma, from Vermont, send a Christmas package, its best gift a big bag of mulling spices for cider. I make mugs of warm spiced cider for Wally all day, and feed him with a spoon. He says, "This is *so* good." It feels to me as if he doesn't just mean the cider; he means the whole experience, the fact of comfort and of pleasure. When did this happen, that he can't control his own hands enough to eat? And suddenly he seems unable to manipulate the buttons on his remote control; he's always saying it doesn't work, the channels won't change. Of course it's his fingers that won't function, though soon he's tired of TV anyway, and prefers silence.

Michael and Thelma have sent, too, a little wooden angel, from Indonesia, designed so that she's looking down onto whatever she floats above. I hang it from the chrome trapeze which dangles above Wally's bed; Paolo had thought it would be good for him, to practice pulling himself up, but by the time it's arrived Wally's not likely to do chin-ups. He adores the wooden angel, and tells me how he loves how she watches him.

That face. The pure self which looks out to the world, essence of Wally drinking it in, being here, with me and with Arden and Beau and Thisbe. Self-consciousness, doubt, circumstances, even history stripped away, he's that awareness, that quality which is most essentially Wally. Its characteristics are wonder and humor, delight in things, a tender regard.

More and more, Wally doesn't want anyone else around, just Darren or me. Where I used to need to get away, and so take advantage of the time the home health aides would come to do errands, to swim or ride my bike or walk, I don't seem to need that now; Wally and I are drawing together into something enormous and quiet, spacious but almost unexplainably intimate.

Christmas, Darren goes home to see his family. The other home health aides are off, and it's just Wally and me at home. It's wonderful to be alone together. I play music, cook and feed him, sit by the bed and read. We talk a little, until he's tired from finding words. I go into the next room and write, working on poems I can't finish but somehow need to be making. Usually I'd only be able to do my work when I'm uninterrupted, but these days are completely different. Every few minutes Wally calls me for water or cider, to change the channel or move the cat or find his Hot Tamales, but it's fine, welcome even. We've arrived at some deep, half-dreaming balance. Outside it snows and snows.

Christmas Eve, I give him packages which I open for him, since the bows and paper represent more labor than he could manage: music videos by the Nashville singers he thinks particularly sexy, fleece-lined slippers decorated with images of bacon and eggs, and a book about breeds of dogs. He says he wishes he had something for me to open, but I don't want anything except to have him here. There's nothing more he could give me than his life, right now, his being with me.

I'm thinking I can't possibly go back to work. What can I do? I'm praying for a grant, which is actually possible, since I've applied for money from the National Endowment for the Arts, that lottery in which every American poet buys a regular ticket. A former student calls to tell me he's gotten word that he's received an NEA fellowship, and he wants to be the first to tell me and to thank me for the help I've given him with his poems. I'm congratulating him and dying on the inside, since I know that this also means I've been rejected, else I would have heard by now. Troubled, afraid, I do what I do when I can't handle things; I take the dogs for a walk. It's snowed till I can't get the car out, so we go down to the bay and clamber over the bluish icebergs that have piled up along the shore. We walk for an hour, during which I renegotiate my relationship with fortune. I think, all right, there must be a reason for this, maybe I'm just supposed to work. I think, This isn't what I'd choose, but we'll get through it, we'll find a way.

And in fact, by the end of the walk, I can't say I'm pleased with the situation but I have arrived at a kind of acceptance; I'll turn my attention to what I need to do today, and something will work out. When I get home the mail's come, and there's a letter from the Ingram Merrill Foundation; they've chosen my work to honor with a cash award. "All you need to do," the letter concludes, "is accept."

Because Paolo's on vacation, just after New Year's, a substitute nurse comes, one we've seen a couple of times before. She takes a look at Wally and acts panicked, horrified.

In the kitchen, she tells me she wants him on morphine. It doesn't matter that he's not in pain, she says it's time, and suggests we start with two cc's. I'm confused. Not that I'm denying that Wally's somewhere late in his life, but can it be time for such a drug? Would I know, would I be able to sense if it were time for such measures?

Putting on her wool gloves, opening the kitchen door, she says, "Have you made the funeral arrangements yet?"

I feel as I've been slugged in the stomach. I'm not naive about what's happening, but I barely know this woman, she has almost no relationship to Wally or to me, and yet she's comfortable being this brusque. Does she think she's helping?

I'm incredibly lucky to have Darren, back from the holidays, to advise me; he's been through this enough times to have a feel for it, to know the territory. Since Wally's losing the ability to communicate, I'm terrified that we won't know how he feels. Will we know if he hurts, if he needs to be eased? Even knowing that face as well as I do, will I be able to read it?

Of course, Darren says, you will. We'll know. He points out to me that one of the things morphine does is make it easier for people to die, to relinquish their hold. Sometimes it seems that pain is one of the few things that doctors and nurses can do something about, and therefore they're very ready to act; here, at last, is something controllable. And he fears, too, that some-times the administration of morphine is about the comfort of the caregiver, about getting the difficult, dying patient out of the way.

Right now, Wally doesn't need morphine. And two cc's, administered all at once, with no gradual introduction of the drug to his system, might have been enough to kill him. What if I'd listened, what if I'd panicked and followed the nurse's advice?

We fill the prescription, so that we'll have the stuff on hand. The substitute nurse returns on Monday, and this time she wants to talk with me first; she's decided to counsel me about death.

Of all the things that have annoyed and troubled me about the medical people Wally and I dealt with, perhaps what I hated most was the seemingly endemic practice of assuming that patients *needed* counseling, and that whoever happened to be around was the one to do it. As people get closer to death, many around them seem to suddenly want to become important, to become experts. And so it doesn't matter if the patient has a lover, a therapist, friends, family, a whole network of support — an expert's here. This expert thinks my resistance to her is about denial; I'm not in denial, I'm just hanging on doing the best I can. In fact what I want to do is protect Wally from her attempts at counseling; already, in her previous visit, she seemed to be hinting around to get him to talk about "letting go."

Doesn't it make sense that we might wish to have these con-versations, if we wish to have them, with people we love?

She seems to think what Wally's experiencing is denial, rather the way Dr. Magnus, on his sole house call, seemed to think Wally more interested in watching TV than in talking about his symptoms. Can these people tell the difference between brain dysfunction and denial? Or are they so hungry for a convenient explanation they'll settle for psychological cliché, because it either gives them something to do or lets them off the hook?

I give Substitute Nurse very firm instructions that she's not to try to counsel Wally, but I decide to hang around and observe her visit with him anyway. Halfway through it, after the requisite vital signs and palpations, she says, "Wally, is there anything you want to do that you haven't done yet?"

At this point, you might as well ask my lover a question in Swahili. Furious, I shake my head at her, mouth "No." She packs up her stethoscope. In the kitchen, she says, "I meant, like, have an ice cream soda."

And so it's clear that I have another job these next few weeks, which is protecting Wally from people who want to help.

Two friends, Ellen and Margie, come to visit for the afternoon, and Margie writes each of us a letter.

1/10/94

Dear Mark,

Halfway home I remembered the Italian sunflower seeds. Ellen said, never mind. Next time. Okay. Your house felt familiar. It felt just right. Ours is barer, which we like sometimes but in the winter doesn't feel cozy enough. We need more winter clutter . . .

I liked so much to see you in your home. That staircase has been in my mind all day, steep and beautiful, and from the bottom unresolved. The resolution's all in the top with those old staircases. There are many more questions in an old house than a new one, many more in-breaths. New ones have to say everything, spell everything out. There's a rigid feeling the minute you walk in the door. Old ones have pulses.

January is sometimes a hard month for me, the month I was born in. Usually the complaint is that things don't move. This winter I have just given up, and it's much richer, much more enjoyable that way. Sitting in the bedroom with you and Wally felt like the heart of my January. Nothing moving fast, but everything moving. Time and room for my heart to really open there on the bed. Wally's looks, his grin. Your big lovingness towards him. All the animals. The garden. The sun pouring in. I felt sort of stunned after that for the rest of the day. Good stunned. The way they would put it in the zendo is: I bow to both of you. There feels like a lot of happiness in your house. I don't know why I didn't expect that, but when I felt it it just made me want to cry.

Love,
Margie

1/10/94

Dear Wally,

After our visit I said to Ellen, "I feel like I just met Wally for the first time." There in the sun with all your wildlife on and around you, in that friendly friendly house, I felt this great big spirit pouring out of you, even as you went to sleep. I didn't want to go. I just wanted to stay and look at you and take you in. You and your plaid covers. The dogs, Thisbe, Mark. Now I can think of you somewhere, now that I know where your bed is. Thank you, Wally. Things move so fast out here. To sit in someone's slow room and drink tea and look out at the rose hips and imagine the garden, what a good moment.

Love to you,
Margie

January 14. W's really shifting now—every day I think he's a little less with us—yesterday looking and looking at me, as if he wanted to fix my face—looking and looking at the dogs. His voice small, trailing away, such effort to speak. Yesterday I washed and rubbed his feet and he said, "I wonder how many people have had their feet rubbed in this house." It felt as if he was in a different kind of sense of time, entering somehow into the house's whole history. So many people must have died there, perhaps in that room—

Yesterday I cried in the pool, imagining his obituary and—worse—imagining the bed being taken away. I called his mother and told her she should come down soon, to see him while he's responsive—we don't know how long that will last. Snow out, more snow . . .

Back from vacation, Paolo gives me a handout titled "Preparing for Approaching Death." A Xerox of a Xerox, it seems to have originated in a hospice program in Florida; it's a description of what death is like, what we should expect, and how to respond appropriately. I hate it. I hate its presumption, its pretense to lay some claim of understanding on a mystery, but curiously what I hate most of all is that it's a sloppy, copied and copied again text, offered to me as if I could use it, as if here the unthinkable's explained, wisdom Xeroxed.

As if any of them knew.

I read a few sentences, flip through the pages, file the paper away, a kind of grim curiosity I think I'll read sometime. I haven't read it yet.

But we have, if not our own understanding, our own experience, and it feels to me sealed, inviolable, ours. We have a last, deep week together, because Wally is not on morphine yet, because he has just enough awareness, just enough ability to communicate with me. I'm with him almost all day and night—little breaks, for swimming, for walking the dogs. Outside it snows and snows, deeper and deeper; we seem to live in a circle of lamplight. I rub his feet, make him hot cider. All week I feel we're taking one another in, looking and looking. I tell him I love him and he says *I love you, babe*, and then when it's too hard for him to speak he smiles back at me with the little crooked smile he can manage now, and I know what it means. I play music for him, the most encompassing and quiet I can find: Couperin, Vivaldi, the British soprano Lesley Garrett singing arias he loves, especially the duet from *Lakmé:* music of freedom, diving, floating. The last picture I paste into my album is an old Polaroid of Wally leaping out of a swimming pool, in a blur of brilliant water, flinging himself into the daylight.

How can this be written? Shouldn't these sentences simply be smithereened apart, broken in the hurricane?

Thursday night, January 20. Wally's smiling. I get the Polaroid and ask him to show me that smile again, and he does, the last time he'll be able to.

Friday, January 21, the last words I'll write for a month:

> *Time's the engine that decks*
> *the world in its beautiful clothes.*
> *And not one, not one is exempt.*

Wally's breathing changes, becomes heavier, regular; breathing's work now, as if it were the audible sign of some transformative process within. He seems turned in on himself, not speaking; I don't think he can speak now. I touch him and talk to him. We know it's time for the morphine, in an eye dropper, on his tongue; perhaps there's no pain, but if there is he couldn't tell us, and the opiate will ease the work for him. Rena comes and says good-bye; his eyes are closed when she comes into the room, but he opens the right one, the still-good side of his face, and takes her in. She tells him she hopes he's not scared, and they spend a long time looking at each other. She says,

"Knowing you has been a great gift in my life," and that she'll always carry him in her heart. Then she's quiet, giving him her love. "And then we looked at each other some more," she told me later, "and I kissed him and wished him a safe and joyful journey, and I left, and I didn't see him in his body again."

I call his mother, who's planning to come Sunday. She comes Saturday morning instead, but by then his eyes are closed. She sits alone with him for a while. He opens his right eye just a tiny bit; we can tell that he sees her. All that afternoon he looks out at us through that little space, but I know he sees and registers; I know that he's loving us, actively; if I know nothing else about this man, after nearly thirteen years, I know that. So into the line of his vision I bring Thisbe and Portia, and Arden, and Beau, and then I sit there myself, all afternoon, the lamps on, since the house is circled in snow and early winter darkness. The afternoon's so quiet and deep it seems almost to ring, like chimes, a cold, struck bell. I sit into the evening, when he closes his eyes.

There is an inaudible roaring, a rush beneath the surface of things, beneath the surface of Wally, who has now almost no surface—as if I could see into him, into the great hurrying current, that energy, that forward motion which is life going on.

I was never this close to anyone in my life. His living's so deep and absolute that it pulls me close to that interior current, so far inside his life. And my own. I know I am going to be more afraid than I have ever been, but right now I am not afraid. I am face to face with the deepest movement in the world, the point of my love's deepest reality—where he is most himself, even if that self empties out into no one, swift river hurrying into the tumble of rivers, out of individuality, into the great rushing whirlwind of currents.

God moving on the face of the waters.

Suddenly I'm so tired I think I can't stay awake another minute. Darren comes in—he's been in and out all day, spelling me, seeing where things are—and says he'll sit with Wally awhile. I say I'll sleep on the couch for an hour. I don't think

I've been lying down ten minutes when I sit up, wide awake. Darren is in fact on the way to fetch me, but I'd have come on my own. I know it's time.

I say to Wally, while the breath comes more shallowly, *All the love in the world goes with you.*

Each breath he draws in goes a little less further down into his body, so easily. He never struggles; there's no sense of difficulty, no sense of holding on.

Arden stands up, suddenly, moved by what imperative I don't know, and falls out of the bed. Darren says, *That's just Arden, he's okay*, not wanting anything to steal Wally's attention from where he is now.

I say, *You go easy, babe, go free.*

The world seems in absolute suspension, nothing moving anywhere, everything centered.

Go easy, but you go.

Twelve Months

I couldn't be in the house when they took his body away, when the workers from the funeral home came, late, in the bitter cold, whiskey warm on one's breath, their coats alive with the chill they wore in from outside. I could hardly be there when Paolo came, to write the death certificate and sit by the bed looking at Wally, filling out a form, saying something bland and consoling to me. I couldn't be in the room when they folded his hands and lifted him onto the gurney and carried him out, so I stumbled down to the harbor with the dogs, so that we might be out of the way of what I could not bear to see because I didn't think I could stand to remember it. Though I remember it anyway as if I *were* there, as I'd watched the strangers bear the wrapped red weight of him away.

The stars over the beach were enormous, dazzling, the night so cold it seemed it might crack wide open to reveal — what? — more of that chill and impossible glitter turning over us, heaven's endless spill of ice? I was shivering and crying out loud and lost in the beginning of raw grief — strange that one can seem numb and in endless pain at once, as if there was so much grieving that I could only feel a little edge of it, though that edge was enough to keep me immobile there on the black shore in front of the empty beachfront houses. The kind of grief that would begin when his body was *gone*, the helpless stumbling in which I'd live. The machinery of care would move in, tomorrow, the friends who'd make sure someone was with me all those first days, who'd help me plan the service and scrub and order the house for the gathering after the service, the hundred ritual things the bereaved do in order to mark the hours of passage. The friends who'd see me through when I could, myself, hardly see the new world I had fallen into.

His wife Camille on her deathbed, Monet writes, "I found myself, without being able to help it, in a study of my beloved wife's face, systematically noting the colors."

What does a writer do, when the world collapses, but write?

The first thing I wrote in my journal, a month after Wally died, was something I'd heard on the radio: *Ninety per cent of the matter in the universe is invisible, unaccounted for.*

> *February. How can I begin, how can I not begin?*
> *I'm not allowed to refuse the task, says a voice in my head.*
> *But then I don't really want to refuse it. It's just finding the strength. I will be swept off my feet, I will be unable to stand up any longer in these great knock-me-over waves of feeling, my legs won't hold me.*
>
> *Then I remember being with Wally, at Herring Cove, some July or August evening, one of those late hours at the beach when the light is long and golden, the air warm, hardly anyone around, so that the two of us, naked, were playing in the surf, Arden swimming out to rescue us, barking, the waves breaking over his head so that he became our sleek seal-eyed companion. The knock and tumble of waves was something we could ride, a rhythm of swell which freed us from earth, our feet lifted up, bodies carried a little of the distance toward heaven by the water's unpredictable undulance. May feeling be like that — may it carry these pages, carry me, and lift me and set me back down again on earth.*

(I never used to save copies of my own letters, in the days of typewriters, but with computers, it's nearly automatic. This one was written to a poet whose work and spirit I love, not the Phil of "Phil and Bill" but another Philip.)

February 26, 1994

Dear Phil,

I'm just getting to the point where sentences start to fit together again, but I've been wanting to write for a while to thank you for your letter, and to tell you how glad I was to spend time with you and Fran at Jane's back in November — that seems like years ago now — and say hello. I've felt you around in the atmosphere here, actually, since I've been reading The Bread of Time and loving hearing that unmistakable voice — passion and good humor, rage at injustice, plain human wonder at the weirdness and beauty of things. I am about halfway through, but that's because I want the book to last — as well as because these days I can read for short bursts of time and then find I fall right to sleep. There's a lot of sleeping to be done, as well as a whole lot of other stuff, two-thirds of which I swear I don't understand at all — all this work going on inside me, necessary, and characterized by these waves of feeling that come out of nowhere, unpredictably, and either immobilize me or fill me with joy.

That's a strange part, that I couldn't have imagined before — how much real joy there is commingled with all this awfulness. I don't know if I can explain it. Partly it has to do with the experience of having been with Wally all through the end of his life, of feeling incredibly close to him, involved in his dying, and how peaceful it was for him, how ready he was to get out of his body and its attendant limitations that he'd put up with (with both grace and frustration) over the last couple of years. The last year especially. I never felt so completely inside my life — no, inside of life — as I did in those last days when despite the fact that he couldn't talk there was such a sense of connection between us. The day before he died all the life in him seemed to move into his face and eyes, just burning there, and he was staring at me and our dogs and everything with such intensity, taking us all in. When he seemed to sail away, or really to leap and somersault away, I felt—I knew—this tremendous sense of liberation, of freedom, and almost immediately, in the devastation of being there with Wally's body, I started to experience this duality. Here was the body I'd loved, the only vehicle through which I'd ever known him, but it so plainly wasn't him—a very good part of him, yes, but not him. And while I felt absolutely stuck in the world where he wasn't, I also felt this terrific sort of secret sense of intimacy with him, so connected. I felt like I had a seat on both sides of the veil, you know—part of me with him, looking back at this world which seemed so radiant and lovely and peculiar, and part of me squarely here and miserable in a place without him, bereft and totally helpless. Ay.

Well, I'm more firmly on earth now, which sometimes in the last few weeks has been the last place I want to be. I found myself walking down the street in town on a weekend when we had tourists here again and thinking, "How much longer do I have to be here?" Not in Provincetown, I mean. And then I've remembered work, which I love. The work of writing. And I've felt restored by all the people who've been around to help me through, and by walking the dogs in the woods and on the shore. And most especially by my sense of having been in ways I can't yet articulate re-educated, about living, by having been through Wally's dying. I keep thinking of Whitman: "to die is different than anyone had supposed . . . "

I've been very grateful, too, for having this time off. I thought I was going to be using it to take care of Wally. Selfishly, I wish that is what I were doing—though I also know that he left the world at exactly the time when he couldn't enjoy this life any more. I have a picture of him, Phil, a Polaroid I took on Thursday night, grinning away—and he died on Saturday!

He—and I—were so lucky that he didn't have one of those awful kinds of opportunistic infections that would have just hurt and hurt him. Lucky, perversely, that he had something that the doctors didn't know the first thing about. They didn't know what to do, so they didn't do anything—no poisonous "therapy" that would have just made the last part of his life more miserable. They left him alone, and we took care of him right here at home, and ushered him out of the world. He never had to go to the hospital once.

Anyway, I was talking about time off—it feels so right to have no obligations except to my own feelings. Which really do constitute a full-time job right now. Some people have said I'd be better off working or something, but I think they just don't get it. I have a feeling your good words and wishes had to do with the good fortune that's come to me. Thank you for that . . . Literary life helps me to have a future right now, a sense of more to do, a world to connect with.

I hope coming back to Fresno's been good for you both—at least you're missing (I am pretty sure) the snow upon snow that's tumbled over the east. I've pretty much liked it, really. All I want to do right now is stay in anyway, and catch my breath, and take time. And three feet of snow is just right for that.

Love to you both,
Mark

Wally had joined the invisible majority, leaping from the bed of which he was so weary. Out of the top of his head, I felt, into the empyrean. Billy enlarged the photo I'd found of him leaping from the swimming pool years before—grinning, arms flung above his head, the droplets of water like rushing lines of energy; the image came to stand, for me, for the way he'd leapt from earth. The photo sat on the table beside the brass box containing his ashes, at the memorial.

He and I both, I thought, were learning to negotiate a new

element. I was learning to breathe, to walk, to eat, to remember to do those things without him.

February 17, 1994

Dear Diane,

Thank you—you've been a welcome and steady presence in the mail, and I know you understand that I'd have answered sooner if I could. I'm at a point of getting my feet more on the ground, feeling back on earth, where I am sometimes glad to be and sometimes, of course, not. When someone that close to you dies it's like having some kind of double vision, part of me being so clearly with him or near him, seeing the world from the other side. For the first week or two things were so lovely to me—fruit in the grocery store, the sky, the big cloth jellyfish-thing in the automatic car wash that sudses up your windshield. Wally was looking out at the world through me. And there was then the other part of me which was just plain bereft, missing him terribly. I'm living much more in that latter part now, which I guess is what happens—we have to come back here where we, after all, live. Oh. It's wildly difficult and at the same time something I seem to be able to do. Everything about this is violent contradiction—my life at its most real and at its most terrible at once, Wally dead but somehow a profound sense of mercy and peace, even joy, around him. I lost him and feel like I've fallen in love with him all over again. Things were never so complicated in my life, yet all I have to do is just feel my way through the day. Days . . .

February 17, 1994

Dear Herb,

. . . I think there are more lessons in the last month of my experience than the rest of my life will allow me to articulate; I've been shown so much that I can't begin to understand, that I am only starting to say. And out of all that I could

enter into here—more time for that, so much time now—I'll say only that Wally's death taught me that, as in anything else, nothing is conclusive. There's no time there, where he is. And one of the many contradictions in this period of intensely lived dualities is that I have felt so close to him, in love with him again in another way, at the same time that I've lost him. Presence and absence tumble together the way time is all atumble now; I'm awash in it. I wonder if dying doesn't make a kind of spasm in time, as if some radiance leaks out of the opening the dying make—at least the opening this dying man made—between worlds, enough of a shine to turn time inside out for a while. Everything poured toward that moment, a watershed, and since then the waters of these hours and days, of years really, have seemed all commingling, and I am not sure if and don't care whether I am in now or then . . .

In some way I had joined the invisible, too. I think that when people die they make those around them feel something like they felt; that may be the dying's first legacy to us. I've had friends who died in confusion or rage or terror, and the living who knew them felt, then, confusion or rage or terror. Acceptance breeds acceptance, as Wally's attitude during his illness had shown; it'd been easy, somehow, for the people who took care of him to do so. He seemed, to those who carried him, to have made himself light.

I don't know what it might have been like for me had I not been present at the moment when Wally died, if I hadn't been there to know that enormous intimacy, that sense of brightness in the depths of the dark, the atmosphere so charged it seemed almost to sing. What if I hadn't felt the movement of energy, the *leap* of spirit lifting from him?

I couldn't have understood what a grace there is around dying, that sort of awe of which beauty is, as Rilke understood, the edge: "For beauty is nothing but the beginning," he writes near the opening of the *Duino Elegies*, "of terror, which we are still just able to endure."

The price we pay for keeping death at such a distance from ourselves is a great one; holding it so far from us, we cannot see its shine.

I wonder now if Rilke's terms might just as easily be reversed: is terror only the edge of a beauty we can hardly bear?

The shine around Wally's dying, the grace of it, was what would carry me through those first months, what would sustain me. Not that I didn't veer crazily, every day dissolving, at some point, into tears and exhaustion, dizzying grief. But it felt possible, out of a kind of connection to him carried *through* death, out of the spirit's sheer shock of recognition at the naked beauty of his dying, to go on.

And what a long season I was given, a time to reflect and to reel, submerged in my own grief.

Time to mark every anniversary; each week, at first, I can hardly bear Saturday night. Each month, the twenty-second looms on the calendar, its pair of two's like black bent-necked swans. I think, Can it be a month? How can it be two?

Time to revisit our old cities, to walk hours every day in the dunes, to begin the work of telling which this book is.

Time to stumble awkwardly back toward the world—into mistakes, failed stabs at single life. Which is not to say there was not respite, in other bodies, the refuge and affirmation of skin and touch, what *could* give comfort and pleasure, in a world where bodies gave such grief, where bodies disappeared.

Time to fall, as whatever it was that had carried me slowly faded, and I found myself firmly on earth, in my body, in my own singular life, into my own illness—of the spine or of the soul. Were they one and the same? Chiropractic, yoga, exercise, rest, acupuncture, massage—everything seemed to help a little, nothing to help enough. A ruptured disk, a rupture of reality? I wouldn't need to draw a distinction, I guess, except that I had to *do* something; and there were days I could barely walk.

Early one summer morning, taking Arden and Beau on the footpath around the forest pond, I hurt so badly, so sharply and insistently, that I can't stand up any longer. Pain shoots down my left leg with a wild, fierce insistence. I lie down on the sandy path, and find myself saying aloud, to no one, Wally's old line: "Now what?"

Patience, slow and careful movements, days of lying in bed and reading, venturing out for treatments. I buy a secondhand laptop computer so I can write in bed, and by August I'm stirring again. I'm a bit delicate but, dosed on anti-inflammatories and visiting a physical therapist two or three times a week, I'm functioning.

I go to New Hampshire to give a poetry reading at a beautiful old meetinghouse in the country. I read a poem there about a neighbor of mine who used to take his elderly springer spaniel for walks in a sort of rope harness he'd made, since the poor old creature used to lie down for a rest and then be unable to lift himself again on his wobbly legs. My neighbor would hoist Charley, by means of the harness, and eventually the walk was more a human endeavor than a canine one, though it seemed to make both parties happy.

An old friend, Nancy, has come to the reading, and we talk about all that's been happening for both of us, and of course she notices how stiff and careful I am in my movements, and asks about my back. Later, she sends this letter:

> Dear Mark,
>
> It was such a joy to see you and hear you read again. Your poems do me good, as though each color, fin and animal pelt had been ground into a homeopathic mash and spooned into my system. Please feel welcome to stay with David and me any time you're in this area — it's quiet.
>
> As I was falling asleep last night, the image of your neighbor lifting his dog in the harness gave me a crazy idea.
>
> You've carried Wally for so long, your back may not realize that earth and sky now carry the weight. I visualized Wally on the floor beside his bed, and you bending over him,

buckling on a harness and leash. You stand, and slowly lift him on his hands and knees and then higher, until he's dangling like a little dog. At first you think he'll be much too heavy to lift from this awkward angle, and he's worried, too, but it turns out you can manage just using the muscles in your arms. He's light, so light that his bones must be hollow, his flesh consecrated bread. You practice raising and lowering him (the harness might need a little adjusting) and then you're ready for some fun. Wally loves the feeling of swinging in the air; he stretches out his arms and legs like a child playing Superman. You go outside and swing him in circles, until his eyes are parallel with yours again, his weight counterbalancing yours, making you both weightless. Effortless play, your back straight—you're both encouraged to try some yo-yo tricks, swirling and arcing—somehow Wally's soaring body has freed you from gravity so that you're flying too, the leash connecting you. If you feel frightened, you know you can always climb on Wally's back; this is his element. He can hold you.

Love,
Nancy

And I do feel, really, that the part of me that resides in the world Wally inhabits now, outside the boundaries of time and space, *can* soar. It's here on earth I'm having trouble.

And it is time, increasingly, to be on earth. I return to teaching, at the beginning of September, at the end of what seems a long period of inwardness. Driving to school, the first day, I almost turn in the other direction. It's been so long since I turned outward, directing the activities of others, putting my energy into meeting people, leading a group. I'm not sure I still *can*; have my resources been drained away, every ounce of me taxed?

Work turns out to be, in fact, fine, and welcome. There are times I feel I'm translating, in my head, from one language to another; I've become a citizen of grief's country, and now I

find I don't always easily speak the old tongue I used to know
so well. Some days I don't feel I have the strength or attention
to be a good teacher, and sometimes I think I'm just going
through the motions, though if the students notice this, bless
them, they don't say so. The best days are affirming, energetic;
I like climbing to something outside myself. Teaching poetry
feels interior and external at once, personal and yet outer-
directed, social yet real.

Working again means I have health insurance, so I go for a
CAT scan to give my doctor a better look at my back. The radi-
ologist, who'd usually just write a report, calls in some alarm,
saying if ever he's seen the scans of a patient who needs a neu-
rosurgeon, I'm him. It's the first time the diagnosis is firmly
pronounced: ruptured disk.

But I am, strangely, feeling better, despite the grim picture
and the definite terms; the sciatica that left me prone on the
path a month or two before seems to be receding, gradually,
though I dimly recognize that I've also gotten used to a drain-
ing level of pain. I make an appointment for a consultation
with a neurosurgeon, though I feel relieved that it takes a cou-
ple of months to even get to see him. Meanwhile, more
acupuncture, more massage.

And I turn myself, for the first time since Wally's death, res-
olutely outward: teaching, readings, travel, a schedule so full
that I hardly know *where* I am, or when, and somewhere along
the way I realize I've done it on purpose, that what I wanted
was a break from my inner life.

Of course we carry ourselves with us everywhere, no matter
what, but working and travel and busyness can make for a
very effective drug, a temporary screen. All through the fall, I
keep myself swirling, staying on the road.

Whenever I stay in hotel rooms on upper floors, I keep my
distance from the windows.

Before I know it I am driving to the clinic outside of Boston
where the neurosurgeon will make a pronouncement about my
future. I sit in the waiting room, my palms sweating, gripping

the envelope containing the mysterious black-and-white films of my CAT-scanned sacrum. I've looked at them in the car on the way, holding up to the light big sheets of negatives, each one bearing groups of circular images of vertebrae, like inscrutable old magic lantern slides.

I am trying very hard not to be terrified. When the doctor taps my knee with his rubber-tipped hammer, there's real and immediate reflex, where three months before my lifeless leg had merely remained still, the reactive nerve pinched off by the rupture in my spine. And looking at the CAT scan and at me, the doctor pronounces me a terrible candidate for surgery, since I am obviously healing myself.

Ironing a shirt, I find myself thinking of Lynda, of a late winter day—how many, three, four years ago? She's staying in a little waterfront apartment in the West End where she's come to write, and visits us every day. Wally is tired, already, his long days of resting on the folding couch begun, and Lynda and I've gone to town for an afternoon walk, and to see what stores are open. Not many, but the reliable oriental imports store is lit and occupied, as it almost always is, and inside we find that the owner's just received a shipment of kimonos, bales of old ones bought in bulk in Japan. They've been dry cleaned but neither pressed nor sorted, and they lie in great heaps of wrinkled, richly textured silk. Here are sleeves of oyster and pearl and smoke, linings patterned with flurries of chrysanthemums or undulations of watery swirls. Laughing at the bounty, overcome by the crumpled luxury, we're trying on robe after robe, playing with things we never would (or could) wear: gossamer sleeves like white moths or frail ghosts, costumes for a Japanese *Midsummer Night's Dream*, tousled fields of sheen the color of hayfields. The owner—who seems himself to enjoy our pleasure in his tumble of wares—gives us a deal, and eventually we settle on three: a short deep blue for Lynda, lined with a secretive orange splendor of flowers; a long scholarly gray for me, severe, slightly pearly, meditative; a rough raw silk for Wally, its thickly textured green weave the color of day-old clippings clinging to lawn mower blades.

Our afternoon, home in the kitchen, is a festival of ironing, of steam and surprise as wrinkles fall away and the drape and soft shine of the fabric reveal themselves. It's raining out and the windows steam up, the room warmed by our work and the heat of our coffee. All three of us are chatting and ironing and happy, wrapping ourselves in our new old robes, thinking of the mulberry leaves spun by silkworms to this unlikely fila- ment, of the endless labor of unwinding the cocoons, of the subtlety and strength of the colors the densely woven stuff is dyed, of our own collaboration, as ironers, in the restoration of beauty. The steam and the rain on the kitchen's new french doors make us feel safe, domestic, inside some familiar child- hood place of warmth and good company.

This memory has about it an aura of intimacy, of an achieved, common warmth—something like what Michael Anania has called, describing the process of reading, "a calm exchange of privacies." It has the time-out-of-time sheen of happiness to it, subtle but unmistakable as the surface of those silks.

So much about Lynda is coming back to me now, as if my subsiding anger made room for the larger sense of who she was to reassert itself. How richly my friend made a life for herself; how much I enjoyed her company. She'd manage to be inti- mate and vulnerable, jazzy and alive, trashy and fun and then achingly and sharply smart, a more incisive thinker than any- one I knew. She was like the elegant, complicated surfaces of her poems: wrought to vibrant life, almost jeweled, no matter how difficult the experiences they described.

That tension between form and content *was* Lynda, in a way—all her glamour's sly or gorgeous gestures lovely because we could see through them to the difficulty and pain they man- aged both to conceal and to acknowledge.

Ruined armor.

One more memory: Wally and I have just moved to

Provincetown, and Lynda's come to visit. We've planned to take her to a drag show, knowing she'll love the illusionists' repertoire of sequins and sentiment, glitz and irony. And since we've decided to sport her out on the town, we both dress in black leather, our hair slicked back, and each of us takes one of her arms, so that she—a deconstructed flapper, in fringe and toque, jet beads and crystal earrings—has a man on either arm like some Broadway ingenue.

The drag show's wonderful; because it's a late autumn night, few people in town, it's been moved to a small room in the front of the hotel/bar where it's held, and we're right beside the stage where Tish de Williams does her signature lip-synch of "You've Come a Long Way from St. Louis." We're greeted, dished, and flirted with by a succession of drags, including a tall black man in a sparkling gown and big Diahann Carroll wig who winds up in my lap (how hard those muscles, what an unexpected weight). The performer asks me what I do for work, and when I say, simplifying things, that I'm an English teacher, the whole place goes up with laughter, the tension between my faux-manly surface and my bookish self revealed.

Lynda is greeted with great regard by the "hostess," who asks, "How are you tonight, sister? Where you from?" It takes me a minute to get it that the reason my friend's getting this extra attention is because the queen on stage thinks she's a man. I'm not sure at first Lynda knows this, or how she'll feel about it— will she be hurt, insulted, to have her gender called into question? I hope not; it's the drag queen's perennial message, after all: *we're all self-made here.*

And then I realize Lynda's utterly delighted, in a sort of heaven: between the two of us, also in disguise as butch men, she is being seen as "in drag" too. And, of course, she is: my unforgettable friend is utterly happy, in her finery, wearing her vocabulary of style and gesture, wearing herself.

I've come to New York to teach a writing workshop for HIV-positive men. Around the seminar table, these eager faces, men leaning forward because they have so much to say. I find myself wanting to sit with each one alone, to hear each story, to find a way to help the narrative of each of these lives make it onto the page.

The next day, in a midtown restaurant, I'm having lunch with R., a new friend. Our professional relationship's almost immediately become a friendship. He's telling me about his boyfriend, how L.'s T-cells have just slipped below the signifying two-hundred mark, into the zone of greater risk. He says this almost casually, as if placing the information on the table beside everything else we've been talking about. And it occurs to me that this is how we deal with terror now; it's so much a part of the daily fabric that we treat it as such, one more fact in a jostling crowd of actualities. R. and I don't even have the conversation about how little the numbers mean, so familiar has that exchange become. We talk instead about our ways of being sick: how tough-minded R. goes on no matter what, smoking and drinking black coffee through whatever, how L., who whines and takes to his bed for days with a sore throat, is not a good candidate for illness. We talk about the way some people make good use of disability benefits, while others find the weight of an AIDS diagnosis crushing, paralyzed by the acronym's bitter weight. I say I think Wally was wounded by the term, by all it seemed to spell for him. I say I don't know that this makes any difference at all in terms of how long one lives, or the course of the illness. But I am sure that how one responds to the "word" AIDS—the numbing blow to the head that diagnosis is, its awful feel of finality—has a great deal to do with the quality of one's life.

And that's when R. casually tells me that, despite his bad habits, his T-cell count remains high anyway; he hasn't seemed to drink or smoke himself out of a single one. The mysterious little things have, in fact, multiplied fruitfully since he abandoned a brief self-punishing bout of macrobiotics.

I feel like the floor of the restaurant has just slid open. But I don't show it, or at least I don't think I do. R.'s placed his disclosure on the table beside what he's said about L., beside the gossip and business of our lunch. To express sorrow or surprise would somehow seem impolite, would seem to underline the gravity of their situation in a way that won't do. This dangerous field of contingency, shiny with threat, is where we live now. It's 1994; of course we're in this condition.

It's later, after we've parted, after my walk through the park, sun gilding the benches and those who rest or sleep there, kids practicing violent or accomplished descents of the slopes on skates, the sparking narrative of casual cruising going on all around, story of possibility and of flirtation I love — it's after all that, back in my hotel room, that it hits me.

Maybe, yes, R. and L. will be fine, maybe the men in the workshop will be all right; the old optimistic line, San Francisco, 1989, plays in my head, *HIV is not a death sentence,* and who knows how any individual will fare, who can predict it. But I've seen too much, I've lived the long corrosive descent, and now I want to moan or cry it out, from the depth of my stomach, I want to double over and push the grief out of me, for R. and L. and the circle of radiant or uncertain faces around that table last night, hopeful, disenchanted, sorrowing, exhausted, still quick with potential. The epidemic opens out and out, endlessly consuming my generation and the one before and the one after me, immense bitter wave, the floor beneath us pulling back, pulling away, a huge gap opening beneath whatever seemed momentarily solid, downward pull, dizzying absence: multiply, endlessly, these human faces.

I can't stop thinking of a line of graffiti in Chicago, spraypainted on a lakeshore wall at the end of Lynda's block:

"Does a snowflake in an avalanche feel responsible?"

Of course it doesn't; of course I do. Not responsible *for* the avalanche, but *to* it, responsible in its wake.

My neighbor's abusing his dog. Not an outright beating, but a kind of nattering, relentless cruelty that must be making the little spotted beagle crazy. It's making me crazy just to listen. Every time the dog makes a yip or bark, the man yells at her.

Soon she's out in the yard, tied to a post, but when she lets out a woof at a passing car or dog he's at the door chastising her. She doesn't seem to be able to stop herself, even though she seems to know what's coming and modulates her barks to little yips I can barely hear.

But her master can hear them, and he comes running out of the house, grabs hold of her collar, and leads her into the back of his four-wheel drive, where her wire cage is waiting. It's a hot day, and it must be steamy inside that black vehicle, but he locks her in the crate. From my front windows I see her fur gleaming in the shady interior, her pink tongue hanging long and loose.

I'm trying not to look, trying to stay away, but I keep going to the window to check on the dog, who still feels like yipping when something interesting passes by. Then the owner comes flying out of the house, the screen door slamming behind him, and he goes to the back of the car and starts to shake the cage.

Something in me snaps then; I don't even think about what I'm doing as I run out of the house and out to the garden, and shout across the fence, "I'm not going to stand by and watch you treat that dog that way! You ought to be ashamed of yourself!"

I don't even know what else I say; it's an outpouring of defense for the animal and condemnation of the man, who stands there and sputters and says something lame like "She's fine."

Which only sets me off again. She's *not* fine, this is not fine, I will not accept this. Wally, who lay nine months looking out these windows, would not have accepted this, would not have been able to bear it, would have spoken. Or would have wanted to, would have been desperate to and perhaps also unsure he had the right to, the nerve; but now he's free, beyond any issues of self-confidence or self-doubt, and that spirit, were it here, would insist on speaking. And does, pouring out through my mouth, passionate and unstoppable—and maybe totally inappropriately, but I don't care, I'm speaking with my love's tongue, I'm speaking for the dead I carry in me, and I will make sure they're heard.

The day of Wally's memorial service, his youngest brother Mark carried the brass box containing his ashes home down Commercial Street, a kind of ritual gesture. Sometime during the next few days I put the box into the nightstand beside my bed, with another box in which I'd collect the letters and sympathy cards people sent, copies of the newspaper obituaries. I needed time to come to terms with the ashes. I imagined that in time I'd know where they should go, whether I should scatter or keep them; Wally had been clear that he'd wanted to be cremated, but the conversation had never really gone further than that. His silence made it evident that the nature of the memorial service and the fate of his ashes were up to me.

In a while I knew that I wanted to spread his ashes in the marsh I love, the wild and open place I walk through, winters, out to the point where the seals are. A part of me wanted to hold onto them, too. But when I meditated about the ashes I imagined pristine urns, sealed off from the world—and then, alternately, the play of light on water, the inward and outward rush of tide, the complex symphonic spectrum of life that the marsh is. What, there, is not part of life? That, I knew, was what Wally would want.

Talking to Wally's mother, I planned to scatter the ashes in the spring, when it would be warm enough for us and whoever else in his family wanted to come to walk out along the dike into the wind-swept field of the marsh. But I could tell she was reluctant, uncertain, even though she agreed. And when the time we'd considered drew close, in May, I offered her an out, saying there really wasn't any hurry, that we should do this when we're really ready. Relieved, she said she'd like to wait, and I didn't know until that moment that I'd be relieved, too. I wasn't ready to relinquish the evidence of his body.

In a while, I began to forget the ashes were there. And then I'd remember them, and wonder if I was avoiding being aware of their presence.

In the fall, Betty and I talked again, and settled on the anniversary of Wally's death. It would be a cold walk in January, but something about the turning of a year felt right. Rather like that Jewish ceremony in which the headstone's unveiled, after the first year, for the family, marker of a year survived, of the actuality of loss.

I'd been tempted, at St. John the Divine, by the walls of little containers bearing the names of the dead, some of them with their small vases, their tokens of remembrance. Wouldn't it be good to have a *place* in which Wally was remembered, an inscription of his name?

But those chapels felt, unmistakably, for the living, even the Christmas cards and flowers and love-tokens there. What these ashes wanted, I felt sure, was not containment but participation. Not an enclosure of memory, but the world.

I brought the ashes out of my bedside cabinet, polished the box, set it on the mantel where I could study it. I still held a fear, a doubt about letting the remainder of Wally's body go. In another box, one I can hardly bear to open, I've saved the little personal things that were around his bed: his glasses, the wooden angel from Indonesia, a toy wooden clown he liked, whose tongue popped out when you pressed on his hat. His silver ring's on my left hand now, pushed against mine. But those accessories, however personal and full of the psychic scent of a man, are not his body. Once I let these ashes go, into their commingling with the world, there was no getting them back.

Relieved to know my back was mending—through whatever agency, Eastern or Western, physiological or medicine of the soul—I experienced a sense of physical freedom which lasted almost exactly a week.

On the last day of November, I stepped out of a shower in Boston, where I was visiting friends, and onto a slick tile floor;

I'd neglected to move the mat nearer the shower. I flew to the floor, breaking the fall with my right wrist. My friends came running to see what the terrible noise was, and the first real indication I had that something was wrong was that, when they asked me if I was all right, I found I couldn't make a sentence. Not that I seemed to be feeling so much pain, exactly, but that pain had short-circuited my capacity to make language.

I'd broken more than my capacity for syntax; the tip of my radius, one of two long bones in my right arm, was cracked clean through. Soon I was immobilized from knuckles to elbow in a white plaster cast.

January 29, 1995

Dear friend Jean,

I was so glad to have your letter this week and your sweet message about the anniversary of Wally's death, too—your thinking of me and of us means so much. This whole month, a year from that last passage in Wally's life, has been something for me, a deep and difficult passage in its own right. I guess Maggie told you I had to have surgery on my wrist; the broken bit of bone was healing in the wrong place and if left alone (they said—who knows whether to believe doctors?) the movement of my hand would have been seriously impaired. So, just after Christmas I went in the hospital and had a bone graft, from my left hip into my wrist, and a titanium plate put in to hold the bone together.

Darren and Michael took good care of me at home, but I struggled—I don't do well with anesthetics and painkillers, I hate that muffled, submerged feeling. And the breaking of a part of my body became aligned for me with the breaking of Wally's body, with his bone being fragmented. I was going back through, in memory, those last days when he was moving into the very heart of things, the depths of last winter when we were more and more deeply inside the house, inside our lives together, approaching that mystery.

As my wrist healed and I got out of cast and splint and stitches I started to do better, as if I'd descended and was climbing up out of the cave again. By the time the anniversary day came I think I had done so much work inside about it that it was okay, sort of odd and numb, like a holiday when you are supposed to feel more than you do but you can't really do anything. I burned the beautiful beeswax candle you gave me that day.

We didn't scatter the ashes—because snow was forecast and his mother didn't want to travel—but waited until yesterday instead, which was a year to the day from Wally's service, so that felt right. His mom and one brother and sister and their partners and I went way out into the marsh, and we read the Whitman poem about the grass from "Song of Myself." I'd forgotten that I would come to the line, "What do you think has become of the young and old men?" And then George and Susan and I threw the ashes into the wind and water in handfuls.

The tide was pouring out of the marsh, out to sea. The lightest dust swirled off in the wind, and the rest made clouds like nebula in the water, and the heaviest parts, the chips of bone, sank to the bottom and looked like pieces of clam shell, like the gulls had been eating there. And of course we had ashes on our hands and skin and clothes. Arden sat and watched. Wally's mom couldn't handle throwing the ashes, so she threw a rose, which Beau decided to fetch—he leapt into the cold water and brought it back about four times, till it finally fell apart. He's the world's court jester. I felt utterly overwhelmed and as if I could hardly bear it but I also felt like I could hear or feel Wally breathing this sigh of relief— as though what he really wanted was for his body to be part of the world, part of the sparkle of all that water. I used to imagine, when I'd walk the dogs before Wally died, that the shining path the sun makes across the sea was the way the dead went, the way home. But now Wally is the path.

So it felt very right. Meditating about it today I felt this *great sense of serenity and light. We did what he wanted and I feel different now—full of grief but less anxious somehow, more—aligned? Certainly my bones are aligned again, in wrist and in back—maybe I needed the physical descent of this break in order to accomplish the emotional descent?*

Things have shifted, with the passage of the whole year, and though sorrow isn't lessened I'm in a different relation-ship to it somehow. Last week in NYC, at St. John the Divine, I was at that wonderful altar for PWA's. I lit a can-dle, and I was crying for a while, and then I heard Wally's voice in the back of my head say, Okay, now let's go to Bloomingdale's . . .

I saved a bit of ash for myself, in a little cherrybark tea canister from Japan I got in New York. I was afraid that there wouldn't be enough intimacy in the family ceremony, although it turned out to be fine. But I am still glad to have this bit of his body with me, though I am not sure what I'll do with it. Maybe take it also out to the marsh, alone—or maybe take a bit to Venice next month—or maybe just wait . . .

What I'd soon feel, about that little canister of ash, was that it was fine to have it with me. There seemed no imperative to take it out to the marsh, and it didn't feel right for it to go to some unfamiliar place. Nor do I feel any need to put it away, to avoid it or forget what it contains. It's a comfortable presence. It rep-resents, perhaps, the way that a part of Wally's with me always, but it's not like I thought—I thought I'd need to hold on to this symbol, this proof of his having been.

I understand, differently, the longing of Antigone to bury her brother properly. Something shifts, with the body where it belongs; Wally's body belongs in the huge sun-burnished field of the salt marsh beside our tiny airport, the first and last of home I see, by the way, when I fly in and out of town. And that smaller part belongs also with me, is, already, part of me.

I didn't know it would make me happy, when Wally's ashes

blew into my face and hair. When, after I scattered them, a fine grit of him was left on my hands, so that I could rub it against my cheeks.

I went back, the next day, and the chips of bone were still gleaming there under the water. If you didn't know what they were, you wouldn't know.

The next day Michael and I walked the dogs at Herring Cove, so I didn't see what had happened.

On the third day, there was an enormously high tide, the whole marsh gone under, and I couldn't see anything beneath that wide, steely expanse.

Epilogue: Consolations

Of course there is no consolation, for the dreadful fact of a death. Nothing makes it right. Nothing can remedy that absence, that break in the continuity of things. Nothing can fill the space Wally occupied in my life; nothing takes his place.

On an absolute level he is gone, utterly, and that absence rings at the core of every one of my days, the aftermath of a struck bell.

And yet. And yet.

There are these gifts, these perceptions or moments or aspects of experience which make it possible, desirable, to continue. Any consolation can and does dissolve, any day, into the lake of grief, that liquid realm where all bright or solid things darken and disappear. One does not lose—one does not *want* to lose, entirely—grief.

We live, instead, into, toward a different relation to loss, a shifting perspective: the grief not as large and overwhelming, not every day, not erasing, not entirely, what there is to praise.

And what is left, when you've lost what you loved most, to praise?

A Metaphor

A portion of a letter, from the poet Alfred Corn:

February 19, 1994

... What I'm working up to is to say how sorry I was to hear about Wally. I didn't know him, but I've heard what a tremendous person he was, and I think I have some idea what you must be feeling. When I call up pictures of friends (none of them lovers) lost, a terrible ache comes over me, so much so that it has to go away on its own, there isn't much by way of remedy that I can do. I remember a letter of Henry James where he said that in times of great grief it was important to "go through the motions of life"; and then eventually they would become real again. Our great enemy Time is also on our side in these matters. And then you have a great resource in your art, which is also a friend and inseparable. I've been trying to write, myself, a poem about those ancient Japanese ceramic cups, rustic in appearance, the property at some point of a holy monk, one of the few possessions he allowed himself. In a later century, someone dropped and broke the cup, but it was too precious simply to throw away. So it was repaired, not with glue, which never really holds, but with a seam of gold solder. And I think our poems are often like that gold solder, repairing the break in what can never be restored perfectly. The gold repair adds a kind of beauty to the cup, making visible part of its history ...

What was can't be restored; I can neither have Wally back in the flesh, nor return to the self I inhabited before his death. The vessel's not cracked but broken, all the way through, permanently.

The break, from now on, is an inescapable part of who I am, perhaps *the* inescapable part. Hasn't it become my essential definition, my central fact: I loved a man who died?

But who can live, day by day, in pieces? Loss shatters us, first, but then what?

Alfred's metaphor offers a possibility: to honor the part of oneself that's irreparable. Not to apologize for it, disguise it, not try to mend it in any seamless way. Studying the cup, the viewer might see the rupture *first*; to fill the crack with gold means to allow the break prominence, to let it shine.

Broken, ongoing, we see at once what it was and what it is. Wearing its history, the old cup with its gilt scars becomes, I imagine, a treasure of another sort, whole in its own fragmentation, more deeply itself, veined with the evidence of time.

A Gift from Bill

Bill died late in the spring, weeks after our visit—at home, amazingly; after the long hospital siege, he'd been allowed some peaceful weeks in his own surroundings, among his own things. And he took care of those things, picking out gifts for people, directing Phil to wrap them.

When Phil came down to Provincetown in the summer, I hadn't seem him since the wake, which was just the extravaganza of white flowers Bill had ordered. The trunk of his car was full of gifts for various people, wrapped in bright paper and bows.

Phil had an alarming story. During the funeral service—its audience half Bill's gay friends and half his Catholic family— Phil had told the story of the green chenille robe, and a tale, characteristically Bill, of how once Bill had played a dress-up game with some very young relatives, nephews or nieces, who were expressing confusion about gender. "Are you a man or a woman?" they'd asked.

"I'm a drag queen," Bill had answered.

Half the congregation had loved this story; half had not been amused. Phil found, suddenly, that the emotional temperature shifted; welcomed by Bill's family for years, he was suddenly given dozens of cold shoulders. When he confronted Bill's mother, after days of this, he learned it was the story that had turned the tide.

"Why," she asked, "did you have to tell people about *that?*" Meaning, of course, why did you have to tell everyone my son was gay, why did you have to talk about it? Meaning, if my son wasn't gay he'd still be alive.

Things changed quickly then. Phil had expected to continue living, at least for a while, in the house the two of them had shared, though Bill owned it. But in two weeks time the house was up for sale, and Phil, in the whirlwind of grief, was also separating their possessions, packing up his things, displaced.

A horrifying story, and it made me grateful for Wally's family, who've expressed nothing but gratitude for the way he was taken care of. Even Jimmy, whose disappearance from our lives rankled me so deeply, said to me at the memorial service, "Thank you for taking care of my brother." And everyone's understood that I still don't feel like cleaning out the attic, sorting out Wally's collection of souvenirs. There's so much there, more than I can keep, things I know his family will want to have.

Bill was wise, to make decisions about those things he wanted to give his friends. And there's something deeply affecting about this gift, across the divide between worlds; here I am, walking back from Phil's car down Commercial Street, carrying in my arms this cheerful package presented to me across the widest gulf in the world. Unbridgeable gap, and yet it's bridged all the time, as gifts pour back to us from the dead: objects full of evocative memory, like the contents of this box, Bill's two-handled blue-and-white Wedgwood cream soup cups, just the thing for *serious* entertaining, and of course he knew I'd treasure them.

Things fill up with us, they carry across time their human store.

And then gestures. Phrases. Ways of seeing the world. Moments so entirely full of the presence of someone gone; an image, an event, the sudden recognition of a quality essentially, unmistakably *theirs*.

The china cups, mementos of a time when people actually required something distinct in which to serve cream soups, relic of a sort of gentility, a pleasure in providing a kind of perfection for guests. *Bill.*

Walking in the evening, along the shore of an Italian lake, under a row of pollarded trees, still bare in the early spring, the line of old iron street lamps curving along the balustrade, glazed in the mist and doubled on the still surface of the water, I think *Lynda*.

In a shop window, in Milan, the most exquisite food I've ever seen, far too beautiful for anyone to eat, a perfection of aspics and gleaming patés, canapés, and little delights resembling not real flowers but glass ones, the gorgeous artifices of Venetian chandeliers: a heaven of display. *Wally*.

A girl in a blue carnival dress, yards of it, and a snowy mask, with softly luminous, silvery pigeons perching on her shoulders and arms. *Wally*.

An outdoor market, in Bellagio, where a vendor's constructed a wall of birdcages, just across from a vendor of candy, the sheen of the parakeets and finches mirroring the colors of the sugary treats in their wooden bins: little blue seahorses, apple-green sour balls, a universe of diminutive produce, in marzipan. *Wally*.

We couldn't keep the dead out of the present if we wanted to. They're nowhere to be found, and firmly here, now. While this is a source of pain, memory's double-edged sword at once wounds and offers us company, interior companionship which enriches and deepens the dimensions of every day.

In an Italian *erbolario*, a fragrance shop full of herbal essences and essential oils, I find a bottle of cologne, a scent called vetiver, one that Wally loved. I lift the tester bottle and spray a cloud of the stuff onto my wrist: the strongest, purest scent of vetiver I've ever known, and Wally's body comes flooding back to me, the scent of his collar, some Boston morning when he's going to work, tying a dotted pink bow tie. In the cloud of the scent is how young he is, how handsome, something hopeful about the morning, something deeply resonant and sexy in the magnetic pull of his body, his physical and emotional warmth. Gleaming chestnut eyes, like good leather or the lustrous wooden case of a violin. So I buy the bottle, and choose days when I want to feel him, physically, that scent close, intimate as skin.

Even the word, *vetiver*, full of him.

They are a way of being in the present, a way of paying attention, these moments when I think, this is *so* Wally.

Or, Wally would *love* this.

Times when I suddenly say, *Oh, babe, look at that.*

When I say to the open air, to the morning, to the ether, *Now what?*

Making

I found myself, without being able to help it, in a study of my beloved wife's face, systematically noting the colors.

When the world shatters, what does a writer do?

David, after Lynda's death, writes poem after poem, bracing, fierce, bitter. My friend Patrick, after the death of his lover Chris, goes into the studio and paints ten hours a day; that work, sheer physical concentration, is what he can do.

The three of us are people who've always depended on our work as a means of negotiating difficulty. A vessel for feeling, an arena in which we give shape to emotion and see it reflected back to us. How lucky, not to have the ability to work desert us. Work is our intangible property, one thing that we individually control. One thing that doesn't disappear.

This book begins as separate essays, pieces written for collections about AIDS and about religion, written because someone invited me to write them. But soon I was impelled, soon I was writing for myself. Writing, in a way, to save my life, to catch what could be saved of Wally's life, to make form and struggle toward a shape, to make a story of us that can be both kept and given away. The story's my truest possession and I burnish and hammer it and wrestle it to make it whole. In return it offers me back to myself, it holds what I cannot, its embrace and memory larger than mine, more permanent.

Always, always we were becoming a story. But I didn't

understand that fusing my life to the narrative, giving myself to the story's life, would be what would allow me to live.

Bitterness

Gridlock in New York; the President's in town and his cordon of vehicles has Fifth Avenue closed, so there's some kind of chain reaction all the way to La Guardia. The taxi driver wants to take an alternate route, so after I agree we wind up on some side street in a particularly beat part of Queens. This would probably help matters except that it seems every other taxi driver in the universe has had the same idea, so that this sad little retail neighborhood with its on-the-skids businesses and wildly graffitied walls is totally choked with yellow taxis, all of them idling and cursing and champing at the bit. Nobody's moving.

Which allows me a really good look at the guy on the corner, a middle-aged black man in shabby clothes, too many layers of them for the weather. He's standing right on the curb, rocking back and forth a little, surveying the air above the cabs, the gridlock, me, and when he speaks, loud as a street preacher, his judgment seems to take in us all.

"The world," he says, "is shit."

It makes me laugh, as well as scaring me a little—he's right outside my window. But all he wants to do is pronounce.

And in fact I know how he feels. Because grief has taught me that bitterness is itself a strange kind of consolation, that clear-eyed, sober bleakness that sees right through the sentiments of consolation, that knows better than all the things that *fail* to console. Time, for instance; my friend Renate, her husband dead three years, saw the wind rocking the chair on the deck where her husband used to like to sit, and the movement of the empty chair tore her apart; she felt, in fact, that her grief had gotten *worse* with the passage of time. Is the way that time "heals" us simply that it encourages us to turn away?

Or memory. People love to say, "Your pain will fade and you

will be left with beautiful memories." But my memories are also a narrative of pain and of diminishment, and that history's vivid to me, too.

Sometimes all that would help would be to allow myself to feel ferocious, to feel like a raging fire burning up the false offerings of consolation, burning right at the dark heart of things. We need, sometimes, to consign it all to darkness. We need to look at the world and proclaim it shit.

Whose ignorant words, says the voice in the whirlwind in Job, smear my design with darkness?

Ours. Because everything around us races toward disappearance. Our brief moment's a flash, an arcing flare which itself serves to illuminate the face of death.

Aren't we always on the verge of vanishing? Isn't the whole world nowhere's coast?

Sometimes all that helps is a deep, bracing breath of emptiness.

The Present

I'm writing in the wild glamour of an early Italian spring, smoke of olive wood drifting up the hill from the grove. This is a world of fragrance: Parma violets, in the shade of the woods, and on days it rains something like eucalyptus, a camphory, resinous scent floating among the trees. Small-cupped yellow narcissus, on the sunny banks. The armoire in my room gives out a deep, contained smell, decade after decade of wools and silks, ancient sachets, long quiet hours when the sun's poured in through the tall windows and heated the redolent wood till it releases something of itself into the atmosphere.

Today is the first of March; I've come here for a month to work in a grand old villa hundreds of steep cobbled steps up the hill from the village of Bellagio. My room is a buttery Naples yellow, thick walls pierced by two windows and french doors opening on to a balcony. My first day, my first moment alone in the room, I opened the doors and stepped out onto the stone shelf suspended above the steep switchback paths of rosemary and lavender, above the green-black cypresses fling-ing themselves vertically toward heaven, above the jigsawed rose-tiled roofs of the village, above the softly luminous hazed expanse of the lake and its distant mountains, behind their smoky blue veils—a landscape like the background in a Leonardo.

How could one not, in that moment, be completely absorbed in the present? What possesses us like the present does, when we give ourselves to it completely?

And then I realized, on that steep little ledge with its lace of iron railing, that this time I didn't imagine myself falling, had no desire, now, to jump. There was too much in the world to see, too much I wanted to pour myself into, to encounter and absorb, too much I wanted to do.

The present begins to hold a possibility, in its thin, luminous edge. It suggests and supports a future.

I want to know how the story of my life will turn out.

Dogs

Dogs, in a way, *are* the present. Animals are infinitely atten-tive to now, wholly present with what's in front of them. Entirely themselves, without compromise or dissembling. Pure directness of being, the soul right in the eyes, brimming to the edges.

Arden and Beau: heart's companions, good boys, eager, steady, always exactly where they are.

And what is right in the present, at this moment's fresh edge, also seems to lead right into the next moment. Last month, with Michael at the animal shelter, I sat in a pen while a dozen puppies climbed over and around us, all eagerness to be just where they were, these dozen new beings come into the world of time, to follow each moment into the next, along the arc that passing through time makes. In those almost identical faces, eyes becoming equal to the light, I couldn't miss it: desire for the next moment, and the next, one at a time, each entirely attended to.

Heaven

Ongoingness, vanishing: the world's twin poles.
Each thing disappears; everything goes on.
The parts pour into nowhere, the whole continues.
And to be nowhere is to be in heaven, isn't it, in the boundless, loose from the limits of time and space?
Isn't the whole world heaven's coast?

Coherence

In his autobiography *Speak, Memory*, Nabokov describes an instance of coherence, the way a book of matches appears as a pivotal image a number of times, in very different contexts, in the writer's life. Delighted, he finds the patterning and coherence of art showing itself in experience, in memory. He writes, "The following of such thematic designs through one's life should be, I think, the true purpose of autobiography."

So we become our stories.

Driving to school, the autumn after Wally's death, I was thinking of something Rena had told me; Wally's therapist had become my friend, the bond between us beginning in our common affection for him, but opening swiftly into affection for each other. In a meditation, she'd seen Wally coming to her on a great white winged horse, a Pegasus.

So I remembered the blue tattoo of Paolo the nurse, that winged horse that Wally had loved imprinted on a biceps he'd admired.

And then I remembered something I'd completely forgotten, something Rena didn't know. Years ago, when Wally and I first met, we had all kinds of endearments for each other, silly little names we liked to play with. The name for him I liked best, Lord knows where I got it, was Skyhorse.

Wind from my love's wings: beautiful shape, threading through a life and afterward, making things whole.

Like Beau and the seals. A year from that first difficult encounter, when he bedeviled the poor sick creature beached high on the edge of the dunes at Race Point, we walked that long fire-road path past the marsh where Wally's ashes lie. (There—glittering beside those rocks where we stood—fragments of shell? chips of bone? Isn't that the point, not to know?)

When we reached the shore he skirted the surf, sniffing at the breaking hemline of foam, and then looking out toward the source of that wild scent he spotted a dozen black heads eyeing him, riding on the crests and troughs of the waves, necks craned up to study the land-creature, brother (cousin?) from the other element. And Beau went into the water, intent, pure purpose. The seals didn't budge. He floated six feet away from the first of them, head to head, studying. Then with a splash of tail the seal vanished, only to reappear a little farther out among the other heads.

Beau was, plainly, enchanted. His aim was play; he swam with abandon into the pod, which continued to await him and then dive, the game continuing, all of them moving farther out.

Until my golden friend was suddenly one of a flock of little heads some ways out from shore, and fear swept over me. How far would he go? Capable of intense passions, utterly single-minded, Beau might simply keep swimming, and what were the currents there? Would he know when he was too tired to go on?

When I could barely see the heads, the black dots of them indistinguishable from distant floating birds, I panicked, standing in the edge of the water myself and shouting his name.

I said to the air, *Wally, bring him back*. And then I couldn't see any heads at all, not even that single one that had no place beneath the surface of the waves.

And just as I am praying and thinking *I can't do this, I can't bear it, I can do it if I have to, don't make me do it*, having said *yes he might disappear, my dog might simply walk into the sea and not walk out,* I see this sleek little arrow shape coming in my direction, the golden fur dark now with salt water, intent on coming back to me.

On shore he's joyous, more than half-possessed. Am I foolish for having been terrified when he's an embodiment of pure delight, having been out there in the strangest of worlds, swimming for half an hour among a tribe he recognizes, though it tumbles in an alien medium? Well, I love him; I want him with me, and yet there's something haunting and perfect about this, too. I think of what Jung said someplace, about children acting out the unconscious wishes of their parents; has Beau been swimming in the wild salt waters of my desire, really, out there among the somersaulting forms unfettered by gravity's constraints?

Perhaps there isn't one meaning to make of this story, of the seal's apparitions and returns, the round of images that a life offers. Maybe only that we aren't *done* with seals; the coherence of the story sweeps us up, stitches and braids the parts of a life together in terror and in joy. How much it helps to think that coherence might be *given* to us, might emerge from things themselves; perhaps our work is to recognize it.

Mystery

We don't know where the dead are. But it's just as true, finally, that we don't know where *we* are. *More things in heaven and earth, madam, than even a lifetime of experience in Abalone, Arizona, could avail you of.*

Whatever this being of ours is, in its depth and complexity, we see only a little of it, and that little bit is too much for us, incomprehensible. If we know so little of ourselves, what could we hope to know about the dead?

In not-knowing, hope resides.

Sex

The comfort and actuality of the body is more poignant, underlined, when we know that the body can only comfort so much, that it will not stay. Sex is a way of entering the present, of moving through this moment's offerings toward the next. Lust as hope: *my dick kept me alive*.

And sex is an acknowledgment of the mystery of flesh, its dimensionality and weight. In touch and touch, feeling the limits of the body with our hands, testing its boundaries.

Aretha Franklin

This voice says, No matter what, I'm here, I hold up, I carry on. And I am not suffering powerlessly; I take charge of what I can, I claim and shout myself, I hold forth, I hold on, take from me what you will. And the song that I make out of my continuing itself sustains.

Longing

No matter what, I want more.

I'm driving on the Cape, listening to our local community radio station, a volunteer effort that is sometimes charmingly amateurish, sometimes annoying dull, occasionally terrific. Today they're playing a syndicated gay and lesbian news program, homos all over the world. Here's a story about newly legalized gay and lesbian marriage in Sweden; at a Stockholm ceremony, couples are exchanging vows, then whooping it up in celebration.

And before I know what hits me, I've burst into tears.

Now I have all kinds of political positions about this. I am not at all sure I like the institution of marriage—look at the difficult, calcified relationships all around us, the predetermined meanings and associations such a sanctioned union places on a couple—and I don't really know, intellectually, that I think this heterosexual model's a good one for gay couples to follow. I turned down an opportunity to edit a book, a compilation of poems and quotations for people to use in commitment ceremonies and the like, because I just wasn't convinced it was a notion I really supported. Didn't we gain from having to make up our own rules, renegotiate and understand our own relationships day by day, year by year?

And yet, hearing these shouts and cheers, my ideas go right out the window. I'm crying because I wish I could have married Wally, because I'll never be able to now. Rationally I know that a ceremony and a piece of paper don't change a thing; we wouldn't have been closer, our connection deeper.

But I want it anyway, I want *more*. Isn't that what we'd want to say of any relationship, I'd have been right there for more, I'd have wanted more?

Whirlwind

This is what happened, my last massage with M.

I was still in pain then, didn't yet feel I'd begun to heal. (I remember, exactly, the day I knew I had turned the corner. It was weeks later, in a friend's cottage, on Long Island, a little studio on a cove which curves inward from the Sound. I'd had days of sleep, reading, walking, more sleep, a sense of restoration, unhurriedness, a luxury and liberty of time. Easy days, the dogs wandering in and out. The day I was to leave, getting ready, picking up the place and stowing things in the car, I suddenly noticed that I didn't hurt. Not with the deep sense of woundedness, the aching fragility way down in the joints. And that knowledge lifted my spirits; I began to feel I had possibilities in front of me again. A few nights later, lying on the sand at Head of the Meadow, a wide Atlantic beach, my head toward a great blond tangle of driftwood, a twisted trunk polished the sheen and hue of moonlight, suddenly I felt so awake, such a sense of freedom of all I could do. How long had it been since I'd felt like that?)

But that was all in the future still. On M.'s table I am fragile, unmended.

He begins with a sort of passive yoga, moving my body into various postures for lengthening, stretching out my spine. I feel pleasure in those movements, even though they also hurt a little, frighten me a bit; couldn't he really hurt me, if I let go too much, or moved the wrong way?

I guess I can't be hurt, really, relaxed as I'm becoming, but there's that fear. Surely part of the stiffness in my back *is* fear, yes? Afraid to be too fluid, to be carried away.

I'm thinking about holding on, about Wally's body. Tension in my arms, resistance. Thinking I didn't want to let his body go, shouldn't have let him go.

M. has me begin a cycle of strange breathing—rapid short inhalations, then holding my breath, expelling it. I do this again and again, the pace increasing, the pitch of my breathing faster, harder, his directions increasingly quick, pointed, intense. And then I hold the breath, and squeeze around it as hard as I can, everything—arms, shoulders, chest, legs, face—everything utterly clenched, as small and tight and singular a point of tension as my body can make, held as long as I can.

And then I let it go.

It feels like exploding, like being born, like breaking apart into a field of stars.

My body has fallen open—arms extended, legs spread, a complete relinquishment—but I feel as if I'm still opening out, extending on beyond the limits of my body; I am spreading out and out, I don't think there's any limit to how far I will go. I'm making sounds, I'm crying, sometimes loud, tears, laughter, groaning. Sometimes I'm thrashing, overtly, and other times what is rippling through me is the slightest wave inside a muscle.

It goes on and on, the self thinning and spreading like spilt oil, endless, beyond any notion of boundary.

I'm hardly myself now, but a great wide field.

And I think, God is *there*, or, there *is* God. I know, through and through. Great grief, great god; where there is one, there is the other.

And I think, all along I've been this, have been part of this great intimacy and light, that immense kindness that was holding me, supporting me, but I hadn't been able to let myself know it. And I'm laughing and weeping at the idea that I had to be forty to find this out. I'm thinking how much love there's been in my life, how much suffering—my mother, my father, Wally, Lynda—and how we didn't know who we were, through the pain, that even that was a part of God.

My hips are vibrating; that's the space, I think, where my doubt has been. And that space is being filled now with this warm loving energy that is healing my body. I know then I'm going to heal, and I feel the increasing fire of a kind of intense vibration, in my belly and chest, energy circling around in me.

A whirlwind.

I hear the border of its enormous, rushing roar.

How long did I stay there?

In a while, in no time, I'm dimly aware of M. on the other side of the room. Slowly, I'm coming back to myself. He says something vague, and after another long time I'm opening my eyes, I'm slowly sitting up, standing up, stretching. M's sitting on the couch smoking a cigarette. It feels so good to stand, feeling my weight balanced on both my legs, my body alive, flexible, light, the life moving in me.

That night I sleep deeply, insensate; the next day I'm still sleepy, a bit sore, sense my body changing, emotion floating up out of nowhere, little tensions coming and going in my muscles, the strange sensation of having been swept up, set down again.

It wasn't that I was healed, right then; the muscles in my spine, my unhappy disk still had its course to run, its process to move through. But something essential, something that reshapes a life had happened to me. How can I explain, moving into that territory where language fails? What have I been doing, through all this story, but moving closer to the unsayable's edge?

I had risen—in the three hours I'd later learn I'd lain on M.'s table—to a kind of awareness above the everyday, above the individual forms of loss and longing, desire and grief, toward a great, benign indifference, an indifference which is the force of life itself. This is one of the paradoxes at the heart of the world:

the Whirlwind is indifferent, but this indifference is utterly, profoundly good.

The Universe doesn't care about Job's suffering, and will not intervene. And the Universe loves Job with the intensity and tenderness with which everything in the world is held. It's Job's vision which is limited, our human eyes which can't apprehend the design, the sense of it. So that when Job cries out against all the grief his life has brought him, the Voice from the Whirlwind says to him:

> *Who is this whose ignorant words*
> *smear my design with darkness?*

That design—ferocious wisdom, implacable light, time's ineluctable unfolding—is too large and brilliant for us to see, though sometimes we can feel the edge of the storm.

After that, I went back to seeing Glen, the sweet, familiar masseur I visit from time to time, who makes me feel relaxed and calm, in my body, in the daily world.

Luckier

This is the story I've been saving.

A week and a few days after Wally died, I took the dogs to walk at Hatch's Harbor, along the long dike that leads across the salt marsh out toward the lighthouse and the far point.

February must have just begun, and the sky was poised on the exact cusp of a storm, half a chilly, bright winter blue and half a billowing dark line of snow clouds. How can something full of so much whiteness be so black? Is it the sheer density of what's contained inside the cloud, worlds upon worlds of snow, which will soon disperse into a perfect, rhythmic scattering, going on and on for hours?

I left the house in sunlight, but by the time I got to the turnout beside the fire road the horizon was layered with deepening bands and swirls of charcoal, grayish violet, smoky black. The distant line of dunes, out across the marsh, was still sun-struck, gilded, a glowing bar beneath the expanse of darkened heaven. Under the storm, that radiance seemed intensified, alluring.

Walking along the narrow road, through the scrub of the low dune lands, then out onto the dike bisecting the marsh, I kept my eyes—like a pilgrim—on that band of hills. I found myself thinking of Whitman, in particular of the part of "Song of Myself" that begins

> *A child said,* What is the grass? *fetching it to me*
>   *with full hands,*
> *How could I answer the child? I do not know what it is*
>   *any more than he.*

What I could remember of the poem began to unroll in my head, with its long-lined marching cadences, its plain-spoken but encantatory, biblical music. In the secondhand college edition of the poem I still read, some long-ago student wrote next to these lines, "Isn't it grass?" which I suppose must be a marker of the demarcation between the poetic sensibility and its pragmatic opposite. For Whitman, plainly, it is not enough to say it's grass. He spins out a stunning series of metaphors, guessing about its nature; is it "the flag of my disposition, out of hopeful green stuff woven"? Or "the handkerchief of the Lord," dropped in order to make us notice the embroidery of the owner's name? Or is the grass a hieroglyph of democracy, growing among all equally, regardless of race or social position?

And then Whitman drops the poem's bombshell, in an image whose yoking of the lovely and terrible still shocks, after a hundred and forty years: "And now it seems to me the beautiful uncut hair of graves."

He imagines, joyously, the origins of the grass in the bodies of dead young men, old people, babies, mothers. It is a meditation both literal (the buried dead are pushing up "so many uttering tongues") and figurative, and it moves Whitman to a question, the core question of our lives, which he answers, in the swift and assured conclusion, with an almost unimaginable authority.

> *What do you think has become of the young and old men?*
> *And what do you think has become of the women and children?*
> *They are alive and well somewhere.*
> *The smallest sprout shows there is really no death,*
> *And if there ever was it led forward life, and does not wait*
> *at the end to arrest it . . .*

I'd been walking with my head down, crying, feeling my way through my shaky memory of the poem. I hadn't read it in years; I don't know where it came from, in my memory, what triggered my recall. The lines, what I could recapture of them, felt like company, like the steadying arm of a companion, a voice of certainty. I was putting one foot in front of the other, not looking up, trying to focus on the words, and I came to the poem's end, those lines I had been traveling toward as surely as I had been walking here, to the end of the dike just before the high sun-washed dunes began.

> *All goes onward and outward, nothing collapses,*
> *And to die is different from what anyone supposed, and luckier.*

And then I looked up, into the face of a coyote.

He was standing only a little ways from the dike, perfectly still, eyeing us with a calm and frank curiosity, and he was utterly beautiful—big, full-bodied, not the scrawny creature of the night supposed to haunt local garbage cans, carrying off the occasional cat, but thick-furred, gleaming, the tips of each gray and blond hair dipped in sunlight. His eyes were golden, magnetic, inescapable. There was a moment when we all stopped—the dogs, the coyote, myself—and the world seemed in absolute suspension, nothing moving anywhere, everything centered around the fixity of our mutual gaze.

I thought, *It's a wolf, a timber wolf,* and then thought no, there are no wolves here, it's a dog. But no dog looks like that, or stands alone with that kind of authority and wildness. Then I thought, *It's one in the afternoon on Cape Cod and I'm staring at a coyote.*

Then, from nowhere, I thought, *He's been with Wally, he's come from Wally.* I knew it as surely as I knew the lines of the poem. This apparition, my—ghost, was it? spirit animal? real creature carrying the presence of my love? Perhaps it doesn't matter. I've never seen one in the middle of the day before or since, and never been so frankly studied from the other side of wildness, from a world I cannot enter. Like my seals, the coyote stared back at us, and I could imagine in that gaze Wally's look toward home—his old home—from the other world: not sad, exactly, but neutral, loving, curious, accepting. The dead regard us, I think, as animals do, and perhaps that is part of their relationship; they want nothing from us; they are pure presence, they look back to us from a world we can't begin to comprehend. I am going on, the gaze said, in a life apart from yours, a good life, a wild life, unbounded.

The coyote was, for me, a blessing: *different from what anyone supposed, and luckier.* That night my friend Mekeel would dream of a coyote wandering the rooms of her house, a powerful and sleek animal who had come to bring her a single word: S*afe.* In the weeks and months after, in the stunned absence, in the hopeless hours, in the immobilized ache those are the words I'd reach for: *lucky, safe.* I think it was this visitation, this story, that most sustained me. The story itself, the image, not what the image means. I don't know what it means, still, only the potent presence and consolation of the animal body, the gaze across the gulf of otherness. To those eyes I would return, over and over: *different, and luckier.*

But I didn't know that yet. I turned to look at the dogs— both of them poised, perfectly still—and turned back just in time to see the coyote loping away, though at a little distance he was suddenly gone.

No watching him take off across marsh and dune; he's vanished. Then Beau takes off after him, my inexhaustible golden rambler who'll chase till he drops—but he merely circles and sniffs the place where the figure has been, and looks into the distance, and does not try to follow, as if he knows the chase is hopeless, that what he'd seen was somehow beyond him, unpursuable.

And I'm suddenly stumbling ahead, toward the stripe of sunlight that remains, gilding the dune between us and the sea beneath a sky entirely given over now to violet darkness. When the snow starts, will my coyote be out there someplace, leaping, nipping at the spinning flakes? Or is he not of this world at all, but a creature of the spirit's coast, passing back and forth between elements and worlds—messenger, emblem, reminder? Whatever he is, he's gone, and the dogs and I have turned up the slope of dune which will lead us to the sea.

We have walked into that golden band of light I've been watching. A wild and bracing wind is blowing off the Atlantic, and suddenly the biting air's alive with big white flakes swirling in a shock of sunlight, and I'm alive with a strange kind of joy, stumbling up the dune into the winter wind, my face full of salt-spray and snow.